An Even Better Way to Zone

An Even Better Way to Zone

ACHIEVING MORE AFFORDABLE, EQUITABLE, AND SUSTAINABLE COMMUNITIES

Donald L. Elliott

ISLANDPRESS | Washington | Covelo

Design and Typesetting by 2K/DENMARK.

Sustainable Typesetting® ID: ST49535052-25-A01
The ID number certifies that this book fulfills the standards and recommendations of Sustainable Typesetting® providing reduced CO_2 emissions.

Library of Congress Control Number: 2025936537

All Island Press books are printed on environmentally responsible materials.

Manufactured in the United States of America
10 9 8 7 6 5 4 3 2 1

Keywords: accessory dwelling unit (ADU), affordable housing, Americans with Disabilities Act (ADA), building reuse, climate risk, co-housing, commercial zoning, cottage, density, duplex, environmental justice, environmental sustainability, exclusionary zoning, Fair Housing Act, fourplex, greenhouse gas (GHG), housing equity, inclusionary zoning, LEED-ND, missing middle housing, mixed-use development, multifamily housing, naturally occurring affordable housing (NOAH), redevelopment, renewable energy, resilience, restrictive covenants, rezoning, triplex, vacant building, variance, zoning inequity

To my parents, John and Joyce Elliott
and
To Beth, Maya, and Ethan, again

Contents

Introduction

Zoning is not an easy topic. But for anyone interested in creating better communities it is an essential topic. In America, we believe in governing ourselves by the rule of law in order to treat everyone fairly and to avoid abuses of government power. And zoning is the system of law that most directly affects the health, safety, and quality of life of American communities. Our residents care deeply about their neighborhoods, and zoning is how those neighborhoods are made and remade over time. They also care about the economic opportunities available to them and their children, and zoning sets the rules on where you can make a living and what kind of living you can make in that location. Unlike many aspects of local governance, zoning affects people's health, safety, opportunity, and happiness in very direct ways. Elected officials know that, which is one reason they guard their zoning powers so carefully. But as the pages below demonstrate, our uses of zoning powers often produce outcomes that we do not want—or that are exactly the opposite of what we say we want. This book is about why that happens and how to stop it from happening.

It has now been more than fifteen years since I wrote *A Better Way to Zone* (Island Press, 2008), and lots of things have changed. So many, in fact, that we need to rethink why we have been given those zoning powers in the first place. In many ways, this book builds on the foundation of zoning history provided in that earlier book, as well as the fundamentals of what is wrong with many zoning codes, and how those problems can be fixed. I still endorse the description of zoning history and the advice provided in that book, but I do not repeat that material in this one. The good news is that you do not need to have read *A Better Way to Zone* to understand the discussions in this book. But if the discussions here make you want to explore other aspects of zoning governance, you can look at *A Better Way to Zone.* Or you can read any of the books listed in "Suggested Reading," each of which I have found helpful.

Over the past twenty years of my professional practice working with more than eighty US and Canadian communities, three key substantive themes keep emerging. Regardless of where in the two nations I work, the project begins with a discussion of how the community wants its new zoning rules to differ from the current regulations. The first answer is generally "We want it to implement our new comprehensive plan." The second is "And we want it to be much simpler and more understandable to our residents." But then most of the communities list three specific things they want to achieve:

- More affordable housing;
- Fairer and more inclusive zoning systems; and
- More environmentally sustainable development.

Not every community mentions all three topics, but a surprising number do. So this book focuses on those three topics, which I think will be among the key challenges facing American cities and counties in the years to come.

The desire for zoning to produce more sustainable and resilient development has been a constant theme for most of my career. It probably began with Vice President Al Gore's focus on climate change and the movie *An Inconvenient Truth*, because all of a sudden nearly all my clients wanted greater levels of sustainability built into their new codes. To my surprise, that trend continued during and after the Great Recession of 2008–2010. Even when development was slow, financing was difficult, and unemployment was high, most communities did not back off from their calls for more sustainable development codes.

Community focus on housing affordability has grown exponentially since about 2010 for two reasons. First, in many areas of the country the housing market never fully recovered from the Great Recession, so we fell very far behind on housing production between 2008 and 2012 and we never really caught up. Second, as the housing supply and demand gap widened, many local governments did not focus on how their zoning regulations might be driving up housing prices. Zoning is not the only culprit, of course, but exclusionary zoning compounded problems with real estate financing, construction trade shortages, and stagnant wages. Because the current "hole" of housing undersupply is so deep, it will take a long time to dig our way out of it, so the focus on zoning housing affordability is likely to remain important for the foreseeable future.

Improving zoning equity has long been a focus of the planning profession. Since at least the 1960s, planners and planning commissioners have been aware that our zoning outcomes often protect the interests of our wealthier residents at the expense of the poorer ones. And we have become further aware that the results of those outcomes are not race, ethnicity, or gender neutral. They hurt households headed by Black and Brown and

Hispanic people, and by women, and by those experiencing disabilities, more than others. The role of zoning in excluding some people from housing and employment opportunities, and from the wealth generation that comes from home ownership in a safe neighborhood, was well documented in Richard Rothstein's insightful book *The Color of Law*. But the publication of that book in 2018 was not the start of concern over zoning inequities; it simply documented what many planners had known for a long time. In fact, concern over zoning equity has grown almost in tandem with concern about housing affordability, because those with the fewest economic resources are those hurt most by unaffordable housing.

But there is an even more important reason to focus on zoning equity: It is the right thing to do. Despite the ebbs and flows of political rhetoric and interest in social equity over time, I think most Americans—and an even greater percentage of planners—understand that structural racism is real and is embedded in many parts of our American economy and culture. But that does not mean that zoning should be used to reinforce it or compound the disparities in income, wealth, and opportunities that our economy produces. In fact, the aspirational principles of the American Institute of Certified Planners call for the profession to pay particular attention to how planning and zoning decisions affect disadvantaged populations and to highlight and change those outcomes. As the Civil Rights Act of 1964 shows, our society becomes fairer when we decide to make it fairer. Since zoning happens mostly at the local level, most of the decisions to make it fairer will happen there, and I want to encourage planners and appointed and elected officials to do exactly that.

This book is about how to address these three key challenges—affordability, equity, and sustainability—through zoning changes. But first, it explores the unwanted outcomes of current zoning systems and the thought mistakes that have led us here. Chapter 1 discusses growing criticisms that current zoning systems have contributed to unaffordable housing, unfair treatment of disadvantaged populations, and unsustainable development patterns. Spoiler alert: They have, and their impact has been significant. For those who do not live and breathe zoning for a living, Chapter 2 outlines how zoning works, not only mechanically but in terms of its DNA of exclusion. Like all tools, zoning was designed to do a specific job, and it is important to understand how and why trying to make it do something else will be difficult. It also breaks down zoning into its component parts: (1) the regulations, (2) the procedures, and (3) the map. In my experience, understanding that zoning involves these just these three elements helps people feel less overwhelmed by the details of zoning and more confident that it can be fixed. Each of these three elements of zoning contributes to unaffordable, inequitable, and unsustainable zoning, and the fixes vary depending on which of these three elements you are working on.

Chapter 3 explores how this happened; how we got into a situation where a very powerful legal tool routinely fails to produce the communities we said we wanted. More specifically, it identifies five important "thought mistakes" we make when we draft zoning regulations and maps. I use that phrase because I think many of the problems with current zoning arise from assumptions about how zoning works and shapes our communities that are not true. Most important among those mistakes is the fact that we overfocus on the forms of new development that we want when most zoning decisions concern reuse, repurposing, and redevelopment of buildings that we already have. We treat the zoning drafting process as if we were checking the boxes of nice things we are ordering on our new car, when we know in our hearts that we will need to drive the current car for many more years.

Chapters 4, 5, and 6 address each of the key elements of zoning in turn: the rules, the procedures, and the map. Chapter 4 starts with the heart of zoning: the regulations and incentives that govern who can do what with their property. Without those rules, there is no zoning. The zoning map simply applies those rules to the face of the earth. Three subsections of Chapter 4 address each of the three key zoning challenges in turn.

Chapter 5 tackles how to fix zoning procedures. In many cases, the procedures used to apply and change zoning rules create barriers to affordability, equity, and sustainability as great as—or greater than—the rules themselves. Because zoning procedures are subject to several constraints imposed by the US Constitution and federal law, we begin with a short overview of these constraints and how they affect the zoning changes available to local government. We also discuss the appropriate role of the public in different types of zoning decisions. Chapter 5 concludes with ways to redesign costly, time-consuming, unpredictable, and unfair procedures to achieve the types of communities we say we want.

Chapter 6 addresses the third leg of the zoning stool: the zoning map. Because maps are visual, many community residents think that the zoning map *is* zoning, and they assume that fixing the map will fix zoning. This is particularly true for those who are focused on the fact that zoning maps often reflect the redline maps produced by the U.S. government in the 1930s.

But it is not that simple—not even close. The maps simply apply the zoning rules. While there are many map changes that could help erase the worst effects of the original redline maps, many of those changes could also be achieved through changes to zoning rules and incentives. More seriously, some of the most obvious ways in which the shadows of redlining might be extracted from our current zoning maps could harm the very populations hurt most badly by redlining in the first place. Chapter 6 discusses how to avoid that result.

Now we get to the fun part. There are inherent tensions between the zoning changes suggested in Chapters 4, 5, and 6. Some changes that would promote housing affordability may do so at the expense of equity or sustainability. And some changes that would improve zoning equity will exact a price in terms of sustainability or affordability. There is no silver bullet that will hit all three targets at once, but that is not an excuse for inaction. All planning and zoning involves tradeoffs between different public goals, and we make those decisions all the time. Because the "right" way to balance these interests will vary depending on the local economy, political will, and the desires of the neighborhoods most affected by the proposed change, Chapter 7 cannot tell you what that answer is. Instead, it lists six principles to use in debating the tradeoffs involved in each proposed zoning change so that the community can move forward with thoughtful zoning changes that avoid perpetuating the mistakes of the past.

Chapter 8 broadens the focus beyond the key challenges of affordability, equity, and sustainability to identify five principles that will lead to more effective and efficient zoning in general. To highlight just two of them, we need to increase our focus on reuse and redevelopment, and we need to remove outdated regulations before thinking about adding new ones. The five principles are drawn from my thirty-year career partnering with communities to draft new zoning codes. If you do something long enough you begin to notice patterns and practices that are helpful for the successful operation of a zoning system regardless of the specific goals of a given community. Chapter 8 is my attempt to summarize those lessons.

The audience for this book are the planners and appointed and elected officials who draft and apply zoning codes on a daily basis. It is not a compendium of research, and its intended audience is not the academic community. So while it contains many observations about our residents, our communities, the global and US economies, and likely zoning and market outcomes, it does not try to prove that each of those observations is true.

Where possible, I have included endnotes supporting why things are the way they are—or why they will turn out the way I think they will turn out. But there will no doubt be statements for which you would like to see a citation and there is none. If you have doubts that the statement or assumption is correct and the lack of a citation bothers you, I suggest you skip over that statement but then see whether the other reasons and sources behind the recommendation still make it persuasive to you.

A few final thoughts before you start reading. First, most of my experience as a zoning consultant has been with medium and large cities, so I think the content of the book is particularly relevant to those types of communities. If yours is a small or rural community, just keep in mind that zoning has to be tailored to the administrative and financial capacities of the government that will operate it. Smaller communities generally need simpler zoning systems.

Second, I have kept the focus of the book on zoning (and in a few cases related subdivision) regulations—that is, the legal system of urban governance that allows the city or county to regulate the use and development of land. Although zoning rules are sometimes accompanied by money incentives (and we discuss the effective use of those for housing affordability in Chapter 4), I am not a fan of "just add money" solutions. Many problems are easier to solve if you pour money on them, but money to fund government programs is always in short supply. With the exception noted above, the book does not assume that communities will be able to add money to make the recommended zoning changes work.

Third, even though I think it is essential that we improve zoning equity, discussing how to do it can be a sensitive subject, because it requires you to name who has been hurt by current zoning systems. I have consulted several sources in an attempt to find appropriate terminology, most of which have encouraged writers to use the most accurate and noneuphemistic terms possible in order to promote accurate understanding of each statement. I have used the terms "Black," "Brown," "Hispanic," "White," and "White non-Hispanic" when referring to specific racial and ethnic and communities affected by zoning. I have used the phrase "historically disadvantaged" to refer to a broader group of communities that I think have experienced disproportionately negative zoning outcomes under our current zoning systems. That phrase includes Black and Brown and Hispanic communities but also women and people experiencing disabilities. As discussed in the pages that follow, it also indirectly includes Americans with low or very low incomes. If the use of these terms gives you offense, I apologize in advance.

Finally, although I have spent most of my career with the firm of Clarion Associates, the opinions and recommendations in this book are mine alone and should not be attributed to the firm as a whole or any individual in the firm. Throughout my career, I have found that most community residents, planners, and appointed and elected officials appreciate clear discussions of difficult zoning topics even if they disagree with my conclusions. I hope you will do the same.

CHAPTER 1

The Dangerous Consequences of Current Zoning

I started my first book (*A Better Way to Zone*) with the line "zoning is not a sexy topic," and I have had that line quoted back to me scores of times since then. But I may have been wrong. In the last few years it seems that zoning *is* a sexy topic—or at least a hot topic (which is not the same). If zoning were a sexy topic, our discussions would focus on how it can help us govern our cities and counties well. Instead, most recent discussion seems to focus on how many problems zoning has caused. More specifically, the discussions often blame zoning for making it difficult for our nation to address three pressing challenges. Zoning is accused of (1) seriously compounding the affordable housing crisis, (2) perpetuating and exacerbating segregation of Americans based on race, class, and income, and (3) failing to make development more sustainable in light of climate change.

Those are serious allegations, and all three are at least partially true. But that does not have to be the case. Although typical zoning powers and the ways we use them have many weaknesses, they are also deeply embedded in most local government operations. Governance laws and practices tend to evolve slowly as the benefits of change become clear—not to planners (who often advocate for change) but to the elected officials who have to weigh the benefits of change against its costs. Although at least one author has argued that zoning as a system of land use regulation is so flawed that it should be abandoned,[1] this book assumes that the majority our local governments will not be repealing their zoning controls anytime soon. Instead, the chapters that follow suggest many ways in which zoning regulations could be drafted and implemented in ways that promote more affordable, equitable, and sustainable development and redevelopment.

At the start, however, we need to recognize that some of the criticisms of zoning seem to target theoretical forms of use-based or form-based zoning that are rarely found in the real world. As an example, critiques based on the fact that use-based zoning separates uses or create single-purpose zoning ignore the fact that many cities and counties have for decades allowed or required mixes of residential types and densities in some zone districts. Many others have adopted mixed-use zones that allow, incentivize, or require mixes of residential and nonresidential uses within a parcel or development. And they often allow these mixes by right (i.e., without the need for special approvals). The most notable example of single-purpose zoning in common use is zone districts that allow only single-family homes as primary uses of land. While that is a serious problem that should be and is being addressed, it is a mistake to visualize current zoning as a collection of zones, each of which allows only one or a few uses, because that is not the case.

Similarly, it is a mistake to think that form-based zoning does not regulate permitted uses of the allowed building forms. All form-based controls currently in use do regulate uses, although they sometimes do so with a lighter hand than they might otherwise. More generally, it is a mistake to mentally categorize current zoning codes as either use-based or form-based, since all zoning ordinances include a mix of both use and form controls regardless of the name attached to them. The differences between what are commonly called use-based and form-based zoning controls are discussed in more detail in Section 2.2. This book discusses the shortcomings of current zoning and suggestions for fixing zoning based on the types of ordinances actually in use—not conceptual models that are not adopted by local governments.

1.1. The History and Law of Zoning

The history of zoning is complex, and somewhat troubled, and discussed in detail in *A Better Way to Zone*. But it is not repeated here. However, one important change to our understanding of zoning history has taken place since that book was published. In *The Color of Law*, Richard Rothstein[2] reviewed in depth the various ways in which racism is embedded in the laws and practices of federal, state, and local governments—and zoning is one of his key examples. That is an extremely important book that should be read by anyone interested in the fairness of US governance. The importance of that book on how we should understand the history of zoning is discussed in more detail in Section 1.3. In addition, key legal principles that affect how zoning can be improved are discussed in Section 5.1.

1.2. Zoning and Affordability

Over the past two decades, the cost of both rental and for-sale housing has risen much faster than American wages, which has led to a serious housing crisis that now affects most low- and middle-income households. By 2024, over 50 percent of the nation's renters were paying over 30 percent of their income for housing, 30 percent were paying over 50 percent for housing, and many households whose income would have supported a mortgage 20 years ago were now far from being able to do so. The national housing deficit is measured in millions of units, and many major metro areas have deficits of over 100,000 units. The most powerful force contributing to this crisis is inadequate housing production. Rent and price increases are unlikely to slow down or fall unless the nation produces many, many more housing units. And while land and material costs, mortgage rates, and shortages of skilled labor all contribute to this challenge, zoning is also at fault. The failures of zoning for affordability include the following:

1. *Too many predominantly single-household zones.* While a home for one family with a large yard may constitute the American Dream for many, it comes at a very high cost. Low-density residential zoning is expensive to build in the short run, provides housing for relatively few people per acre of land, requires longer pipes and wires to serve, and is more expensive to maintain over the years. All of that drives up housing costs.
2. *Too much land in predominantly single-household zones.* As documented by a National Zoning Atlas compiled for many states over the past few years,[3] 50 to 70 percent of the land in many American communities is reserved for single-household homes, which means that land is not available for more affordable and mixed-income forms of housing.
3. *Too little inclusion of accessory dwelling units (ADUs).* Despite strong evidence that allowing accessory dwelling units does not significantly

change the character of neighborhoods or create negative impacts on their neighbors, many codes still do not allow ADUs, allow them only after complex review procedures, or impose strict design and parking requirements that discourage their construction.

4. *Too little inclusion of missing middle housing.* The helpful term "missing middle housing" was defined by Opticos Design founder Dan Parolek to include triplexes, fourplexes, cottage courts, co-housing, and small apartment buildings. But despite much research showing their potential to dramatically improve housing affordability, few zoning ordinances list or allow these types of housing, or they allow them only in high-density zoning districts or only after discretionary approval procedures.
5. *Too little inclusion of manufactured housing and tiny homes.* Despite the popularity of tiny homes as a discussion topic and the documented affordability of manufactured homes—both in parks and on individual lots—many codes do not mention either type of housing, and some codes that do have a manufactured or tiny home district have not mapped any lands into that zone.
6. *Too many occupancy restrictions.* Many codes include limits on the number of unrelated people—usually between two and five—who can occupy a dwelling unit, regardless of the size of the dwelling unit. As rents or mortgage payments rise, the ability to take in additional renters or to rent out rooms is not available.
7. *High off-street parking requirements.* Although evidence shows that requirements for one or two (or more) off-street parking spaces have a very significant impact on housing costs, many codes still retain these types of standards and do not offer adjustments based on the urban or suburban context in which the housing is located.
8. *Artificial limits on residential density.* Many codes still apply minimum-lot-area-per-dwelling-unit standards to multihousehold development, or apply low floor area ratios (FARs) to both single-household and multihousehold development, both of which artificially limit the number of dwelling units that can be constructed on a parcel even if the proposed development complies with all other zoning standards.
9. *Discretionary approval processes.* Although some communities allow missing middle housing and multihousehold development by right in medium- and higher-density zoning districts, others still require

an unpredictable discretionary approval process—even for housing that matches the intended development character of the district.

10. *Add-on design review requirements.* Instead of adopting objective design standards for different types of development, many codes still require an additional layer of discretionary design review even if the housing use itself is a by-right use in that location.

1.3. Zoning and Equity

In *The Color of Law,* Richard Rothstein[4] accurately points out how land use zoning was originally proposed—and successfully defended as a constitutional exercise of local authority—as a Plan B. Land use zoning was a response after the US Supreme Court invalidated overt racial zoning (i.e., local prohibitions on Black people owning property in some zoning districts) in the case of *Buchanan v. Warley.*[5] The use of zoning regulation to promote and perpetuate racial and class segregation did not just occur soon after the *Buchanan* decision. Those motives were explicitly stated and highlighted as reasons why the use of land use zoning should be upheld as constitutional, and in the 1926 case of *Village of Euclid v. Ambler Realty Co.*[6] the US Supreme Court agreed that it was constitutional.

The power to exclude unwanted land uses and forms of development has always been the core strength of zoning, but *The Color of Law* helped us understand that racial and class exclusion was a driving force in the design of those tools. Whether or not individual local officials have been motivated by desires to exclude races or classes, zoning has been remarkably effective in creating land use patterns that do just that. That should make today's planners and appointed officials very sensitive to who is being excluded by zoning and how each proposed zoning change perpetuates, increases, or decreases segregation in our communities.

The key ways in which zoning has created or perpetuated racial, ethnic, or class segregation in America's communities include the following:

1. *Redlining.* Many current zoning maps look suspiciously like the maps issued by the federal government beginning in 1937 to guide

residential lenders to areas of perceived lower lending risks; maps that were themselves explicitly based on the race, ethnicity, income, or class of the populations in each area.

2. *Concentrating polluting land uses.* Many zoning ordinances concentrate polluting land uses in a few areas but then allow residential development in or close to those areas, resulting in documented higher environmental risks and poorer health and longevity to the disproportionately Black, Brown, Hispanic, and poor residents of those areas.
3. *Limits on entry-level commercial activities.* Many zoning ordinances still prohibit or significantly limit the ability to engage in disfavored businesses in many zone districts based on their perceptions of the clientele or operators of those businesses, even though there are few if any documented negative impacts of those uses. Disfavored activities sometimes include hair and nail salons, tire shops, thrift stores, check cashing facilities, day labor halls, or hookah bars, all of which can provide needed services and employment to historically disadvantaged communities.
4. *Strict limits on group homes.* While the federal Fair Housing Act prohibits many types of discrimination against people experiencing physical or mental disabilities, many codes still try to exclude group homes from low-density residential neighborhoods or apply expensive additional standards, or they require complex (and often contentious) approval procedures. In addition, many codes make it difficult to locate group living facilities for those not protected by the Fair Housing Act, such as the homeless, those being diverted from or released from the criminal justice system, or victims of domestic abuse.
5. *Strict limits on home occupations.* Those with fewer financial resources often cannot afford to pay for housing for their families and also pay for a separate place of business to earn the money they need to keep their families housed and fed. While newer zoning codes often take a more flexible approach to income-earning activities allowed in the home, many still prohibit the very types of activities or uses of accessory structures and yards needed to make a home business viable.
6. *Complex development and design standards.* While intended to improve the appearance of a community, complex development and

design standards make it harder for smaller developers and businesses to compete with larger and better-funded companies.

7. *Complex and time-consuming development approval procedures.* The longer and more complex the development approval procedure, the harder it is for those with limited English proficiency, limited financial resources, and no professional help to get a development approval. The complexity and uncertainty of zoning procedures discourage many from even applying.

In addition to the types of regulations listed above, almost any zoning regulation that increases the cost of housing, development, or opening or operating a new business creates disproportionate impacts on households headed by Black or Brown people, women, and people experiencing disabilities. That is because each of these populations has significantly lower incomes than the American population as a whole.[7]

Because of the seriousness of these zoning outcomes, the American Planning Association has produced both a *Planning for Equity Policy Guide*[8] and an *Equity in Zoning Policy Guide*[9] listing specific changes that local governments can make to their planning and zoning policies and regulations to address these issues. In the chapters that follow, I present some of the ways in which zoning can be changed to reduce the very negative impact zoning has had on historically disadvantaged populations.

1.4. Zoning and Sustainability

The ways in which zoning regulations discourage environmentally sustainable development are many and serious. At a minimum they include the following:

8. *Not allowing enough mixed use.* Many codes still discourage healthy mixes of residential and nonresidential uses that require longer driving, biking, and walking distances between the places where we live, work, play, educate, and consume public services. Avoidable driving is a significant contributor to greenhouse gases.
9. *Missing connections.* Many codes still do not require the types of sidewalk, trail, path, and bicycle connections that would encourage

walking and biking as alternatives to driving for shorter trips. This, too, increases greenhouse gas emissions and discourages forms of safe exercise that could help address America's obesity challenges.

10. *Limiting renewable energy.* Many codes unnecessarily restrict the locations in which wind, solar, and geothermal energy can be produced, distributed, and used, as well as failing to support the rising need for electric vehicle charging stations and alternative fuel stations. Allowing more and easier use of renewable energy can accelerate the retirement of fossil fueled generating plants.
11. *Limiting local food production.* Because growing food was long considered a rural rather than urban activity, many zoning codes still restrict or prohibit community agriculture, farmers' markets, and other venues where local food can be sold to the public. This contributes to greenhouse gas emissions by requiring more food to be packaged and shipped over greater distances and increases reliance on processed or packaged foods that may not be good for your health.
12. *Failing to reflect rising climate risks.* Many ordinances do not take into account predicted sea level rise, increased likelihood of flooding due to more intense storms, or the increased risk of wildfire due to climate change. They still allow new development to occur in areas that we now know are risky and even allow rebuilding in the same areas after a flood or fire occurs.
13. *Not adequately valuing the existing built environment.* Too often, zoning codes include standards that are easier to meet by demolishing an old building and replacing it with a new one. They ignore the energy, labor, materials, and carbon embedded in the existing structure and the environmental cost of disposing of those materials and then bringing in construction materials for the new building.

CHAPTER 2

How Zoning Works

It is hard to fix something that is broken until you understand how it was designed to work. This chapter describes the foundation of how zoning works, so that the following discussions about fixing it can be more focused and productive. Section 2.1 clarifies the DNA of zoning, and Sections 2.2, 2.3, and 2.4 describe the mechanics of three key components found in all zoning ordinances.

2.1. The DNA of Zoning

To understand zoning, you need to understand what it was designed to do, because it does that very well. And you also need to understand what it was *not* designed to do, because trying to make it do that can feel like trying to push water uphill.

2.1.1. Zoning Was Designed to Exclude

Zoning was designed to exclude, and it is very effective in doing so. That sounds like a simple statement, but understanding its implications is key to fixing zoning. Zoning regulations can rarely make someone build what they do not want to build—but it can absolutely prevent them from building what they want to build. The power to exclude anything—buildings above a certain size or height, buildings that do not match a defined form, businesses or land uses that are disfavored, or development that does not meet desired quality or parking standards—opens up opportunities for overexclusion by local governments.

At best, the list of things excluded from a zoning district reflects a balance of the opinions of rich and poor, Black and Brown and White, employed and unemployed, single and partnered, families and singles, youth and elderly, and both current and potential residents in the community. If and when that happens, the exclusions may not produce many unintended consequences. They may exclude development and activities only from some areas while allowing them in other parts of the community that everyone agrees are where and how they should occur and that are fair to all involved. At worst, the power to exclude can reflect the values of only a limited slice of the community while ignoring those who would like to see different forms of development, types of buildings, or business and employment opportunities that are not allowed or are allowed only after an expensive approval process. At very worst, the power to exclude types of development and business activities is an effort to exclude the racial, ethnic, lifestyle, or income groups that community leaders fear would operate and patronize the excluded types of buildings and activities.

The word "exclusionary" should not be confused with "bad," however. It is simply the way zoning works. Excluding lower-income residents from the right to live in neighborhoods with high levels of amenities, schools, housing, and services is certainly bad. But excluding an investor from building a large retail building on a small-scale neighborhood retail strip may not be bad. Excluding high-end residential development from a lower-income community with a strong desire not to be gentrified may not be bad. Excluding commercial parking lots from low-density residential neighborhoods is almost certainly not bad. One key to fixing zoning is to take a much harder look at who and what is being excluded from each district and the actual impacts (not the stated intent) of that exclusionary regulation.

While zoning can also include incentives—discussed in more detail in the Section 4.1.2—they work only if the incentives are large enough to make development profitable. It is an exception to the basic exclusionary power of zoning, but a limited one, as evidenced by the fact that many zoning incentives go largely unused.

2.1.2. Lines Are Usually Necessary

Because zoning establishes some of the rights, opportunities, and obligations of property owners, they need to be enforceable, and for them to be enforceable, lines must be drawn. Each zoning regulation must apply to either the entire community or a defined area of the community, and the areas in which they apply need to be understandable to property owners, neighbors, potential investors, and everyone else. Many zoning regulations apply to a defined zoning district whose boundaries are shown on a zoning map. This is another fundamental point for those involved in fixing zoning. Zoning is almost never effective without lines, and the drawing of lines is how exclusion happens.

There have been a few scattered efforts to implement zoning without lines, however, often under the general heading of "performance zoning." For example, the City of Fort Collins, Colorado, once adopted a Land Development Guidance System that allowed (in theory) any land use to be located next door to any other land use as long as all the unwanted impacts of the new use on the existing adjacent use were mitigated. But it had a short life, because it turned out that many property owners want to know what will be built and what will happen in the building next door. The desire for predictability based on zoning districts with lines and known rules turned out to be stronger than the desire for the flexibility provided by a code without lines, and the Land Development Guidance System was repealed. In other cases where zoning has tried to avoid drawing lines, it has replaced those lines with highly discretionary review and approval processes that can increase the time, expense, uncertainty of development and further disadvantage our poorest residents.

The need for specific lines is one of the features that distinguishes zoning from planning maps. But each of the lines is drawn by humans, and humans are imperfect and subject to a wide range of motives in drawing those lines. Except in extreme cases, zoning lines are not arbitrary, but they could certainly have been drawn a block east, or west, or north, or south of where they were drawn. Because each line is inherently imperfect, it may be wise to avoid drawing more lines than necessary. In fact, the more lines you draw (by creating more zoning districts or by applying each district to smaller, dispersed areas of the map), the harder it is to explain to the public why that line is important to protect the public interest.

At best, zoning district lines reflect break points in the historic patterns of development that need to be reinforced or changed, or the limits of where a new type of development is to be encouraged. At worst, they reflect someone's desire to "wall out" or "wall in" certain types of development or the people who are likely to operate or use them. Because line drawing is the tool by which the exclusionary DNA of zoning operates, it is very important to evaluate who bears the burden, or reaps the benefit, of the change in opportunities represented by a zoning district line. This is one reason why many newer zoning ordinances strive to replace many finely differentiated zoning districts with fewer zoning districts that each allow a wider range of building forms and uses. When drawing lines, the important question is not "Can we find a difference between these two sides of the line?" but "Is the difference between these two sides of the line so important to the public interest that it is worth enforcing through zoning?"

2.2. The Rules

Many of the ways in which zoning thwarts the achievement of affordable, equitable, and sustainable development are embedded in the rules of the code itself. So we start there. If zoning operates through rules, then the most direct way to get different outcomes is to change those rules. Keep in mind, however, that there are at least two other ways in which zoning outcomes can be changed. The second way is to change the procedures by which those rules are drafted, applied, changed, and enforced, which is discussed in Chapter 5. The third way is to change the zoning map so that the zoning rules apply in different areas of the community, which is discussed in Chapter 6.

The most basic of zoning rules are those that regulate both the forms of buildings that can be built and the uses of land and buildings that can occur in each district. For convenience, we refer to these as "form controls" and "use controls," and almost all zoning codes apply both types of controls throughout the community. Although there are no "pure" form-based codes or use-based codes currently in use, it is helpful to discuss them briefly as concepts.

Before I start, however, it is worth clarifying what the term "by-right" development means, because it is used frequently. It means that the application will be reviewed and approved without the need for a public hearing. But it does not mean that anything goes. By-right development still needs to meet all the zoning regulations that apply to that type of land use and building and site. By-right means the decision will likely be administrative (assuming all the rules are met) and will be largely insulated from political influence.

2.2.1 Permitted Form Standards

Form-based codes emphasize regulation based on the form of the building as more important than listing the uses permitted in that building. They often organize their substantive rules into zoning districts based on the shapes and sizes of buildings permitted in each district. Some form-based codes assign names to particular building types (e.g., "apartment building," "mixed-use building," or "suburban house"), but many others do not. Similarly, some form-based codes define specific forms of building frontages (e.g., "arcade," "shopfront," or "stoop") that are permitted in specific zone districts or with specific defined building forms, but others do not. Even if they do not name building or frontage forms, most form-based controls still contain rules addressing the design or placement of doors and windows facing the street and the articulation of the façade in general, since these are important to public perception and usability of the building, but many use-based codes do the same. While some model form-based codes also define forms of public spaces (e.g., parks, plazas, greenways, playgrounds), thoroughfares (e.g., streets and sidewalks and the spaces that people and vehicles use to move around), and subdivision blocks, those are rarely adopted as local zoning regulations.

Permitted uses are treated as a secondary concern, but (regardless of labels) usually categorize uses as permitted, permitted within limits, permitted as a supplement to a more important use, or not permitted. Some codes go further to specify which of the allowed uses may occur in different building forms, and not all allowed uses can occur in each of those forms. Although not really a part of form-based zoning theory, many form-based codes currently in use still require public hearings for the approval of some allowed uses, simply because elected or appointed officials did not want to give up control over individual approvals of those uses. Most form-based codes also include development standards that apply in some or all of the form-based zoning districts to address things such as landscaping, lighting, and signage.

While over 400 communities have adopted form-based controls for some or all of their area, this tool is most often used in downtowns and dense areas where the shape, form, and fit of buildings matter a lot to the creation of a walkable urban environment. These are areas where a wide variety of uses are going to be allowed anyway and where the location of specific uses in specific buildings does not really matter and will change over time without significantly changing how well the area works. Despite the focus on form over use, many form-based codes make an exception for low-density neighborhoods and often limit the use of single- and duplex-household building forms to single- and duplex-household uses. When triplex, fourplex, or other missing middle housing forms are permitted, they too are often limited to those numbers of dwelling units. When it comes to the low-density residential areas that make up over half of many communities, use and form controls often coincide, and a creative design that allows three units to occupy a building that looks like a duplex may not be permitted.

Because the lines drawn for form-based districts focus more on building forms than on listed uses, they may be less frequently used to exclude unpopular land uses. However, the fact that some codes still require conditional use approvals, and the fact that lower-density residential forms are often limited to favored lower-density residential uses, shows that the desires and the ability to exclude are still there. In addition, drafting complex form standards that require expensive construction can exclude small or innovative developers just as effectively as complex use standards that exclude desired land uses.

2.2.2. Permitted Use Standards

Use-based codes (sometimes called Euclidean codes because use controls were the primary subject of the *Euclid v. Ambler* Supreme Court decision), look at development regulation differently. They define lists of uses that are permitted, conditionally permitted, permitted with objective limits, permitted only in support of other uses, or not permitted in each zoning district. They often start with the districts in which the list of permitted uses is narrowest (e.g., open space or low-density residential districts) and ending with the broadest (e.g., the downtown commercial or mixed-use districts).

The shape, size, and form of buildings in each district are a secondary concern. At their simplest, each district includes a set of dimensional standards defining the minimum dimensions of lots, the maximum heights of buildings, and the minimum building setbacks from property lines. These very basic controls are sometimes called "the invisible box" because they define a volume (not too tall, not too close to your neighbors or the street) within which any building design and location is permitted. Other codes go further to include maximum setbacks (to keep new buildings near the street) or minimum required heights (to avoid the construction of small new buildings in areas designated for dense development). Having addressed permitted uses in detail and allowed building forms in much less detail, most use-based codes generally do not go the extra step of defining which allowed uses are permitted in which allowed building forms, but some do.

Although the basic dimensional standards that govern the form of new buildings often do not address the details of building design, many codes include development standards that address the same issues covered by form controls. These often include requirements for doors and windows facing the street and for articulation of street façades to avoid boring blank walls. In newer codes, development standards for parking often require that parking be placed behind or beside buildings (rather than in front of them), a topic that many form-based codes address in a different way.

Until the last twenty-five years, most zoning codes focused much more heavily on regulating uses than on regulating building forms. As a result, the fundamental power of zoning to exclude things was exercised primarily through the exclusion of unwanted land uses. That often included exclusion of most housing other than single-household homes from much of the community, but it also included exclusion of unpopular commercial uses from some commercial and industrial districts. It is often easier to list examples of exclusion that lead to unaffordable housing or limited business opportunities in use-based than in form-based codes. That is because it is easier to name a particular unwanted land use than to describe the building form that usually contains that use and because use-based controls have been in use much longer than form-based controls.

Since many communities want to see the same general types of street-oriented, pedestrian-friendly, mixed-use, multistory building forms in dense commercial and mixed-use areas, many newer codes require that type of development, regardless of whether they are labeled as a form-based or use-based zoning code. They just do it in different ways, and in most cases the label does not determine what winds up being built. Most importantly, both form-based and use-based controls can contribute to unaffordable, inequitable, and unsustainable development if they exclude needed land uses and building forms.

2.2.3. Development Standards

In addition to whatever combination of form and use standards they contain, most codes include development standards that apply to some or all of the zoning districts, and some or all of the land uses, and that are unrelated to specific land uses or building forms. Examples include minimum or maximum parking requirements, minimum landscaping and streetscaping standards, outdoor lighting regulations, and sign regulations. They may also include internal site layout standards, site access and circulation controls, or on-site open space standards.

Development standards can operate as a third form of barrier to more affordable, equitable, and sustainable zoning outcomes. In other words, even if the community's building form and permitted use regulations would allow the types of development we want to encourage, overly strict, detailed, or rigid development standards can stop that development from happening. And when development standards increase the costs of development, the added costs usually affect smaller and less experienced builders the most. The types of barriers created by different types of development standards are discussed in Chapter 4.

When I was learning to drive, my father taught me never to drive with one foot on the accelerator and the other on the brake. He said, "In an emergency, you may push on the wrong one or on both at the same time, and the car will not do what you want it to do." Allowing specific building forms and land uses and then attaching complex or expensive development standards to them is a lot like driving with one foot on the gas and one on the brake.

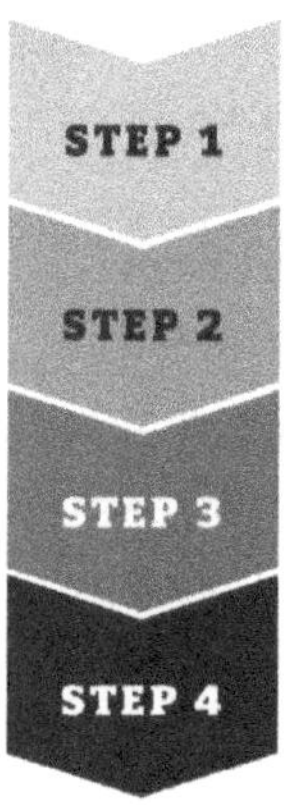

2.3. The Procedures

While most public discussions of zoning impacts on affordability, equity, and sustainability focus on exclusionary form and use rules, the role of zoning procedures receives too little attention. Developers often point to complex, unpredictable, and time-consuming procedures as the key barrier that prevents them from achieving more sustainable and affordable development. And advocates for greater zoning equity point to zoning procedures as a key way in which current practices exclude historically disadvantaged residents.

Almost all zoning ordinances include at least five different types of procedures:

1. A zoning text amendment procedure;
2. A zoning map amendment procedure to change the boundaries of base and overlay zoning districts;
3. A development review procedure (or more than one);
4. A procedure for granting a hardship variance to individual properties; and
5. A procedure for appealing decisions made by staff or appointed bodies in administering the zoning code.

In addition, some codes include separate procedures to review the architectural design of proposed projects or to review their environmental, transportation, or health impacts. Others have a procedure to allow deviations from code standards for reasons other than hardship (e.g., neighborhood-sensitive design or protection of mature trees). Failure to coordinate all the procedures required for a particular development, or to ensure that they are consistent with each other, is a major source of frustration for both zoning applicants and their neighbors. It is also one reason why builders often prefer to design and submit projects with which the community has lots of experience and where the procedural outcome is more predictable. Overlapping and unpredictable procedures act as a brake on innovative housing solutions, new forms of mixed-use, and creative approaches to environmental challenges.

Importantly, zoning procedures almost always include criteria that the staff or appointed or elected body must use in making their decisions, and these criteria are often another major barrier to innovation and to reversing past inequities. Stated bluntly, the more criteria there are, and the more vague or complex they are, the smaller the chance that any project out of the ordinary or significantly different from what is around it will be approved. That is a good way to preserve the status quo and exclude projects and people that have been excluded in the past, but a very bad way to create better communities for the future.

2.4. The Map

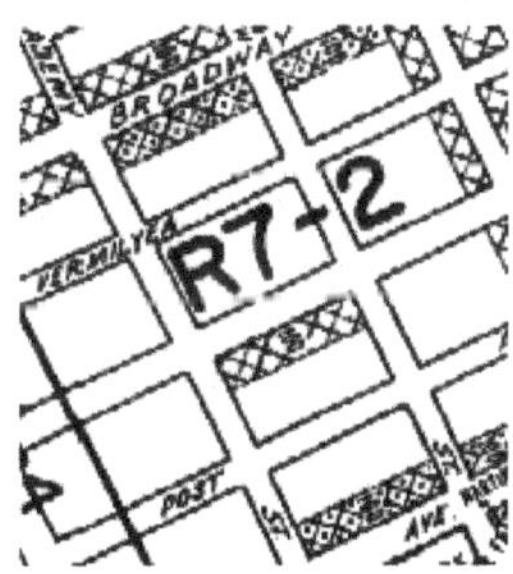

Form controls, use controls, and development standards operate when the zoning districts where each regulation applies are shown on a zoning map. In older cities the zoning map is often eerily similar to the maps published by the federal government in the 1930s to redline and discourage housing investment in some neighborhoods based on race, ethnicity, income, or class. Of course, in newer communities that did not exist in the 1930s (including most postwar suburbs) and smaller communities for which federal maps were not prepared, that is not the case. Importantly, the resemblance—or not—of a zoning map to a redline map is mostly irrelevant to the sustainability and affordability impacts of zoning. The exclusion of most forms of housing except single-household dwellings creates all the negative environmental impacts of low-density development, increases long-term maintenance costs, and acts as a barrier to living in those zoning districts regardless of whether there ever was a redline lending map for the community. So although it is tempting to discuss fixing zoning maps by "removing redlines," the need for reform is much broader than that. This complex topic is discussed in more detail in Chapter 5.

While it is tempting to think there is only one zoning map that shows which zoning district applies to each property, that is often not true. In many communities there are not only base zoning districts but overlay zoning districts whose regulations supersede the base regulations. This happens when the community wants to apply special protections to a defined area (e.g., a steep hillside area) or allow additional activities (e.g., a theater zone allowing more exciting signs) without changing each of the base zoning district in the area. In many communities the zoning maps show this as a hatch or pattern on top of a base zoning district color. But in some cases overlay zones or other forms of supplemental land use controls are contained in a separate map posted or available somewhere else in the local government (e.g., a fire risk map located in the fire department). For purposes of this book, however, I will discuss the zoning map as if it were one map.

CHAPTER 3

What Is Wrong With Our Current Approach

Why—and how—does zoning make it so hard to achieve affordable, equitable, and sustainable development? The answer to that question lies largely in how we think of zoning. As anyone who has tried to pound a nail using the handle of a screwdriver knows, how you think about using a tool may be different from what the tool was designed to do. The pages that follow describe how the ways we think about zoning influence how we use it and why the results are not always what we wanted. And each of these thought mistakes influences the discussion in the chapters that follow.

3.1. Too Focused on First-Time Development

Almost every comprehensive plan I have reviewed in recent years concludes that one key way to address the challenges of affordability, equity, and sustainability is through better, more compatible, more contextual infill development and redevelopment. That is true because no matter how many times experts study the issue, more compact and efficient development patterns produce more economic and environmental benefits than the alternatives. That should not surprise anyone. But while preferring infill development is easy to say and defend, it turns out to be very hard to do. To paraphrase the book of Romans, "What I want to do I do not do, and what I want not to do I do."

Infill development is often redevelopment but not always. Infill could be new development of never-developed land, and redevelopment could occur on land that is not surrounded by other development. But the discussion that follows focuses on redevelopment in infill contexts, because that is by far the most common scenario. Generally, a property that has plenty of neighbors has already been built on or used for something, but that something is no longer viable or the property has become vacant. Once land has been developed and used, the question is not "What should this property be?" but "What should this property be next?" Like planning discussions, zoning discussions often assume that the rules will be applied to an empty parcel of land when that is very often clearly untrue.

3.1.1. Most Development Is Redevelopment

Most of what goes on in American cities—and a fair amount of what goes in more urban areas of counties—is redevelopment. Building permit officials know this. City councils and planning boards know this. Most of the builders and residents who want a land use approval are interested in changing a land use or a structure that has already been established or built so that it better meets their needs or the needs of the market. Although many cities have less raw land and more developed land, changes to the zoning code are often drafted as if raw land development were the norm. Even when a lot has been developed with buildings, and those buildings are later demolished because they are damaged or obsolete, the land itself has been developed. It often has pipes and wires installed up to the boundaries of the lot—or right across it. It may also have remnants of lead paint, heavy chemicals, or other pollutants in the soil. Those site constraints significantly influence the best and most feasible reuse of the lot.

The predominance of changing and fixing old buildings rather than building new buildings is borne out by building permit data. In 2022, for example, the City of Des Moines, Iowa, issued a total of 321 building permits for new residential and nonresidential buildings and additions, while it issued 2,670 permits for residential and nonresidential remodels, alterations, repairs, and other residential changes.[1] That's about a 9 to 1 ratio. So unless you are a brand new suburb with no old buildings that need renovations or repurposing, most of your construction activity is probably improving things that have already been built.

Despite knowing that most development is redevelopment, many planners think in terms of desired patterns or details of development that can happen only when raw land is developed for the first time. To be clear, this mismatch between vision and reality is very much a part of the comprehensive planning process. We want citizens, planners, and property owners to think beyond current reality to imagine a fairer, more livable, and more sustainable future, and we want to see those aspirations embodied in comprehensive plans. The problem occurs when a serious mismatch between aspirational visions and economic reality gets translated into zoning and development standards. More specifically, the trouble happens when the vision cannot be supported by market forces today or in some reasonably predictable future.

As an example, many zoning codes try to "raise the bar" on development standards. They require private developers to invest more in site and building quality than they otherwise would have in order to raise the image or the community and property values in surrounding areas. That is one of the primary reasons we have zoning: to implement planning goals for a better future and to prevent individual property owners from starting a spiral of lower quality development. But zoning standards that far exceed what the market can support and what is technically possible on the ground tend to discourage redevelopment or result in a steady stream of requests for exceptions and variances. Neither reflects good governance policy. The gap between zoning based on aspirational development thinking and zoning that will work for real-world redevelopment needs to be narrowed.

This mismatch between land use dreams and possible future realities occurs because zoning has always reflected an underlying tension between the goals of good design and good governance. Good designers have always considered site constraints when they create a site plan and have always considered the surrounding built environment when they create a building design. Often this requires the designer to refine the design several times in order to optimize the relationship between the building and its site and context. Unfortunately, it is difficult to codify site-specific design principles.

On the other side of the tension, zoning ordinances are administered by local governments that have limited staff and budget to review each site and building design. While they can support an iterative design review process to optimize design in a few areas of the community (usually the more historic or downtown areas), they do not have the time or resources to review an evolving design many times before granting or denying each approval. In addition, in economically depressed areas where profit margins are thin, private builders often cannot afford an iterative review process. The economics of the project depend on a fairly quick and predictable approval.

Zoning should be written so that a property owner can read the rules and be fairly certain about the outcome of their application. If their use and design meet those rules they get an approval, and if not then they do not get an approval. The pressure to balance good design with predictable review often results in zoning that does not adequately reflect the site or market constraints of developed lots. We need to allow much more flexibility for redevelopment to reflect and accommodate unique site conditions and constraints than we have in the past.

3.1.2. Most Challenges Are in Developed Areas

A second reason to focus on zoning for redevelopment is that infill projects are where the impacts of unaffordable, unfair, and unsustainable development are felt most acutely. Because America is about 70 percent urbanized, most of the Americans affected by unaffordable housing, gentrification, and climate change already live in developed areas. Even the largest new greenfield subdivision or mixed-use development will house and provide workspace and schools for only a small portion of the population. Unfortunately, many zoning codes tend to reflect greenfield thinking because those new development sites provide lots of opportunities to design innovative solutions for water use, stormwater treatment, and missing middle housing. That is true not only because the state of these arts continues to improve but because there are fewer neighbors around raw land projects to object to the innovative aspects of the development. Even expensive sustainable utility or mobility systems can become financially feasible for the developer if the costs can be spread over 100 or 1,000 homes. In addition, less popular uses or buildings can be hidden within the overall greenfield development, and their potential negative impacts on neighboring properties can be minimized.

In contrast, infill and redevelopment sites almost always have more neighbors, some of whom may not like innovative designs or engineering or types of housing. And since infill development often has to connect to and work with existing utility and stormwater systems, the options to incorporate new and more sustainable designs and technologies are more limited. Infill sites also tend to be smaller than greenfield sites, so the costs of innovative technologies and the internal subsidies needed to produce more affordable housing can only be spread over a smaller number of future homes and businesses.

The impacts of inequitable zoning rules and procedures also tend to fall most heavily on and around infill and redevelopment sites, for several reasons. Developed areas tend to have more neighbors, and some of those neighbors may face rent increases or displacement caused by nearby redevelopment projects. In addition, the opportunities for successful redevelopment often turn on the ability to buy land at a lower price, and those opportunities often appear in lower-income neighborhoods with greater concentrations of Black, Brown, or historically disadvantaged people. Finally, the smaller and more constrained nature of many infill and redevelopment sites means that it is often difficult to hide less popular aspects of the proposed redevelopment uses or buildings or to make them less visible to neighbors. By refocusing on redevelopment opportunities, zoning can not only influence many more sites and buildings; it can also focus on the potential impacts of zoning changes on more disadvantaged communities.

3.1.3. The Greenest Building Is the One Already Built

A third reason to draft zoning to facilitate redevelopment is that it tends to promote more sustainable communities. The alternative to redeveloping already-used land or buildings to accommodate a new use is to locate the new use on raw land, which is generally located farther from population centers. Greenfield development sites generally offer fewer biking and walking connections and require longer driving or transit trips back to the rest of the community, and that often means more carbon dioxide emissions and other pollutants. Several studies have estimated that about one third of carbon dioxide emissions comes from buildings, and another one third from vehicles with internal combustion engines.[2] Those buildings and vehicles are located predominantly in developed areas where redevelopment can incorporate newer and more sustainable technologies without requiring residents to drive out to find them.

Over the past decades, federal and state regulations have done a fair job of forcing new vehicles toward lower emissions. As older, more polluting cars are exchanged for newer, cleaner or electric cars over time, the greatest impact will occur in the urban areas where most of those cars operate. So far so good. But what about building-related emissions? Many of the carbon dioxide emissions related to those buildings come from the energy loss in heating and cooling them, and the biggest impacts will come from replacing or retrofitting those inefficiently heated and cooled buildings with more efficient buildings. That does not happen when a new building is constructed on raw land and the old building is left in place. It happens when an older, poorer-performing building is replaced by or retrofitted to be a better-performing building, which happens in developed areas. I once heard a conference presenter quip, "The green agenda is the gray agenda," meaning that those who seek a greener future need to focus on improving the environmental performance of already developed grayfield sites rather than greenfield sites.

In addition, redevelopment takes advantage of the infrastructure, utilities, materials, labor, and energy that have already been invested in existing sites and buildings. Everything that exists on the landscape today got there through the expenditure of energy, the consumption of materials, and the sweat of labor in the past. The existing water mains use steel that was fabricated in steel mills that consumed iron ore and significant amounts of energy. Then they were shipped to the city on trucks and rail cars that consumed lots of energy, unloaded using machinery that consumed energy, and installed using machinery that consumed energy. And every step involved many person-hours of labor.

Even a tear-down-and-replace redevelopment project often takes advantage of the water, sewer, power, and telecommunication lines that extend to the edges of the developed lot and at least part of the existing site grading and the investment in streets along the parcel boundaries. That avoids the consumption of materials and labor needed to construct new infrastructure on a greenfield site, as well as avoiding emissions from the trucks needed to transport pipes, wires, concrete, and equipment needed to install the new infrastructure. These savings in energy, materials, and labor realized when existing sites and buildings are redeveloped have led architect Carl Elefante to coin the expression "The greenest building is one that is already built."[3]

That tagline was attached to a study completed by the National Trust for Historic Preservation in 2011 that compared the materials, time, and energy needed to reuse an existing building with those needed to construct a new, energy-efficient building to accommodate the same use. More pointedly, that study asked, "Given that the new building will be more energy efficient than even an energy-efficient renovation of an existing building, how many years will it take for the energy savings in *operating* the new building to offset the energy losses incurred in *building* the new building?" (as compared with an energy-efficient renovation of the old building). That question was analyzed by comparing energy and environmental impacts for commercial buildings, mixed-use buildings, and warehouse-to-office conversions in Atlanta, Chicago, Phoenix, and Portland. To simplify the conclusions of a fairly complex study, the answer is between ten and eighty years. In other words, for a pretty long time, renovating and operating an already-built building to be as energy efficient as possible would result in a net energy savings compared with building a very energy-efficient building from scratch and operating it for that time period.[4]

While there are no doubt exceptions to these rules, they are still exceptions. For example, some buildings just cannot be retrofitted for the property owner's intended use of the site. Others may contain asbestos or other hazardous materials that can only be sealed or remediated at great expense. And there are scenarios where new construction on a never-developed vacant infill parcel with good transit services produces fewer overall emissions than redevelopment of a greenfield self-storage warehouse without transit. But those cases are not the norm. The more common tradeoff is redevelopment of an existing building closer in versus new development on an outlying greenfield parcel. The former has a greater chance of being reachable by transit than the latter, and rules that would facilitate the inner parcel redevelopment would tend to require fewer car trips and related emissions.

The fact that redevelopment almost always turns out to be more sustainable for a significant period of time when both the building and operating impacts are considered is reflected in the LEED-ND standards. When the US Green Building Council and the National Resources Defense Council developed the Leadership in Energy and Environmental Design for Neighborhoods (as opposed to buildings) scoring system, they made "Smart Location" within or adjacent to existing development or in an area of low vehicle use a threshold requirement for sites. The LEED-ND rating system does not just give more sustainability points for sites that have or are adjacent to existing development; they require that type of location as the price of admission. This was a controversial decision, because it required the rating system to say to builders, "No matter how energy efficient and sustainable your development is all by itself, if it is located far from existing developed areas, we think the energy inefficiencies and resource consumption involved in building out there and then getting residents and occupants to and from the completed development are so substantial that we decline to rate the sustainability of your new neighborhood all by itself." You can have an extremely efficient and sustainable freestanding development in the wrong location, and it will not get a LEED-ND rating. Focusing on redevelopment tends to focus zoning rules and regulations on the right locations: those where increased efficiency and sustainability will be offset less by the emissions and energy used to get to and from a greenfield development site.

3.1.4. Redevelopment Reduces Commuting Costs

Unfortunately, greenfield sites are also the places where public transit and ride-hailing services that can provide cost-effective alternatives to auto ownership are least available. While it is true that some less expensive urban redevelopment sites are found in historically disadvantaged neighborhoods that are viewed as less desirable places to invest, the other place to find relatively inexpensive land is in on the far outskirts of cities. But when new development occurs on the outer edges of cities, the savings on housing costs are often undercut by the higher transportation costs necessary to get to and from your home.

Although this factor has become less significant as rates of working from home have risen in the post-COVID era, it is still important to many households. It is particularly significant for low-income families and those whose employment requires on-site physical labor, jobs that cannot be done from home. These types of work include retail sales, nursing and medical support, care for children or the elderly, and in-person social services, many of which tend to be low-wage positions filled by those with fewer employment options. Warehousing and fulfillment services also fall into this category, and they often require workers to drive to large facilities on less expensive suburban land far from transit and nondriving options. The further housing and employment centers are located from each other, the greater the cost of commuting, and the greater the burden on the low-income earners we count on to provide these services. This is why the US Department of Housing and Urban Development has for decades understood that the true cost of housing includes not only the cost of the dwelling but the cost of getting to and from the dwelling from jobs, schools, and shopping sites.

After the Great Recession of 2008, home mortgage rates skyrocketed, but some of the areas with the highest rates were those with newly developed "attainable" housing far from employment centers.[5] In general, these were areas where rapidly rising housing costs may have led some households to "drive until you qualify," to expand their search for housing farther from employment centers to where lower land costs help make housing more affordable. Households that lost one or two incomes had to find ways to cover both their rent or mortgage payments and the costs of transportation, and that combined burden proved too much for many families. The obvious answer is to find ways to develop affordable housing where cheaper forms of daily transportation are available and the distances from home to schools and jobs and shopping are shorter—in other words, in existing developed areas.

3.2. Blank Sheet Thinking in a Highly Constrained World

A second flaw in our thinking about zoning is to assume that each site, lot, or parcel is a "blank sheet" on which the property owner can be required or induced to organize the location of land, buildings, open spaces, and amenities to match our picture of what ought to be on that site. Examples include rigid dimensional standards for building setbacks and parking space sizes and locations. In practice, most redevelopment sites are much more complex than that. To start with, a previously developed lot or a passed-over vacant lot in an urban area often has utility easements running along the property lines (or worse, running through the lot itself), and locations of those easements for pipes, wires, and cables may make the desired locations for buildings, parking, or landscaping unavailable.

This is a slightly different thought mistake than the focus on first-time development discussed in Section 3.1. Blank sheet thinking can occur even for redevelopment projects when planners or neighbors or stakeholders start a visioning process that assumes the prior development and the existing context around the site does not affect its realistic prospects for successful redevelopment. But they do, for the following reasons.

3.2.1. The Challenge of Existing Utilities

Recently, I had the opportunity of working for a Midwestern city that had very ambitious redevelopment plans that ran afoul of this reality. The city already had a quaint, walkable historic core, but much of the surrounding land was occupied by large, auto-oriented, low-density residential developments, corporate campuses, and shopping centers. The city wanted to expand its walkable urban fabric over those auto-oriented campuses and complexes, so it commissioned a redevelopment plan showing a fine-grained pattern of prewar-like grid streets and blocks that largely ignored the existing streets and land assemblages.

While laudable in a visionary "what if" world, it had serious drawbacks in the world we live in. One problem is that almost all of the existing streets had water, sewer, electric, and telecommunication facilities under or beside them. So erasing an existing street means either that the expensive infrastructure beneath it will also be torn out or that the infrastructure will remain in place and make the new nonstreet parcel above it harder to redevelop. And each new street (and there were many of them) will probably need to install new utilities to serve the new lots. Once utility lines have been installed in streets, it is expensive to move those streets and utilities. Zoning for the real world needs to recognize that existing patterns of streets and infrastructure often need to be respected, because most applications are for one- or two-lot projects financed by smaller businesses and individuals that do not have the financial ability to cover—or even contribute their "fair share" to—an expensive relocation of those existing streets, pipes, and wires.

Imagining away that infrastructure because it is in the wrong place to fit our preferred street and block pattern for the future assumes that the benefits of the new street and block pattern exceed (1) the value of the embedded energy and materials and labor in the existing infrastructure and (2) the cost of the new infrastructure we will need to build to replace the old pipes and wires in the new street pattern. That may be true, of course, but it is far from obvious. The value of a new street and infrastructure network may unlock the development potential of previously landlocked areas, create public health benefits through increased walking and bicycling, reduce the length of motor vehicle trips, and increase tax revenues to a point that justifies tearing out and disposing of the existing infrastructure. Too often, however, redevelopment plans assume that will be the case without actually considering the saved energy and material costs achieved by retaining or refreshing the existing infrastructure.

While the decision to replace an individual building is usually made by a private property owner, decisions to replace an old street and infrastructure network with new a new network usually involve the public sector—either as the builder or through subsidies to private developers. In some cases, of course, a private developer may assemble enough land that it can afford to replace the old network with an expensive new one without subsidies from the city, but that is not the norm. The norm is that redevelopment in even a two-block area will involve multiple property owners with different operating and investment goals, so the chances of them ever agreeing on their own to fund the replacement of old infrastructure to make their respective properties more valuable is very low. So if the city wants the new utilities to happen, it will have to make that happen, either by paying for part of the infrastructure or by creating a taxing or assessment district to which the property owners contribute. The way to reduce those costs is to avoid blank sheet thinking and take into account the on-the-ground realities of existing buildings and street and infrastructure systems.

3.2.2. The Challenge of Existing Land Ownership Patterns

A second and related problem is that each parcel of land is already owned by someone. In a perfect world the nearby landowners would meet each other and decide they want to redevelop their properties in a way that is consistent with the blank sheet plan. In practice, however, abutting and nearby landowners usually do not want to redevelop the lands at the same time. In fact, their plans (if any) to redevelop their lots may differ by decades. In addition, they may not like each other and may in fact be economic competitors. Blank sheet thinking ignores the fact that relocating an existing street to the planned location may result in my developed or currently developable lot being bisected by a new street, leaving me with two remainder parcels that are too small or irregular to develop. Making plans that do not take into account the current land ownership patterns is imagining away one of the most serious challenges to sustainable redevelopment. Imagining it away does not make it go away.

Early in my career, I thought that developing a plan without consideration for the existing property ownerships and assemblages was a "purer" form of planning because it was untainted by the messy realities of historic lot, parcel, and ownership lines that might interfere with the design principles I was trying to implement. But I was wrong. The further redevelopment plans diverge from the reality of where utility lines run, drainage patterns flow, and who owns which parcel of land, the less likely they are to be implemented and the more they will cost to implement.

As noted earlier, most redevelopment occurs on a lot-by-lot basis. When the owner of lot 7, block 7, wants to replace an old building with a better one, it is difficult to tell her, "Actually, we cannot issue you a building permit because we're planning to put a new road through your lot at some time in the indefinite future." One of the obvious engines of redevelopment is current property owners who want to redevelop and holding them off in the hopes that maybe their neighbors will assemble the land and dedicate a new street to the city is usually not a winning strategy.

This is another mistake I made early in my career: assuming that "bad" land ownership patterns (i.e., those that got in the way of the redevelopment desired by the city) would solve themselves over time as new and wealthier property owners bought out the existing owners. It could happen, of course, but it often takes a very long time, and the strategy can easily be stalled by a single property owner who doesn't want to sell. Many of the communities most in need of reinvestment in old and underused properties are also short of real estate brokers and developers who are willing or able to invest the time and money to persuade abutting landowners that it would be in their interests to sell their land sooner rather than later.

Of course, blank sheet thinking is a problem only if money is in short supply. If there is plenty of city or developer money, then buying out reluctant property owners, tearing out old infrastructure, building new streets, and installing new infrastructure under or beside the new streets may not be a problem. But almost all cities lack the funds to do everything they want to do, so money is often a constraint, and planning and zoning that assume the availability of money are always vulnerable to the likelihood that it may not be available. More importantly, zoning that allows and encourages private redevelopment to happen without waiting for public money or new and wealthier investors is more likely to weather the ups and downs of economic cycles.

3.2.3. Complicating Redevelopment Feeds Sprawl

Finally, making infill and redevelopment harder feeds environmentally damaging and costly sprawl. When greenfield development standards are applied to redevelopment sites, the difficulty of meeting those standards tends to make potential redevelopers start looking farther out. The same is true when iterative design and negotiated approval processes that may be appropriate for a major new subdivision on the outskirts are applied to approval of individual small redevelopment projects. One answer to the frustration of saying we want creative infill and redevelopment but not getting much of it is that we are our own worst enemy. As the cartoon character Pogo said during the environmental movement in the early 1970s, "We have met the enemy, and he is us." In fact, zoning standards and procedures need to be made easier—not harder—if closer-in redevelopment is to have a chance of competing with the lower-priced land and fewer objecting neighbors that building on outlying raw land provides.

As professor and author Robert Bruegmann once quipped, "The only thing Americans hate worse than sprawl at the edge is higher density near themselves,"[6] but we have to get over that. Low-density residential development—for example, development at net densities of ten dwelling units per acre or less—is bad for all three of the values addressed by this book. Its harm to the environment is well documented, not only because it leads to the avoidable loss of farmland but because of the resources consumed in the longer pipes, wires, and roads necessary to serve them and the greenhouse gases used in moving people to, from, and through them.[7] But it is also bad for affordability because of the higher public and private costs of building that larger infrastructure network and maintaining it over time. Even if all the costs of building and maintaining longer-than-necessary infrastructure networks are placed on the developer through the use of development agreements and special taxing districts, those costs are passed on to the residents of the new homes, resulting in higher housing prices. And to no one's surprise, low-density single-household development is also bad for equity, because systemic biases in our mortgage lending and property appraisal systems make it particularly difficult for people of color to qualify for the same levels of mortgage lending available to White purchasers.

Just to be clear, not all new development can be infill or redevelopment. Closing our huge housing supply gap and accommodating new population growth and household formation will require many cities to expand outward into new greenfield areas. The need for more housing is so great that it will not be filled with only one type of development or neighborhood. The question is not whether America's cities will need to expand outward in the future. The question is whether zoning should be revised to remove the inherent biases that often make greenfield development easier than infill and redevelopment despite its social and environmental costs.

3.3. Wealthy Thinking in a Lower Income World

A third flaw in our thinking about zoning for redevelopment is ignoring equity. We ignore the fact that every regulation, standard, or procedural step we add to the development regulations makes it more difficult for small property owners, small investors, small contractors, and historically disadvantaged businesses to upgrade their properties or participate in the development process. Instead of assuming that the current property owners should be able to make their way through the development process without professional assistance, we sometimes assume that redevelopment will occur when a new owner (with more money) buys the property or invests to help the existing owner build something more or better. The regulations do not say that, of course, but they often raise the bar on future quality or design in ways that will make it difficult for the existing property owner to meet that standard without an infusion of someone else's money.

The rising tide of concern over this issue is long overdue. For decades—in fact, since the advent of urban planning as a profession—most planners have assumed that their job was to make neighborhoods nicer than they were before. When it comes to poorer neighborhoods or those with lots of vacant or rundown property, we hope our actions and investments will make the neighborhood *much* nicer than it was before. And until recently, citizens and residents who attended public meetings and workshops to make the new neighborhood plan assumed that they would be the ones to benefit from the better, nicer neighborhood that resulted from the plan. As a result, neighborhood plans often called for better public investment and more private investment to make the place "nicer." But both planners and neighborhood residents have increasingly realized that with each notch of neighborhood quality improvement, we increase the chance that some of the existing residents will no longer be able to afford to live there. We have begun to experience public meetings in which neighborhood residents ask the city to please *not* make further investments that can only attract more money into a lower-income neighborhood.

3.3.1. Ignoring the Human Cost of Gentrification

Unfortunately, those who bear the cost of wealthy thinking are not the wealthy. They are often smaller, independent property owners and the residential or commercial tenants who do not own their properties. If they owned the property, they could just decide not to redevelop or sell the property, continue operating their current home or business, and enjoy watching the neighborhood improve around them.

However, tenants are usually at the mercy of their landlords. When the landlord wants to raise the rent because of the nicer surroundings, the tenants will have to pay or move out. If the landlord decides to sell the property, the tenants may have their leases terminated. So the tenants who can least afford to pay the higher rents are often the first to move out. As more public and private investments are made and the area improves, more rents are raised, more existing property owners decide it is time to sell the property, and the neighborhood mix continues to shift toward residents and tenants who were not there when the process started. The whole process is often called gentrification, but the real pain comes from the involuntary dislocation of the existing residents and businesses. If the neighborhood improved and no one was forced to move out to make way for someone with more money to move in, the topic would not be so controversial.

Responses to the challenge of gentrification tend to fall into two categories. The first says, "That's just how the process works. People are always moving around in a city, and the poor are often forced to move out when rents increase, even if the change occurs due to market forces that have nothing to do with planning or zoning. The planner's job is to improve the city, and it's naïve to assume that people won't move around as different neighborhoods become 'better' or 'worse.'" The second insists, "Planners should care about people as well as buildings. It *is* the planner's job to consider who can afford to live in different neighborhoods, as well as the quality of the buildings in those neighborhoods. While people may always move around by choice, the government should not be spending the taxpayers' money to make improvements that will make citizens move when they don't want to." It is high time we adopted the latter approach – especially when working with poor and disadvantaged populations.

While it is tempting to think of large real estate companies scouring the internet to pick up bargains in rundown neighborhoods (or neighborhoods where new public investments will probably raise property values), that is only partially true. Many rental homes are owned by the people who used to live in them before they moved to another neighborhood or by people who live in one of the homes while renting out the other. I learned this lesson when I assisted tenants in landlord–tenant disputes during law school. Many landlords own only one or two properties, and in many cases, they are not much wealthier than their tenants. The point is not that all landlords are wealthy, but that those who own rental properties are generally wealthier than their tenants, who may get displaced when property values increase and rents are raised.

Redevelopment planning that does not take into account the limited financial resources of current property owners often means those with the least money will need to move. In recent years, urban neighborhoods near bus and rail transit have become more popular with empty nesters, retirees, and those who do not want to own a car. The current urban renters displaced by those who can pay higher rents have often had to move further from the centers of our cities, which generally have fewer bus and rail transit lines. As a result, regardless of whether the new rent is higher or lower than it was in the old urban neighborhood, the displaced family often faces higher travel time or costs. In some cases, they may need to walk or bicycle further to a bus or rail transit stop. In other cases, they may need to call a ride-hailing service more frequently or buy a car (or a second car) in order to reach jobs and schools. Redevelopment policies that result in increased travel burdens for lower- and moderate-income households exacerbate an already serious affordable housing problem.

3.3.2. The Expanding Donut of Poverty

Although these dynamics of displacement play out differently in different neighborhoods, the overall result is a well-documented "suburbanization of poverty."[8] It is likely that the United States is moving toward the spatial distributions of poverty often found in large Asian, African, and South American countries. Throughout the world, more affluent households tend to live in central locations and in distributed neighborhoods that are desirable because of topography (e.g., high ground and views) or amenities (e.g., parks, trails, or transit). In contrast, lower-income households are generally found farther away from the center and in the tendrils of less desirable land (e.g., low-lying and flood-prone areas, or polluted lands, or land involved in title disputes) closer to the center. Each major city is different, of course, but the poor are generally not found in central locations unless those central locations have environmental problems or title disputes that prevent the owners from putting them to a more profitable use. In many large Indian cities, up to half of the population lives in these areas, often in informal settlements that lack the security of tenure or occupancy found in more formally developed areas.

Through much of its recent history the United States has been the exception to this rule. During the postwar years, households with money often moved out to new developments and suburbs far from the city center. Whether the driving force was federal subsidies for roads and highways, the lure of more land for children to play, racism, or classism, the pattern was the same. The poorest neighborhoods were often those located near city centers where residents could not or did not move out to the newer neighborhoods. In the United States this trend was compounded by the ineligibility of Black households to qualify for mortgage loans that were available to White households with the same levels of income and educational achievement.

While it is easy to point to examples of rich neighborhoods in central locations, for decades it was more difficult to find poor neighborhoods in the suburbs. Lower middle income, perhaps, but not the poorest. Income maps looked like irregularly shaped donuts, but the poorest urban neighborhoods were usually somewhere near the center. Some of those poor neighborhoods were in terrible shape, but others were fine, affordable places to live. They make up what some have called naturally occurring affordable housing (NOAH), places where housing was affordable not because of legal income limits or subsidies but because the property values and rents, and sometimes housing quality, were low.

Now, in the twenty-first century, we are watching the donut hole of less affluent households breaking up and being pushed into neighborhoods farther away from the center and its greater concentration of transit and services. If so, it is due to many powerful forces beyond the control of planners (or any other single profession), but that does not mean planners should not try to address it. Very important among those causes is the high concentration of wealth in White, non-Hispanic households. Among those families, there is an additional concentration in older households that are past their child-rearing ages and free to choose where they want to live without worrying about the size of their yard or the quality of neighborhood schools. Since about the year 2000, those more affluent, often White, often older households have shown a remarkable desire to move into urban neighborhoods near transit, and they often have the money to outbid existing renters or to buy naturally occurring affordable housing and rebuild it as something less affordable.

Just to be clear, concentrations of extreme poverty have long been bad places to live. We can probably all replay visual images of the Pruitt–Igoe urban renewal project in St. Louis being demolished when it became clear that the social problems created through high concentrations of poverty far outweighed whatever shelter value those buildings provided. But that is rarely what we are talking about. Most neighborhoods where naturally occurring affordable housing is found are not extremely poor; they contain a mix of incomes from very poor to lower-middle-income households, and studies documenting the impacts of concentrating extreme poverty do not apply to them.

Obviously, planners cannot significantly influence the distribution of US wealth between racial, ethnic, or age groups, so the trends that have pushed gentrification of lower-income neighborhoods are likely to continue. The point is that plans and zoning regulations that raise the bar of redevelopment quality tend to reinforce these trends by making it harder for current property-owning residents to reinvest in their own properties and by increasing the incentives for outside buyers and investors to purchase and redevelop properties and charge higher rents than the current residents can afford. There is no right answer, of course, and many cities have implicitly or explicitly decided that displacement of lower-income households is an acceptable price to pay for reinvestment and redevelopment of their poorer neighborhoods. Others may decide that avoiding displacement of existing residents is a priority, and they may want to avoid adopting redevelopment plans and policies that create unintended incentives for buyouts and displacement.

3.3.3. Using the Law to Protect Privilege

Unfortunately, wealthy thinking has often been used to protect privilege in the United States. From the earliest days of zoning, many ordinances have begun by stating that one of their key purposes is to "protect property values," and there is little doubt that they can do so. Reducing the unpredictability of what investments will happen near your property almost certainly stabilizes property values.

But zoning controls over building forms and uses, as well as development review procedures, tend to become more complex and detailed over time. As that happens, allowing opportunities for new forms of housing, new types of employment, or creative designs becomes more difficult. The original goal of zoning was to avoid major differences between nearby uses that differed significantly in size, scale, character, or impacts but stopped far short defining required minimum qualities or forms of development. The early New York City distinction between "residential," "commercial," and "industrial" zones, for example, stabilized the investment climate while leaving significant flexibility for innovative or unexpected buildings and development within each of those categories. In contrast, many newer codes impose development design standards that seem designed to ensure that no one nearby will build a building that is less beautiful than, or less expensive than, yours. The goal of protecting property values has been used to justify zoning that tends to lock in the economic and social level of both residential neighborhoods and commercial or mixed-use areas.

3.3.4. Zoning for Tax Revenues

A final form of wealthy thinking is the assumption that new development can somehow be made to pay its own way. The hope in this case is that the public taxes and revenues generated by some parts of a development can be managed in a way that offsets the public costs of serving other parts of that new development. That is seldom the case. In most communities, state restrictions on local abilities to levy taxes and fees or political opposition to paying higher fees, assessments, and taxes mean that most development does not pay its own way. As with many other public facilities and services, the local government collects what it can and then makes up the loss from unrestricted public funds (if it can find some) or outside grants, loans, or assistance.

While the desire to make development pay its own way may be well intentioned, it has serious consequences for the sustainability, affordability, and equity of the resulting development. Only nonresidential development, and sometimes very high-priced residential units, generate more tax revenues than they cost the community in services provided. That leads many communities to overzone for commercial and industrial development that it hopes to attract, both because they are sources of employment and because they generally pay higher taxes and assessments than residential development. This can and often does result in vacant commercial lands or commercial buildings with low occupancy rates (due to oversupply). But it also results in an undersupply of land available for residential uses, which can be a significant contributor to high housing costs.

The unpleasant truth is that zoning does not create market demand. Zoning more land for office development does not increase the number of offices if there is little demand for them. Zoning more land for coffee shops does not induce more residents to drink coffee. Zoning more land for retail development in hopes of collecting more sales tax does not result in more revenue unless the market needs that retail space, and the rise of online shopping has made that a riskier assumption than it used to be.

Trying to balance local government costs and revenues through zoning also ignores the changing nature of real estate markets and development economics. Assumptions about appropriate (and economically supportable) mixes of residential and nonresidential land uses that applied before the Great Recession changed dramatically as both housing supply and average incomes increased slowly after that event. And those assumptions changed again, dramatically, after the worst of the COVID-19 pandemic receded. They also ignore the fact that real estate market demands are generally regional rather than local. Many shoppers, residents, and business owners have a choice of where they locate, and a community that could (somehow) zone for a perfect mix of net-revenue-producing and net-revenue-consuming land uses could easily find its perfect solution undermined by an oversupply or undersupply of zoned land in a neighboring community.

One of the most visible examples of the weak relationship between zoning and market forces is the rise in vacant ground-level shopfront space in many cities. Regardless of whether they were promoted by elected officials interested in increasing sales tax revenues or by planners interested in adding visual interest and activation of the street, many communities now have more ground floor retail and service space than the market can support. In many cases, that unleased or unused space came at the expense of residential units that could have occupied that space. And even a short walk through many older mixed-use neighborhoods and corridors will show that allowing ground floor residential units instead of shopfront uses often helps meet housing needs while creating no adverse impacts on street life.

Zoning for tax revenues is trying to make the revenue tail wag the land use dog. Throughout our nation's history, local governments have had to find ways to pay for the services their citizens need (and at least some of what they want), and the types of taxes they can and do impose have adjusted to do that. They had to, and they will need to again in the future, because zoning is too weak to work as a revenue generation tool over the long run.

Fortunately, the United States has fifty states and over 38,000 general-purpose local governments that serve as laboratories for how to balance revenues and expenses. Eastern states generally rely more on property taxes to balance their budgets, while Western states tend to rely more on sales taxes. About thirty-eight states have some form of local taxing limits, while some do not. Some states still do not collect income taxes, and some do not collect sales taxes, while most others do. In some cases, local governments can approve special taxing and assessment districts so that the financial burdens of supporting new development in a defined area falls mostly on the landowners in that area. In other states they do not have that power. In some states, professional services can be taxed; in others they cannot.

In each case, lack of authority to collect one type of public revenue requires cities and counties to rely on others instead. With so many possible ways for local governments to pay for needed public services, it is much more likely that we will adjust our taxing and assessment systems to do so than that zoning systems will somehow develop the superpowers needed to be effective revenue generators.

3.4. Slow Thinking in a Faster World

A fifth challenge with our current zoning systems is that we tend to think that development processing time is less important than it really is. We overuse conditional and discretionary approvals, which add significant time, expense, and risk to the development process. As a point of reference, it is interesting to remember that when zoning was created back in the early twentieth century it was designed to be by right. In each defined zone district, each use was either allowed or not allowed, except for a very short list of "Special Uses" that could be approved on a case-by-case basis, usually by the Board of Adjustment on a quasi-hardship. Those were often things like hospitals or police stations or other public health and safety facilities that pretty much had to go where they had to go. So the codes included a process to cover those rare situations. Buildings sited too close to their neighbors or too tall for the neighborhood were not allowed. Of course, you could apply for a use or dimensional variance, but that reflected the applicant's choice to enter into a discretionary approval process, not a requirement for development.

Although now very common, the middle-ground concept of "conditional uses" did not become a common zoning tool until after World War II. Conditional uses are those that might—or might not—be approved in a specific location depending on an evaluation of how well they fit in that location. Usually, the evaluation occurs after a public hearing at which the public (mostly the neighbors) are allowed to offer their thoughts on whether the conditional use does or does not fit in their neighborhood. In most communities, the public hearing is held by either the Board of Adjustment or Appeals or the Planning Commission, but there are exceptions. In some (generally smaller) communities the city council makes conditional use decisions, and in some (generally larger) communities city staff or a hearing officer is allowed to make some of those decisions. Regardless of who makes the decision, the conditional use process usually adds time, expense, and uncertainty to the process, because the alternative was a faster and simpler "yes" or "no" answer.

3.4.1. The Unpredictability of Discretionary Reviews

Conditional uses are just one example of how zoning evolved from a "yes/no" system to a "yes/no/maybe" system through the twentieth century. Other examples include requirements for traffic impact studies, environmental conditions studies, transportation demand management plans, habitat conservation plans, and review procedures that involve a discretionary decision based on additional information about those impacts. Obviously, conditional reviews and discretionary zoning decisions have many advantages. Just look back at the previous sentence; they allow closer consideration of the traffic, environmental, and habitat impacts of proposed development, all of which are worthy goals. They also allow the neighbors and property owners closest to (and potentially most affected by) proposed development to bring to the attention of decision makers information about local conditions that they might not otherwise know.

But conditional and discretionary zoning approval procedures also have some downsides. The need to assemble more background information about why the project fits can add expense to the application process, the need to schedule a public hearing and to provide public notice in advance of that hearing adds time to the process, and the need for a discretionary decision adds unpredictability to the process. All those factors can discourage applicants from pursuing projects they would otherwise pursue. This is particularly true for infill development, where the costs of completing the zoning approval process need to be recouped through anticipated future value or revenues from a relatively small project. In contrast, applicants for raw land development approvals on larger projects can often plan on spreading the costs of the approval processes over more lots, more houses, or more buildings. In addition, infill development by definition has neighbors, many of whom may have opinions that they want to express about the future of an undeveloped or underdeveloped parcel in their neighborhood. Raw land development often has fewer neighbors and elicits fewer comments just because some of its impacts will occur farther away from current residents.

I call the time, expense, and unpredictability of discretionary approval processes the "negative trifecta." It's a trifecta you do not want to win. It is a lose–lose–lose that you want to avoid if you can. Getting this wrong affects not only the feasibility of infill development but the affordability of the resulting development.

3.4.2. Mixed Motives Complicate Things

Unfortunately, the prevalence of conditional approval processes tends to increase over time—sometimes for good reasons and sometimes for not-so-good reasons. As mentioned earlier, the good reasons include an increased understanding of the complex and incremental impacts of many types of development on the environment. As we gain more detailed information about the earth and its natural systems through geographic information systems and environmental studies, it seems only reasonable to use that information to try to understand holistically all the direct and indirect impacts of each development approval. The not-so-good reasons sometimes include the reluctance of decision makers to make hard decisions when writing zoning regulations. Even if it is clear that the comprehensive plan promotes wider availability of day care centers, there could be opposition to individual projects by immediate neighbors, so making day care centers uses-by-right in a wider variety of zoning districts is a harder decision than saying, "Let's make them a conditional use and look at them one at a time."

In recent years, another not-so-good reason may be an unspoken desire to evaluate what types of businesses or tenants are likely to occupy or patronize specific types of housing and businesses. Recorded testimony at conditional use hearings often contains statements about personal desires or assumptions about the likely residents and business owners rather than the land use impacts of the proposed use. But zoning is about evaluating consistency with planning goals and the impacts of proposed land uses and buildings, not the individual human beings who may own or patronize those businesses. Wanting to avoid a hard decision that will clearly promote city policies and instead make an easier decision that adds time and expense to that process is not obviously in the public interest, but in many communities that has been the trend.

This trend toward more discretionary approvals is what I call "slow thinking in a faster world." In addition to the good and not-so-good reasons mentioned above, there are many mixed reasons, those in which the good and not-so-good reasons are mixed based on whether you take a citywide or neighborhood perspective. Infill development is one of those areas. In my experience, most recent comprehensive plans endorse efficient and sustainable infill development. And the community really meant it when they adopted the plan. However, each infill project represents change—and sometimes an unexpected change—in the neighborhood where it occurs. So projects that everyone supported in the abstract in the comprehensive plan become controversial when they are proposed in a specific locations. In this case, a by-right approval system would be good from a citywide perspective but not so good from a neighborhood perspective. On the other hand, a conditional development approval requirement would be good from a neighborhood perspective but not so good from a citywide perspective.

Let's go back to the day care example above. There is no always-right answer to the balancing of citywide and neighborhood interests, of course, but few would disagree that the conditional approval system adds time, expense, and risk that will probably result in fewer day care centers being built than under a by-right system. To be blunt, by-right systems are built on the premise that the benefit of having more day care centers in operation ten years from now is worth the pain of having individual day care centers created in locations where the neighbors may not have expected them.

3.4.3. State Legislative Reactions

The tension between the citywide and neighborhood perspectives is mirrored in the tension between statewide and local land use control in places such as California, Oregon, and Maryland. Many local governments want as much land use control as they can get, but sometimes the exercise of that control tends to slow down the achievement of statewide planning goals. So some state governments have started limiting local control in areas where the statewide interest is strong, and one rapidly growing example is affordable housing. In the abstract, all but the most affluent and exclusive of California's residential community plans say that they want to promote affordable housing, but cities and counties have routinely adopted conditional approval requirements that tend to result in fewer affordable housing projects being built. As a result, California has passed a long series of statewide laws, each of which removed another plank of local discretion to deny types of housing needed on a statewide basis.

Similarly, several studies indicate that accessory dwelling units (ADUs) can be a significant contributor to the affordable housing stock over time,[9] but many communities have adopted conditional approval processes that make it easier to deny individual applications for ADUs. As a result, potential applicants know that they will have to survive a public hearing process that will potentially put them at odds with their neighbors, and fewer property owners apply for ADUs. So in 2019 California adopted Assembly Bill 68, which requires local governments to approve up to two ADUs on single-family lots through an administrative (not a conditional public hearing) process. Simply put, the California General Assembly recognized that local actions were undermining a state housing goal and decided that the benefit of many more ADUs was worth the pain of local government disappointment over their loss of local control or neighbor unhappiness about a particular ADU.[10]

The point of these examples is not to endorse California's actions. In fact, many (perhaps most) state governments would reject those solutions, and in some states the courts might decide that they are illegal due to state constitutions or home rule systems. The point is that when the achievement of broader state or community goals is being undermined by local decisions, one potential response is to reduce the number of conditional and discretionary approval systems. In the post-COVID era a growing number of states—including Connecticut, Massachusetts, Washington, Vermont, Montana, Rhode Island, and Colorado—have enacted legislation limiting the ability to delay or deny some types of housing projects through discretionary approval procedures.[11]

For all these reasons, slow thinking in a faster world is one additional barrier that many current zoning ordinances place in the way of infill development, one that many local governments have the ability to remove without changes in state enabling law. Doing so can promote all three of the key values addressed by this book: affordability, equity, and sustainability. Replacing conditional approvals with by-right approvals subject to objective standards could result in more frequent approval of less expensive housing, more affordable types of housing often excluded from wealthier neighborhoods, and more mixed-use development that reduces greenhouse gas emissions.

3.5. Picturebook Thinking in the Real World

Because a picture is worth a thousand words, it is often much easier to explain planning goals and intended outcomes with a picture rather than words. Much of today's planning and zoning practice relies on visuals to help the public see what the different possible outcomes are, so they can choose the one they like best. Unfortunately, when planning moves from the citywide scale down to a smaller scale, those visuals can get very detailed. In recent years, this trend has become more pronounced as the use of community planning charrettes has expanded and 3D visualization software has enabled us to "fly through" a computer-generated image of an area or a proposed development.

3.5.1. Zoning to a Picture is Usually Unwise

Our increased reliance on visual technology to show desired outcomes has a downside. The end result in many cases is "zoning to a picture," a planning process that embeds a particular picture of future redevelopment in the public mind and then drafts zoning rules to make that happen. Historically, that is not how zoning worked. Zoning established rules based on some basic public interests (size and scale, light and air, and maybe building orientation) and allowed private developers to fill in many of the details of exactly what the site and building would look like. Zoning rules were treated as a framework rather than an outcome; the result was more predictable (approval if you meet the basic rules) but the built outcome was more flexible. The path toward more prescriptive and predictable zoning has been long and steady, with gains in predictability generally treated as improvements—at least until the rules become too rigid. The problem is that redevelopment requires flexibility, and zoning to a picture often results in a beautiful picture that no builder can afford to build or no tenant can afford to rent.

More seriously, zoning to a picture runs the risk of becoming outdated—either because the market changes or because we no longer like that picture of the future—much faster than zoning based on a less detailed framework. This has negative impacts on affordability (because those who do invest have to charge higher rents and sales prices to cover the added costs), equity (because smaller investors cannot hire professionals to create something that matches the picture of desired development), and sustainability (because developers decide not to redevelop the infill parcel because of overly prescriptive rules).

3.5.2. Life Seldom Turns Out Like the Picture on the Box

We seem to have forgotten one of the basic rules of life: It seldom turns out exactly the way you planned. We have also forgotten its corollary: Things do not have to turn out exactly how you planned in order to turn out well. It is important to have a vision for the future, but it is also important to leave breathing room for that goal to evolve as property ownerships, capital markets, and economic cycles change. This is particularly important for redevelopment, because property ownership patterns, utility locations, and individual investment and operational goals often do not fit well with the planner's visions for the area. The more detailed the picture, the more likely it is that the current property owner's goals for reinvestment (let alone a potential investor's goals) will not match that picture.

Zoning to a picture should be applied only to medium- and large-scale land ownerships where negotiations with a single property owner can lead to a shared vision or to sale of the property to someone who agrees with the community's vision for the future of the area. For smaller areas with multiple property owners and significant utility or environmental constraints, zoning to a picture often prohibits the type of creative revisioning needed to reuse hard-to-use infill and redevelopment sites. More seriously, zoning to an overly detailed picture can result in no investment at all.

3.5.3. Places and places

All this points to one of the fundamental challenges of zoning for redevelopment: getting the level of detail right. Zoning that requires the redeveloper to build "exactly this" generally has too much detail and runs the risk that no one will come to your party. Potential developers decide they cannot achieve all those details, or finance them, and they stay away. In addition, many builders are builders because they have dreams too. They want to build certain types of development, and too much detail can create a gap between the local government and developer visions of the future that cannot be bridged. Some developers decide to stay away even though they could build and finance the project, but they would rather work on projects that are closer to their personal goals.

On the other hand, too little zoning detail and you get a second- or third-rate development or one that does not help achieve the community's vision for the area. People come to your party, but you wish they had not. The key to finding the right balance is to remember that zoning was created to protect and enhance public interests, not the private preferences of individual planners or neighborhood groups or developers. Urban economies are complex, and any approach to redevelopment that suggests a single model of what success looks like creates rigidity that discourages investment. It also runs a significant risk that what we think is pretty or desirable today will become dated faster than we think. Future residents of the neighborhood may well have different desires or needs, and they may wonder why vacant or underused properties remain that way simply because no builder can satisfy zoning details that are not important to the new residents.

Throughout the planning and zoning process, it is often helpful to distinguish between Places—with a capital "P"—and places. Although this issue was mentioned in *A Better Way to Zone*, it bears repeating here. Not every place needs to be a Place. That does not mean that zoning should not apply to all areas of the community, that neglected areas should be allowed to remain that way, or that the inequities created by zoning tools to protect wealthier neighborhoods should not be addressed and reversed. It means that zoning rules do not need to address all areas of the community at a similar level of detail.

In his groundbreaking work *The Image of the City*,[12] Kevin Lynch showed that people perceive and understand cities through mental maps of five elements: paths, edges, districts, nodes, and landmarks. Those generally need to be treated as Places that are planned and zoned with a greater attention to detail. Over the past decades, this reality has given rise to a new subspecialty of Placemaking, and the art of making Places that people will use, remember, and love continues to improve. As with any new focus, however, it is easy to apply it too broadly or to contexts in which it has unintended consequences, such as decreasing housing affordability or equity.

For example, transit nodes need to work both functionally (to allow easy transfer between different lines or modes of transportation) and visually, because lots of people pass through, understand the city, and form their opinion of the community by what they see and experience there. Historic districts, character protection districts, and entertainment districts are Places too, for much the same reasons. People remember them, and their success depends on residents and visitors being able to visualize where they are and what they are likely to see there.

Educational and medical districts are Places for a different reason. They are often major economic drivers that need the flexibility to add, remove, and change the purpose of their various buildings without each change requiring a public debate and approval. The highly specialized nature of their operations makes it unlikely that elected officials can move fast enough to allow the institution to make the changes they need to make to remain successful. But while their internal operations require a lot of flexibility, careful zoning at the edges of these districts is very important to the surrounding communities. That is true wherever areas of intense activity abut less intense residential areas.

Unlike these examples, however, much of a community is not a path, edge, district, node, or landmark. They are places that can succeed—and often succeed better—with less detailed zoning. They form the background on which Places are remembered. While places often cover much of the community, they are often found in lower-density residential and mixed-use areas and in higher-intensity industrial and service areas. All those are crucial to the economic and human success of the community, but that success does not depend as much on the application of detailed zoning controls.

As an example, most US residential neighborhoods constructed before roughly 1960 are not subject to either public or private design controls. They are often subject only to lot size limits, minimum house setbacks from streets and other properties, maximum height limits, and in some cases a maximum lot coverage limit. Many are considered highly desirable neighborhoods despite the lack of design controls or the relative unpredictability of the type of house your neighbor may decide to build. In addition, most of those neighborhoods are not subject to zoning that requires that specific corners or areas be designed as gathering places or that a convenience store be allowed to locate at the corners of two collector streets. The community's comprehensive plan may include guidance to that effect, but the zoning rules generally do not reflect every detailed outcome that the local government would like to see happen. For these neighborhoods, their status as a place rather than a Place is a plus; it means that they are not destinations that will be frequented by tourists or large numbers of visitors. And that is exactly what they want.

This distinction between Place and place neighborhoods is important for both affordability and equity. While architects sometimes say that "it costs no more to design and build an attractive house than it does to design an ugly house," some design controls do increase housing costs. And since incomes and ability to buy in America are closely correlated with race, ethnicity, gender, and levels of physical ability and disability, increasing housing prices have a disproportionate impact on non-White and non-male-headed households. Whether this was the intent of those who adopted strict design controls for residential neighborhoods is irrelevant, because the impacts on historically disadvantaged populations are the same.

At the other end of the density spectrum, industrial, manufacturing, and employment centers often do not need to be Places. Their primary need is to make it convenient for employees to get in and out so they can do the work that adds value to goods and materials, and then to move those goods and materials in and out efficiently. New buildings in highly visible locations—for instance, along highways or community edges or near residential areas—need to be well designed. But the design and appearance of other assembly facilities, warehouses, fulfillment centers, and call centers is often not very important to their function or to the image of the community. They are generally not designations for visitors, tourists, or most of the general public, and they do not need to be regulated as Places.

CHAPTER 4

Fixing the Rules—and the Rewards

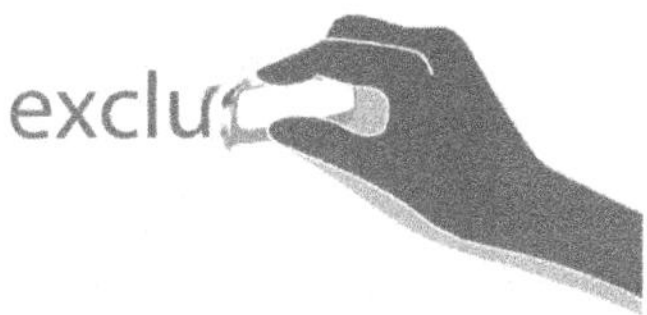

Despite all the weaknesses and unintended consequences of current zoning regulations and practices, zoning can be fixed. Really it can. At least one recent analysis of zoning came to a different conclusion.[1] After describing in detail the racist and classist outcomes of current zoning codes, including those listed in the previous chapter, the author concluded that a system of restrictive covenants and agreements (perhaps like the one used in Houston) would produce better and more equitable land use outcomes. I respectfully disagree with that conclusion. After discussing many of the ways we can fix zoning to achieve the three primary goals of this book, Section 4.4 addresses why restrictive covenants are not a substitute for good zoning.

Although this chapter addresses ways to improve the zoning rules (i.e., the text and regulatory illustrations in the code), it is important to remember that there are usually at least two other ways in which new zoning goals can be promoted. Those alternatives are discussed in Chapters 5 and 6. These three approaches are not mutually exclusive. You can mix and match them to achieve the zoning outcomes you want, or you can try a different approach to get around political opposition to one type of change.

Let's start by emphasizing one overarching principle that applies to all changes to substantive zoning rules: Keep it simple! More words and more standards and more steps in the review process often make only minimal (if any) contributions to mitigating the impacts of development or achieving important planning goals. But they clearly do exclude development that cannot meet the standards, as well as residents and business owners who cannot even understand complex standards without the help of professional architects, engineers, or planners. This is one important way the DNA of exclusion discussed in Section 2.3 shows itself in modern zoning ordinances. Pages upon pages of use-specific restrictions and building design, site design, landscaping, and lighting standards make it unlikely that individuals or companies with limited understanding of development, limited English skills, or limited experience with local government will even attempt to create the new types of housing or businesses many Americans need. In addition, many construction and home improvement companies owned by members of historically disadvantaged communities are small businesses, and complex regulations penalize small and startup businesses.

Too often, the debate about zoning regulations seems to focus only on "Would this make the project better?" The better questions are "Is this necessary to protect public health and safety?" and "Would this make a contribution to public welfare and the achievement of planning goals that outweighs the costs of administering and enforcing the standard and the likelihood that it will discourage historically disadvantaged groups from investing in their properties?" In other words, is the new regulation worth the societal costs of adding one more gene to the DNA of exclusion? Complex zoning rules come at a high price, and that cost is disproportionately paid by individuals and small companies that do not have the time or expertise to unravel that complexity. Perhaps the old advice about the use of commas applies here: When in doubt leave it out.

4.1. Improving Affordability

It is no surprise that housing has become unaffordable for many Americans, and that is true regardless of whether you are looking for a place to rent or buy. The gap between wages and housing prices only seems to get worse each time a new affordable housing study is released. And while many factors have contributed to this crisis, one key contributor is simple microeconomics. The United States has seriously underproduced housing for over fifteen years. The gap between how much housing our population needs and how much housing we have may now total over 4 million dwelling units. A hole that deep cannot be filled quickly, but it can be significantly narrowed over time.

One key to tackling this problem is to realize that there is no one correct strategy. In many public meetings and debates it seems citizens and experts are hoping that an obvious, most powerful, single strategy will emerge and that pursuing that strategy will mean we do not have to pursue other (more politically painful) strategies. That is not the case. The US housing market is so large and diverse that what looks like one shortage is really many discrete shortages in many types of housing. Each one requires different resources and types of housing construction skills and is subject to different housing production barriers. Addressing those many separate shortages requires a "yes, and" approach. For almost every suggested fix to the housing affordability challenge, the answer needs to be "Yes, and we should also do several other things."

Unfortunately, zoning is a big part of this problem. Regulations that slow down housing production and make the resulting dwelling units more expensive are routinely identified as a key contributor to our current crisis.[2] On the bright side, zoning is one of the causes of unaffordability that can be fixed. We, collectively, wrote our zoning, subdivision, and land development regulations, and we can change them. Unlike the local costs of housing inputs such as wood and concrete, the cost of land, the cost of labor, and mortgage interest rates, which are largely beyond local government control, zoning is not. This is a key point worth emphasizing: Zoning is not only an important cause of the housing affordability crisis but also one of the few big causes that we can address very effectively, and the results of undoing some of the zoning barriers we have erected can be very significant. This is not a technical challenge; it is a political challenge. And it is a political challenge that can effectively be addressed at the local level even without the cooperation of state or federal governments.

Consistent with this "yes, and" approach, the pages that follow address housing production strategies (i.e., increasing the supply of all housing) and housing affordability strategies (i.e., increasing the supply of housing affordable to low-income households). We need to stop arguing about which of these to do, because we need to do both.

4.1.1. Housing Production Strategies

The single most important change that zoning can make to improve affordability is to allow more types of housing in more places. Simply put, increased housing supply alone will not solve the affordability crisis, but there is no solution to the affordability crisis that does not include a big increase in housing supply. Although there are many ways for zoning changes to spur housing production, the following four represent the biggest targets:

- Allowing missing middle housing in single-household neighborhoods;
- Allowing medium-scale multihousehold development in commercial zoning districts along collector and arterial streets;
- Allowing medium-scale multihousehold development on properties zoned for religious, educational, and institutional uses; and
- Removing artificial restrictions on residential density that tend to push developers toward fewer, more expensive housing units on each parcel of land.

Allowing More Missing Middle Housing in Low-Density Residential Zones

The key reason to include low-density residential areas in a housing production strategy is that there is so much low-density residential land out there. In many communities, a full 50 to 70 percent of the developed land area is devoted to or reserved for single-household dwellings, and there is a belief that this has always been the case because it is an authentically "American" style of housing. That, too, is untrue.

The proliferation of single-household zoning emerged after World War II, which means that it has been a dominant form of housing for only about 75 of the 250 years of American history. Before World War II, one of the predominant forms of urban housing was multihousehold apartments, so there is nothing distinctively American about dispersed single-household development. It emerged with postwar national wealth, and like that wealth its availability was not evenly distributed among the nation's residents. Single-household dwellings became so common because they were affordable to so many, in part because of federal subsidies. But as that affordability has evaporated, the usefulness of this one type of housing as a distinctively American way to house people has also declined.

Interestingly, single-household zoning has often been applied to neighborhoods that contained other types of housing as well. Rather than zoning each parcel of land to reflect what actually existed on that property, single-family zoning was often applied based on the predominant form of housing in the neighborhood or based on plans that (implicitly) hoped the other types of housing would disappear over time. As discussed in Section 8.4, however, making a property "nonconforming" by applying zoning different from the current use is usually not an effective way to make that property redevelop the way you want it to. Nonconformities—and particularly nonconforming housing—have a surprising ability to stick around over time. So maps of single-household zoning often cover up the fact that duplexes, triplexes, small apartments, and accessory dwelling units (ADUs) are already present and have been for decades. I recently had the chance to point out to a neighborhood of single-family homeowners that the exclusionary zoning area they were defending already contained 264 duplexes, triplexes, and small apartments that they somehow thought were incompatible with their own homes. If there are that many exceptions to your rule and you still love your neighborhood, then the exceptions are probably compatible with a great neighborhood.

In many cases, opening up single-household zoning to ADUs, duplexes, triplexes, fourplexes, and small cottage and co-housing developments—so-called missing middle housing—will not significantly change the nature or feel of the neighborhood but will just allow more of the types of housing that actually exist in that neighborhood. In fact, that is why some proponents of missing middle housing refer to these types of housing units as "invisible density" or "gentle density." The newly allowed types of housing will generally appear over time and on scattered areas as property owners decide to redevelop or to sell to someone who sees the opportunity to redevelop the site.

As a side note, allowing ADU or duplex development in current single-household neighborhoods is likely to result in more housing development in the short run than allowing triplexes or fourplexes. That is because many local fire codes apply the same fire safety requirements to a two-household structure that they apply to a one-household structure.[3] In contrast, many fire codes treat a building with three or more residential units as a multi-family structure subject to more extensive and expensive fire protection standards. That is why in many cities one- to two-unit conversions are much more common than one- to three-unit or one- to four-unit conversions. The latter are substantially more expensive to accomplish, particularly in older structures. In the long run, allowing triplexes and fourplexes may produce significantly more housing, but that housing may be rented or sold at higher prices than duplex units because of the higher construction and conversion costs. Incidentally, the two-unit cutoff is not cast in stone. Fire codes can and do change over time as fire protection techniques improve. Our current codes provide an extremely high level of safety at a not-insignificant cost to housing production, and that balance of interests may change in the future.

In addition, legalizing missing middle housing often does not increase the actual density of a neighborhood at all, because the existing structures were in the past occupied by more units, and those units each contained more people than they do today. In Denver's historic Capitol Hill neighborhood, for example, the low-density housing stock changed very little between 1950 and 2020. It was made up mostly of one-, two-, or three-story prewar homes in a variety of styles and sizes. However, in 1950 many of the homes contained more than one apartment, and the citywide average occupancy of a dwelling unit was 3.51 persons per unit.[4] As postwar wealth made its way through the Denver residential market, some of those single-family structures were converted back to single-household occupancy, and by 2020 the average occupancy of a Denver housing unit had fallen to 1.5 persons per unit.[5]

In some ways, this trend toward lower household size and lower occupancy simply mirrors nationwide patterns, but it sometimes received additional help from exclusionary zoning. Between 1956 and 1989 many parts of Capitol Hill were zoned R-0, which not only required that a housing unit be occupied by a single household but that the adults in the household be married to each other.[6] While largely unenforceable—and later invalidated by US Supreme Court decisions[7]—the designation almost certainly had the impact of discouraging any group of people not related by blood, marriage, or adoption from moving into the area. In addition, between 1989 and 2021, Denver allowed only two unrelated adults to live together in a single-household dwelling. This was also difficult to enforce, and there is some evidence that requests for enforcement were sometimes ethnically or racially motivated and targeted lower-income populations where occupancy by multiple families was sometimes a financial necessity. In 2021, Denver increased the maximum number of unrelated persons in a dwelling unit to five, and in 2024 the Colorado legislature banned occupancy limits based on family relationships.

In the case of Capitol Hill and many similar neighborhoods, allowing missing middle housing types back into the neighborhood may not significantly change the number of people actually occupying the neighborhood above what it was in the past. It would allow new development and redevelopment in which new residents offset the declining occupancy of existing structures that has been happening for decades.

As noted earlier, the strongest rationale for allowing more missing middle housing is that there is so much land currently restricted to prohibit it. Not allowing missing middle housing into low-density residential neighborhoods means that communities have to fill the housing production "hole" in the 20 to 30 percent of land currently zoned for medium- and high-density development. While significant additional housing can and should be included in those denser areas, trying to solve the entire housing production shortfall on a minority of the existing developed land is like fighting with one hand tied behind your back.

However, proposals to allow missing middle housing in low-density residential areas often face strong opposition from current neighborhood residents, and housing market logic is often not enough to change those minds. In the face of such opposition, fallback positions are sometimes necessary. One is to require that missing middle housing occupy structures that are the same size and height and that occupy the same percentage of the lot as single-household dwellings. For example, an existing single-household dwelling structure could be modified to include three units but could not be physically expanded to do so, and someone buying a vacant lot to build a triplex would also have to fit the units into a building the same size as a permitted single-family home. A variation on that strategy is to allow minor expansions of existing structures—say 10 or 20 percent—to accommodate a missing middle housing use because of the need to construct new stairways or install additional fire protection, utilities, or trash and recycling enclosures.

Allowing More Medium-Density Housing in Commercial Districts

The second key zoning change to promote housing production is to allow medium-scale (three- to five-story) multihousehold uses in commercial zoning districts, particularly along arterial or collector streets. And the reasons are several. First, most communities have significantly more commercially zoned land than they need to meet the needs of local (or even regional) consumers. Second, land along bigger streets is often well suited to accommodate any increases in traffic caused by residential development. Third, medium-density housing along arterial and collector streets often imposes the lowest impacts on nearby lower-density residential neighborhoods and can buffer some of the impacts of larger roads on surrounding areas.

By the way, a three- to five-story scale is discussed here for the same reason duplexes were discussed above: fire codes. In many communities, buildings up to about 75 feet in height are required to meet less restrictive fire protection requirements, because fires in those buildings can be fought by commonly available firefighting equipment and because it is easier to get residents out of buildings of that height. Taller buildings have stricter fire safety requirements because of the need for more specialized high-rise equipment and the greater difficulty of evacuation. In some cases, creative architects can manage to get six stories within the medium-rise height limit, and in some cases, communities have fire codes with higher limits, but it is important to align housing production thinking with the relative costs of providing adequate fire protection. However, fire codes do change over time, and new options for housing under midrise fire codes could arise in the future.

In many cases, zoning districts named "commercial" already allow these types of housing uses. This is sometimes a carryover from early pyramid zoning approaches in which residential uses were considered "higher" (in terms of image and protection) uses, to be protected from the impacts of "lower" commercial and industrial properties. But many early codes allowed the "higher" uses to voluntarily locate in "lower" districts if they wanted. At the time, this was a crude and incidental allowance for mixed-use neighborhoods. Crude because commercial and industrial development had more noise, air, water, truck, and rail impacts than it does today, so the adverse impacts on residents of allowed housing uses could be serious. Today, most commercial and industrial uses are federally regulated to produce minimal air, water, dust, and odor impacts, and only the largest, heaviest, and most vehicle-oriented commercial and industrial uses create significant truck or rail transportation impacts. In fact, these days some residential neighborhoods have more truck traffic impacts from frequent online shopping deliveries and service calls than commercial areas have from transporting goods to and from the facility.

By the way, online shopping is one reason why America is overzoned for commercial uses and why future needs for arterial and collector street strip centers and small shopping malls will continue to decline.[8] Our urban history is one of continued locational and functional obsolescence of commercial lands. In the past, locational obsolescence usually occurred when cities expanded and the more affluent shoppers in outlying housing preferred to shop closer to their homes, leaving many older and smaller strip centers and malls to decline or die. These days, it may also occur as more dense housing is built in more central locations and America's aging population chooses to live closer to downtown, transit centers, or dining and arts venues. Either way, dying commercial centers are an outcome of having more commercially zoned land than necessary to meet our needs.

Functional obsolescence occurs when shoppers choose to obtain goods in a different way than they did before. In the past that meant preferring enclosed malls to freestanding stores. Then it meant preferring large, enclosed malls with lots of choices to smaller malls with fewer choices. Then it meant preferring outdoor "lifestyle centers" to indoor shopping malls. And since about the year 2010 it has meant online shopping, which has replaced a growing percentage of all of the above. Online shopping will never replace all in-person shopping, but it does not have to do that in order to hasten the decline of many marginal strip centers.

Both locational and functional obsolescence have produced an excess of vacant or low-occupancy commercial centers that represent the low-hanging fruit for three- to five-story townhouses, apartments, condominiums, and cooperative housing developments. Zoning should allow that type of redevelopment by right in most locations, and many communities have done so.

As we move in this direction, however, we should not try to force vertical mixed use where it is unlikely to survive. Unfortunately, too many communities have required that midrise housing on arterial and collector streets contain retail or pedestrian-active uses on the ground floor in locations where there is little or no demand for those uses. This is one of those cases where—to paraphrase French philosopher Émile Chartier, "There is nothing more dangerous than a good idea if it is the only one you have." While many residents and elected officials like the image of small-scale shopping and dining uses installed on the ground floors of residential buildings, the retail and dining market cannot support that everywhere. When we see this type of relaxed, interactive urban lifestyle on vacation and then envision it for our hometowns, we often forget two key facts.

One is that it does not occur on every street or on every part of every street. Shopping and dining tend to be nodal, and despite our memories of a charming ground-floor shopping or dining experience, we forget or never saw the nearby streets or portions of the same street where those uses did not exist because the market would not support them. Second, we often forget that these areas were supported by tourist economies or by residential development far in excess of the three- to five-story multifamily housing we hope to achieve on our arterials and collectors. And much of that higher residential density occurs in purely residential apartment or condominium buildings without ground floor retail that we never saw because they were not on the tourist destination streets we visited. Our country is rife with vacant ground floor spaces created by well-intentioned but market-disconnected desires to have a mixed-use experience everywhere. While it may be wise to require it in key nodes, tourist destinations, arts and entertainment districts, or other types of "Places" discussed in Section 3.5.3, it is generally a mistake to use a broad brush to apply it to most medium-scale housing. The better practice is to allow (but not require) those small-scale ground floor retail and shopping uses in medium-scale residential buildings and allow the market to decide when and whether they can be supported by the nearby residential and pass-by markets.

Allowing Medium-Density Housing on Institutional Properties

The third key zoning change that could spur housing production is to allow (by right) the construction of housing on excess land owned by churches, synagogues, mosques, gurdwaras, and other religious entities, as well as schools, colleges, and other institutions. The key rationale is twofold. First, those institutions collectively control an enormous amount of land in the United States, and in many cases that land is no longer needed for its original intended purpose. Second, the use of excess property for housing often aligns with the charitable or nonprofit missions of those institutions, in some cases because the housing is to be provided to the general public, and in other cases because the housing will be used for their own employees, workers, or visitors.

Collectively, religious institutions own millions of acres of land across this nation. The Church of Jesus Christ of Latter-Day Saints alone owns 1.7 million acres of land, worth an estimated $16 billion, making it the fifth largest landowner in the nation, although much of that land is devoted to agricultural rather than worship-related uses.[9] However, one recent study found that in California alone there were approximately 39,000 acres of land in religious (not agricultural) use and potentially developable.[10]

Similarly, many public and private schools, universities, and other institutions own significant amounts of land that they may or may not need for future educational purposes. And, of course, local and state governments often acquire lands intended for a specific uses or facilities that later turn out to be unneeded or unfeasible to develop. Taken together, these landholdings—some of which may be needed for their original purpose in the future but many of which will not—represent a substantial potential supply of land that could be used to increase housing supply. That alone makes institutional land ownership worth considering as a potential source of sites for housing development. Proponents of this form of religious institutional land development call themselves the "Yes in God's Backyard" (YIGBY) movement. At least two states and cities including Atlanta, San Antonio, San Diego, and Seattle have passed legislation to help them achieve this goal, and several more are considering similar legislation.[11]

These lands are also worth focusing on for a second reason: They are owned by nonprofits that are often mission driven. The lands are important as a means to advance the religious, educational, or civic purposes of the institution, perhaps not as an asset for which they need to earn market-rate returns. Make no mistake, however; these are not "free" lands. If the institutions that own these lands decide they are not needed for their primary mission (e.g., for parking or for a new church or educational building), they may see the excess lands as a source of income to support the existing buildings, programs, or operations. But they may not need to make the same levels of financial return from the lands that a profit-maximizing landowner might expect.

Religious institutions may view the provision of income-restricted affordable housing as a secondary mission, or as consistent with their primary mission, for which they are willing to accept a less-than-top-dollar return on investment. Educational and civic organizations may view the provision of housing for their own teachers, staff, or employees as a way to save money on salaries for those employees or a way to hire more skilled and experienced staff. A job offer that comes with reasonably priced housing may make the difference between hiring and not hiring the teacher, principal, or public works manager that you want to hire. To accomplish that, the institution may be willing to partner with a builder and make the land available at below-market prices.

Although the reuse of excess institutional lands for housing purposes has grown significantly in recent years, actual housing production faces several significant barriers. While school districts, colleges, and universities often have staff devoted to property development, management, and reuse, churches and religious institutions often do not. The creation and operations of religious institutions have strong constitutional protections, but church leaders and administrators often have little experience with property development or even the basics of the zoning regulations that apply to their properties. But zoning reform can help solve that problem.

Zoning ordinances can be revised to provide that excess lands owned by religious institutions that already have street access and utility lines in place may be used for housing development by right.[12] Mild forms of these ordinances require that the religious institution maintain enough land to meet minimum parking requirements. Stronger ordinances sometimes remove that requirement, either because the community knows that its minimum parking regulations are excessive or because it trusts the religious institution to keep (or arrange to share with the housing developer) any parking areas needed for their staff and congregations. Similarly, mild forms of YIGBY ordinances sometimes limit the maximum height or density of housing to that in the surrounding neighborhood, but stronger forms sometimes allow taller buildings, particularly if the resulting housing will be affordable.

Incidentally, many religious institutions are already located in "residential" zoning districts, because those districts sometimes list churches, mosques, and synagogues as allowed uses of land. Even in these cases, however, YIGBY ordinances can be helpful for two reasons. First, many zoning ordinances state that each lot in a residential zone district can only contain one primary use of land, and if the religious worship center is that primary use then another primary use would not be allowed. While housing for church employees or staff might be considered a valid accessory use of land, housing for the general public would not. Second, the low maximum housing density of the district in which the synagogue or mosque or gurdwara is located might limit the reuse of excess parking areas to only one or two or three single-household homes, which the church and the community would not consider a significant contribution to the affordable housing challenge. To make a meaningful difference, the housing development would need to be larger or taller or denser than otherwise allowed in the zone district, and a YIGBY ordinance can make that possible.

Removing Unnecessary Density Limits

A final zoning change that could significantly increase housing production is removal of unnecessary limits on the density of residential development. One common example is single-household minimum lot sizes above those necessary and already existing in the neighborhood and not necessary to protect access to light and air and prevent the spread of disease. This does not mean that all residential density limits need to be removed but rather that decision makers focus more on public health and safety and less on public welfare when setting minimum lot sizes and on-lot open space requirements.

While the protection of public health and safety is clearly a worthy goal that should be at the heart of zoning decisions, the protection of public welfare has a much more troubled past. The term "public welfare" came into greater use in the postwar period as US wealth expanded and Americans wanted to know that their neighbors would be occupying properties that were more or less like theirs. In some cases this was due to expressed or unexpressed desires for class or racial segregation, but more often it was defended in public as a way to protect property values. The term "public welfare" was used to defend minimum lot sizes, maximum building coverage limits, minimum landscaping requirements, and design requirements intended to assure property owners that nearby development would not diminish their property values. In some communities, the term "public welfare" has come to mean "protection of the existing community character" or "protection of the existing relative distribution of wealth." That turns what was supposed to be a guiding principle to distinguish between necessary and unnecessary uses of the police power into a tool of class, race, and ethnic exclusion. And it does so at a significant cost to housing affordability.

A second example of unnecessary density-based controls is in the common requirement that multihousehold apartments and condominiums contain a minimum amount of lot area for each dwelling unit. While often well intentioned (few would object to requiring on-site open space for children to play), these too have become an engine of housing unaffordability. This is also true when the requirement is expressed as a maximum floor area ratio (FAR)—no more than *x* square feet of building area per *y* square feet of lot area—rather than as a square-feet-of-open-space-per-dwelling-unit requirement. If a developer can successfully build, provide parking for, and rent or sell ten dwelling units on a parcel of land, but open space requirements limit her to seven dwelling units, those units are likely to be bigger and more expensive than the ten units the builder really wanted to construct. Not only does the regulation deprive the community of three dwelling units, but the remaining seven units will be affordable to a smaller number of households.

Regardless of whether a zoning code emphasizes traditional use-based or form-based zoning controls, the better practice is to define permitted building sizes, heights, or forms based on protecting public health and safety and then allow the market to decide how many units can be created within those limits. While this is likely to result in more, smaller multihousehold apartments and condominiums, that can promote affordability. Providing smaller units for smaller households to occupy allows them to free up larger units for larger households, and there is little likelihood that builders will oversupply small units that they cannot sell or rent.

When it comes to housing production, communities should be particularly wary of setting density limits based on "public welfare" or "community character," not only because of their impacts on affordability but because those affordability impacts fall most heavily on historically disadvantaged populations. For the same reason, if increased housing production is the goal, communities should be wary of adding minimum dwelling unit size or bedroom requirements to basic use standards. If more dwelling units of a certain type are needed, requirements to build units that the market would not otherwise build should probably be accompanied by incentives, as discussed below.

4.1.2. Housing Affordability Strategies

Chapter 4 began with a discussion of zoning changes needed to increase housing production, because shrinking our current huge deficit of housing units is the most powerful and necessary step toward long-term affordability. It is also the easiest way for zoning to be effective, because it involves "erasing" some of the current rules rather than writing and administering new ones. In the absence of zoning controls, each of the new housing uses listed in the previous section would have been allowed, so the changes recommended really involve erasing the prohibitions on the uses that we adopted earlier. Similarly, the final recommendation in the previous section involves erasing the density limits that feed the underproduction of housing and encourage builders to construct fewer, more expensive housing units. Each time we erase an old rule that is no longer needed or is counterproductive, we simplify the job of urban governance, because there is one less thing for staff or appointed bodies to check or consider, which speeds up the development review process.

In this section I move past strategies to increase the construction of housing to address the affordability of the housing being produced. I shift from housing production strategies to affordability strategies. But make no mistake: These are not alternative strategies, because there is no alternative to increasing housing production. Choosing to focus on housing affordability instead of housing production is often counterproductive, because many housing affordability strategies can discourage or even stop housing production. Trying to force builders to build only "affordable" dwelling units can easily result in builders declining to pursue uneconomical projects or leaving the market altogether. Remember, we are in a "yes, and" world now.

It is hard to design housing affordability controls correctly—that is, so that housing production increases *and* more of the housing produced is more affordable than it would be otherwise. And it is good to recognize that all mandatory (as opposed to incentive-based) housing affordability strategies except one are likely to slow down housing production to some degree. When it comes to mandates, there is usually no free lunch; the price of greater affordability is often fewer new units. Fortunately, that almost inevitable impact can often be offset by carefully designed incentives. The bottom line is that, if designed correctly, the strategies discussed in this section can be helpful when used in addition to the housing production strategies described in the previous section—but not in lieu of them.

There are three types of housing affordability strategies: affordability incentives, affordability mandates, and preservation of existing affordable housing. I will discuss them in that order. However, first I will discuss the most direct incentive of all: money.

The Role of Money

This is a side trip from the primary topic of this book—zoning—but a necessary one, because laws and money are both key to solving the affordability problem, and zoning cannot solve the problem all by itself. To recap something you learned a long time ago, government has three essential powers: the power to regulate behavior (police power), the power to tax the public and spend tax money for public purposes (taxing power), and the power to force private property owners to sell their land to the government for public purposes at a fair price (the power of eminent domain). This section is a side trip from the police power to discuss the taxing power.

Money is important because zoning can only do so much to promote affordability. It can offer carrots (i.e., land use incentives) to induce builders to build more affordable housing units, but if the carrots are not big enough, builders will not respond. Or government can use sticks (i.e., land use mandates) to require builders to build a portion of their housing at affordable rents and prices. But in both cases the builder can decide not to build the project, and when that happens neither housing supply nor affordability improves. Or government can prevent the replacement of current affordable housing units with more units or newer units—but only at the cost of slowing housing production and investment in those areas.

Every government strategy that may improve housing affordability has a weakness that may undermine its effectiveness, and when that happens money can offset some of those negative impacts. More specifically, money can increase the size and attractiveness of carrots and can induce builders subject to mandates to build projects they would otherwise not build. Money can also subsidize the maintenance of existing affordable housing when housing preservation strategies slow down market investment to preserve that housing.

That is why governments in many Western nations spend much more money to create and preserve affordable housing than the United States. They have come to the conclusion that in today's global economy many workers will never earn enough to rent or buy the housing they need to house their families. And that remains true despite minimum wage laws that try to push wages up and social safety nets that reduce the amount of earnings households need to spend on nonhousing goods. As an example, over 16 percent of the United Kingdom's and 14 percent of France's rental housing stock is in "social" (i.e., subsidized and income restricted) housing. The average for the over 100 members of the Organization for Economic Cooperation and Development is about 7 percent. In the United States that figure is under 4 percent.[13]

As a second example, Finland, France, Germany, and the United Kingdom all spend between 0.35 and 1.25 percent of their gross domestic product (GDP) on housing allowances (subsidies or vouchers) for lower-income households. That figure for the United States is about 0.15 percent of GDP.[14] And Austria, Australia, France, and New Zealand all spend between 0.20 and 0.35 percent of their GDP on support for social rental housing, while the United States invests about 0.10 percent of GDP for that purpose.[15] While it is always difficult to compare public support for housing across the prosperous countries in the world, it is clear that many of those countries with a standard of living at or near that of the United States spend significantly more on housing subsidies to maintain that standard of living.

In the context of the affordability strategies discussed in this chapter, the good news is that many of the unintended negative impacts of housing affordability strategies can be offset by increased public spending. The bad news is that historically the United States and its states and local governments have been unwilling to spend significantly more on housing affordability, and without increased spending each of the following strategies may have limited effectiveness or unintended consequences.

Offering Affordability Incentives

In my experience, almost everyone involved in trying to address the housing affordability problem would prefer to use the carrots of incentives rather than the stick of mandates. Incentives are voluntary and politically much easier to adopt. If you don't like the size or color or shape of the carrot, don't bite. The problem is that the economics of producing affordable housing are often very challenging, so the carrots often need to be very big to be effective.

That isn't surprising. Most new housing in a given location is more expensive than existing housing in the same location, just as most new cars are more expensive than the same car a few years old. There is a general market premium for newness in most products. But that means that zoning incentives to include a certain percentage of affordable units in a new apartment or condominium building need to be big enough to offset the costs of new construction of those units. When costs are high, the incentives to alter behavior need to be big.

Over the years I have drafted numerous zoning incentives for affordable housing and have talked to many housing developers about what sizes and types of incentives would modify their behavior. Obviously, the answer depends on local market prices and conditions and how much affordable housing you need to provide to earn the incentive, but more than one builder has said some version of the following: "I start paying attention if the incentive allows me to build about 30 percent more units or reduces my cost of building the same number of units by 30 percent." As an alternative, some say, "I pay attention when you dramatically reduce the time, expense, and uncertainty of getting the project approved," and we will discuss that more in Chapter 5. Passing this information on to my clients often elicits a groan, because they were thinking of a 10 percent (or very rarely 20 percent) incentive. Ten percent seems to be the default number for all types of incentives offered by local governments when they have not studied the economics of the project. The point is that it is often a waste of time to talk about affordable housing incentives unless the local government is willing to talk about very big carrots.

When it comes to land use (not money, not process) incentives, and assuming the artificial density controls discussed in Section 4.1.1 have been removed, those carrots usually take the form of allowing the builder to build a bigger building, or more dwelling units, than they could under applicable zoning without the incentives. That usually means (1) allowing additional building height or mass, (2) requiring less on-site parking, (3) allowing smaller setbacks, (4) allowing higher lot coverage or less on-site open space, or (5) some combination of the these. In my experience, items (1) and (2) on this list are the ones of most interest to developers because they operate most directly on building construction economics. Items (3) and (4) make a lesser contribution; they are generally smaller carrots. The same can be said for incentives that simplify building design (e.g., removing requirements for upper floor stepbacks and expensive facing materials). They are nice but not likely to result in a significant change to the building economics. Just as importantly, the more things you have to do to earn the incentive, the harder it is to design the building to achieve them all and the more time and expense it takes for planning staff to check compliance. When it comes to zoning incentives, it pays to focus on the items that will make the biggest difference and ensure that they are big enough to modify builder behavior. And an incentive that is based on objective standards – if you do *x* we will give you *y* – is much more attractive to developers than one that has to be negotiated for each project or is subject to a discretionary public hearing process.

Tailoring Affordability Mandates

When incentives have proven ineffective, many communities consider mandates as a possible way to ensure that at least some of the new housing produced is more affordable than it would be otherwise. One form of mandate is a general system of housing rent controls on new and existing housing, but since those are illegal in many states and are generally not considered zoning regulations, they are not discussed in this book. Because zoning generally regulates only new housing construction, the most common form of mandate is an inclusionary zoning ordinance. Before discussing the pros and cons of this tool, it is important to understand how it works.

Inclusionary zoning regulations generally apply to new multihousehold construction projects above a stated size (often five or ten or twenty units) and require that a certain percentage (often 10 or 15 percent) of the new units constructed be rented or sold at or below a stated percentage of the Department of Housing and Urban Development (HUD)-published area median income (AMI) for the area. As an example, inclusionary zoning could state that all new apartment and condominium projects containing over ten dwelling units must rent or sell at least 10 percent of the new units at prices affordable to households earning no more than 100 percent of AMI for the area. To ensure that at least some of the new units are usable by families rather than individuals and couples, some communities might also require that at least one half of the rent and price restricted units contain more than one bedroom. To make the math simple, let's assume that the ordinance is applied to a proposed project to create 100 apartments or condominiums. In practice, both the definition and administration of inclusionary zoning ordinances is much more complex, since some types of projects (e.g., transitional housing or group living projects) are often exempted from the mandate, and since AMI levels vary based on the number of people in the household, which is often related to the number of bedrooms in the project.

In practice, our example ordinance means that the builder will have to create an internal cross-subsidy. If ten of the units need to be rented or sold below the market rate, and that price is below the builder's construction cost, then the builder will need to raise the sales or rental rates on the other ninety units to make up for that loss and still allow the builder to make a profit. If the required rental rates on the ten "affordable" units are above construction costs but below the builder's planned profit on those units, then the builder will need to raise the rental or sales prices on the other ninety units to make up the lost profit. If the builder concludes that it may not be able to rent or sell the ninety units at the higher rates necessary to offset the loss of revenue on the ten regulated units, the developer may well decide not to pursue the project. If that happens the community loses not only the hoped-for ten affordable units but also the ninety market-rate units that could have helped increase the general housing supply and bring down overall housing rents and prices in the community.

Incidentally, it is usually a mistake to try to solve this economic challenge by simply blaming builders for wanting to make a profit or for not just absorbing the cost of the lost revenue by accepting a lower profit. In my experience, many market-rate builders plan for about a 10 percent profit on their projects, and even mission-driven affordable housing builders often plan for about a 4 percent profit. That is because a lot of things can go wrong in a housing construction project. It may take them much longer than expected to arrange project financing and get through the development approval process, and they may need to agree to a lower project size, height, or density during that process. Even if the cost of land is known at the start, the costs of labor, materials, and transportation may increase during the project. They may encounter unexpected site conditions or environmental challenges that slow down the project, and each month of delay increases the costs of holding the property before the rental and sales price revenue begins to arrive. Because construction is a risky business, construction financing interest rates are higher than the mortgage interest rate the owner of the building will face after construction is completed and the construction loan is paid off. For all these reasons, builders know that in practice they may earn more than 4 or 10 percent on some projects and lose money on others. Because you cannot lose money on many of your projects and still stay in business, builders need to plan on some level of profit. Earning the profit you need to stay in business is not greed.

The details as to how inclusionary zoning will work in a given community is often a matter of significant debate. In hot residential markets, the builder may be able to pass on the costs of this internal subsidy onto the ninety market-rate units without any problem. Note that this does not mean the subsidy is "free." There may still be households that could have afforded one of the ninety units if the price of those units had not been increased to make up for the revenue lost on the ten subsidized units. In other markets, inclusionary housing requirements may slow down the production of market-rate housing. The new affordable units are achieved at the cost of fewer market-rate units, because some builders decide they would rather build somewhere else without inclusionary zoning requirements. Where the multihousehold real estate market is weak, inclusionary zoning requirements could even stop market-rate multihousehold development until the requirements are adjusted or repealed. And these types of ordinances almost always result in many more projects being proposed with one dwelling unit less than the threshold for applicability of the ordinance. If the ordinance applies to projects containing ten or more housing units, you can expect to see more applications for nine-unit projects.

I have worked in two different cities where, despite the advice of housing economists, the city council adopted strict inclusionary zoning regulations for political reasons and then quickly suspended the operation of the regulation when it became clear that the economists were right and that few builders would develop under the new regulations. The question of whether the benefits of inclusionary zoning outweigh its costs is a factual question of economics, but unfortunately the local government's answer is sometimes based on political arguments for and against that are not grounded in good economic data.

One more important point: Because the internal subsidies required by inclusionary zoning generally need to be funded through price increases on the market-rate units, the resulting price and rent subsidies achievable through inclusionary zoning tend to be "shallow." A shallow subsidy is one that results in only a few income-regulated units or that requires regulated prices and rents only modestly below market prices and rents. While the greatest need for affordable housing in many communities involves households that earn less than 50 or 60 or 70 percent of AMI, inclusionary zoning generally cannot be used to produce housing at those levels—or can only do so for very few units. That is because, in most markets, the revenue loss to the developer needed to achieve those prices and rents is so big that it cannot be made up through price increases on the market-rate units. Or the local government may be worried that the price increases imposed on the market-rate units would be so large that many moderate-income residents will not be able to buy or rent those units. There is often both an economic and political limit to how much market-rate prices and rents can be increased, and that limits the depth of the subsidy available to the regulated units.

In spite of the mixed bag of advantages and disadvantages inherent in inclusionary zoning, a growing number of cities and counties across the United States have adopted these types of regulations. One study found that over 1,000 ordinances were in place as of 2019.[16] I think this is happening for three main reasons. First, the housing affordability crisis requires a "yes and" approach; it is one of the many tools that might increase the supply of affordable housing, and we need to use all the tools we can. Second, it happens because the internal subsidy needed to create the new affordable housing units is off the books; it does not need to be funded as a public subsidy. In other words, if the builder were not subsidizing the affordable units through higher housing prices on the market-rate units, the city could obtain those units only by making up the builder's lost revenue through cash payments, and there is never enough public cash to go around. Builders often argue that cash payments would be more efficient and transparent, and local governments respond that avoiding cash payments for the types of shallow subsidies possible through inclusionary zoning allows them to preserve their limited resources to subsidize housing for poorer households.

The third reason for the continued popularity of inclusionary zoning is that, in theory, it leads to better economic integration than market-rate housing alone. Several studies have shown that integration of lower-income households in medium- or high-income areas results in better household health, education, family stability, and economic success.[17] Requiring that 10 percent of new income-regulated housing units be mixed into the same housing development as higher-income units seems like a good idea. In practice, however, these benefits may be limited, because the studies demonstrating the benefits of integration generally focus on benefits to households with very low, low, or low-moderate income, whereas the shallow levels of integration achievable through inclusionary zoning often mean that the occupants of the regulated units have incomes not all that much lower than those of the market-rate families in the same building.

In addition, most economic integration studies focus on the results of mixed-income neighborhoods, not buildings, and it is not clear what benefits (if any) accrue to having a single building with a mix of incomes. Stated another way, inclusionary zoning tries to achieve the social goal of mixed-income neighborhoods through mixed-income buildings, because zoning influences happens on a building-by-building basis. A second challenge with the economic integration argument is that many ordinances include buyout provisions, which are discussed in more detail below.

To make things even more complex, four additional aspects of inclusionary zoning need to be discussed: incentives, buyouts, geographic targeting, and administration. Because inclusionary zoning can generally achieve only shallow subsidies, or because of political opposition to the regulations, or because of state law requirements, many inclusionary zoning ordinances are paired with development incentives. To build on our previous example, the ordinance might provide that in return for including 10 percent income-regulated units, the builder will be allowed to increase the size of the project by 30 percent. That way, the revenue loss can be offset through smaller rental or price increases spread over a larger number of market-rate units. If the builder accepts the mandate-plus-incentive and completes the project, the community also gains a bigger increase in the overall housing supply than it would have without the incentive. In my experience, a clear majority of inclusionary zoning ordinances include some form of incentive along with the mandate.

A second key aspect involves buyout provisions, which can take a variety of forms. At their simplest, many ordinances allow builders to buy their way out of the inclusionary zoning mandate by paying a fee to an affordable housing fund, which will then be used to build or subsidize income-restricted housing elsewhere. More complex versions also allow the builder to agree to build the income-regulated units (or have another builder build them) in a different project in another location. Unfortunately for those looking for economic integration, sometimes builders take advantage of buyout options when the proposed housing is in more prosperous areas. Although in theory these are the locations where price increases on market-rate units can be most easily absorbed and deeper cross-subsidies might be achieved, in practice the higher profits on market-rate units in wealthier locations often make it more worthwhile for the developer to pay someone to fulfill their affordable housing obligations elsewhere. The more serious challenge is that it is rare for the buyout cash values to be set at levels that actually allow the local government or another developer to subsidize the same number of units at the same AMI level elsewhere, plus covering the costs of administering the transfer of obligations from one builder to another. Many buyout payments are set at bargain rates that undermine the intent and effectiveness of the ordinance.

As an example, my hometown of Denver, Colorado, adopted its initial inclusionary zoning ordinance in 2002, but the buyout price charged to allow developers to opt out of the obligation was so low that during its fifteen years of operation almost every developer used the buyout option and only about 1,116 units of income-restricted housing were actually produced. That's about seventy-seven units a year, not nearly enough to make a dent in the housing affordability problem. In light of its meager success, in 2016 Denver repealed that system and enacted an alternative based on a pure cash system with a roughly fifty–fifty split of developer and city contributions to an affordable housing fund.

When that resulted in the development of few affordable units, the city moved to an "expectation" that developers would include a negotiated number of income-restricted units at negotiated AMI levels (meaning that rezoning proposals for housing projects that did not include a side agreement for affordable housing would probably fare poorly at city council). That produced more units, but the negotiations were time-consuming, and the commitments varied in ways that were sometimes hard to explain to city council. So in 2022 Denver again made inclusionary housing mandatory, generally requiring between 8 and 15 percent (often 12 percent) affordable units in new multihousehold projects. This time the price to buy out of the duty to construct affordable housing was set significantly higher. Because of the large backlog of projects approved before 2022 through negotiated agreements, plus a significant number of applications submitted just before the new system came into effect (in order to avoid the stricter requirements), it is too soon to know how many affordable units will be produced by the new mandate or whether fewer builders will use the buyout option. I think

Denver's circuitous journey from mandates to a cash contribution system to negotiated incentives and back to mandates demonstrates that the affordability challenge requires a "yes, and" approach. There is no single answer to the affordability challenge, and even imperfect tools will be used and refined despite their weaknesses.

A third key issue in inclusionary zoning design is geographic targeting. Many early mandate ordinances applied throughout the community, based on thinking that new affordable housing was needed everywhere, and economic integration is always a good idea. In practice, however, many of these ordinances resulted in few new units being constructed in medium- and upper-income neighborhoods, particularly if buyout options were available. Most new units were built in neighborhoods that were generally more affordable anyway. In a few cases it resulted in new "affordable" units being built in lower-income neighborhoods where it was unclear whether the neighborhood would benefit more from a handful of affordable units or from more market-rate units, which might actually result in more economic integration of the neighborhood as a whole (if not the project itself). As experience with inclusionary zoning has grown, some newer ordinances limit the applicability of the mandate to moderate- and upper-income neighborhoods.[18]

One final issue for both zoning incentive and mandate-based housing affordability programs is administration. Income-based housing restrictions are probably the only way to ensure that the benefits of public and private investments in affordable housing continue to be focused on households at their intended AMI levels. But they require that someone continually monitor rentals and sales of income-restricted units. That is hard, and it's made harder by the need to verify the incomes (and in some cases the assets) of residents. Given the variety of ways in which people can earn money, the increasing number of people with more than one job, and the hard-to-monitor nature of the internet and gig economies, this would be a challenge even if everyone involved was honest. But experience shows that is not always the case.

And the administrative challenge gets even harder when the income-restricted units are scattered in many locations, or when a building owner's obligations to keep 10 percent of the units affordable is not tied to particular apartment or condominium units in that building. Although often ignored in affordable housing discussions, this is a key point. Affordability requirements are only as effective as the administrative capacity to monitor and enforce them over time. And the required effort is often higher than expected.

Although the housing affordability challenge has now existed for many years, and almost all of my zoning code clients want to discuss some form of income-based incentives or mandates, I am continually surprised at how many communities do not understand the administrative complexity of managing affordable housing. That complexity is probably unavoidable, so the challenge is to consider administrative staffing and funding implications in the design of zoning approaches to affordable housing and to avoid writing regulations so complex that they cannot be consistently and efficiently administered to achieve their goals.

Oh, and keep in mind that the more housing production can be increased by using the tools described in Section 4.1.1, the more likely it is that housing supply and demand can come into better balance, and the less we will need to design and rely on income-restricted housing mandates to house our more vulnerable residents.

Although inclusionary zoning is perhaps the best-known type of zoning affordability mandate, other mandates can be envisioned. For example, a zoning regulation could limit the maximum size of a studio, one-bedroom, or two-bedroom housing unit in an effort to reduce construction costs per dwelling unit and encourage builders to create more housing units within a defined building envelope. As with all other market interventions, however, this approach has weaknesses.

Most obviously, lower construction costs do not mean lower sales or rental prices. Small does not necessarily mean inexpensive. In hot markets, builders may respond by creating small luxury units and renting or selling them at high prices. And smaller units tend to be occupied by fewer residents, so some communities see them occupied primarily by single students and elderly singles or couples. That is a fine outcome if those are the populations that most need housing. The low-income elderly are one of the fastest-growing segments of the population in need of affordable housing. However, students often have outside financial support. Students may have little income, but parents or relatives may be providing financial support, making them less in need of housing assistance than other groups with low reported incomes. As stated above, almost every form of governmental mandate comes with a caveat that may compromise its effectiveness. That caveat can often be successfully addressed through incentives or careful project design, but it should not be ignored.

4.1.3. Housing Preservation Strategies

A third type of housing affordability strategy focuses on preserving existing housing rather than trying to hold down the costs of new housing. It is important to think hard about preserving the affordability of the current housing stock simply because there is so much of it. While the United States has a huge stock of existing housing—about 145 million dwelling units—the total number of housing units expands at only about 2 percent per year. While we build new units at a rate higher than that, we also lose units to demolition, damage, and aging (they are no longer habitable). So about 80 percent of the housing units that will be available ten years from now are already built. Focusing on incentivizing or mandating affordability in new construction means we will affect—at the very most—the 2 to 3 percent addition to the housing stock built each year, and if incentives or mandates are applied to only 10 percent of new construction (which is much more that the current ratio), then we will be increasing affordability for only 0.2 or 0.3 percent of the housing stock each year. So limiting zoning reform to apply only to new construction is a very slow strategy. Focusing on preserving the affordability of the existing housing stock gives us a much bigger target: the 97 to 98 percent of the housing stock that already exists at the beginning or each year.

More specifically, zoning regulations can be designed to discourage speculative investment in neighborhoods with naturally occurring affordable housing (NOAH). Not all older housing is more affordable, but some of it is. Smaller, older bungalow homes in habitable but unrenovated condition can be affordable if the neighborhood has not yet been targeted by speculative investors interested in replacing, expanding, or updating the houses to meet current market preferences. The same is true in older apartment buildings where little updating or renovation has taken place. America is full of neighborhoods that were much more affordable ten or fifteen years ago than they are today, and zoning can be used to discourage price and rent increases from happening in existing affordable neighborhoods.

Learning from Our Experience with Manufactured Homes

Some states and local governments are already doing this, particularly when it comes to manufactured housing. Manufactured homes that meet the federal safety standards adopted in 1974 represent America's largest source of housing affordable to households with low and low-moderate incomes. There are currently about seven million manufactured housing units in use throughout the country, which represents about 6 percent of our housing stock.[19] In fact, Congress passed the Manufactured Home Act in that year specifically to promote the production of manufactured housing by requiring everyone to accept a single safety standard.

Unfortunately, in most manufactured home parks the residents of the homes do not own the land under their homes; they lease it. That makes them vulnerable to displacement if the owner of the park decides to redevelop it for another purpose. In many cases, older and more affordable manufactured homes cannot be safely relocated to a different site or park due to age, settling, and deterioration, so when the park is redeveloped the homeowners have to walk away from their housing investment. Because the housing units that they are forced to abandon are often not only habitable but very affordable, it would require very deep subsidies to buy down rent or sales prices in other types of housing to the same level of affordability. Allowing this market-created and unsubsidized form of affordable housing to disappear when it cannot be efficiently replaced seems like a very poor choice.

The exceptional vulnerability of these residents to displacement (not to mention the loss of their investment in buying the home) has led some states and communities to give them higher levels of protection. Sometimes that protection comes in the form of requiring longer notice periods before land leases can be terminated, requiring landowners to assist residents in finding new housing, or requiring owners to pay residents some cash compensation (but usually far less than the value of their investments or the costs of relocating to new housing elsewhere). In other cases, however, it comes in the form of zoning changes that make it difficult for the owner to redevelop the property for another use. Communities as diverse as San Jose, California, and Fort Collins, Colorado, have revised their zoning to create new districts allowing only manufactured housing and related accessory uses. This is an exception to the rule that, in general, zoning is moving toward fewer, broader land use categories that allow significant market flexibility to redevelop for different forms of housing.

In Fort Collins, for example, manufactured home parks were for a long time one of several types of permitted land use available in a single mixed-use zone. That meant that a manufactured park owner could redevelop the park for another more profitable use without needing to get the property rezoned. After the closure of five manufactured home parks in ten years, the city studied the problem and decided to rezone the remaining viable manufactured home parks to a zoning district that would allow only for continued operation and new investments to prolong the life of the park (plus a few community uses such as childcare).[20] Putting the property to a different use now requires a rezoning by city council, which can weigh the advantages of the (presumably) higher tax revenues likely from the redevelopment against the loss of very affordable housing that it would be difficult to replace. San Jose, California, and numerous other cities have done the same.[21] These steps are often accompanied by other resident protection measures and sometimes by low-interest loan and grant programs to allow manufactured home park owners to replace failing facilities and keep the park habitable and attractive.

While these protections have been motivated largely by the exceptional vulnerability of the park residents and the very high levels of affordability of the homes themselves, the logic of preserving very affordable housing can be expanded to other forms of housing. In many cases, this job has been taken on by local housing authorities or nonprofit community funds operating without the help of zoning changes. For example, a growing number of community land trusts have made it their business to raise funds to buy current housing units (usually freestanding homes) and then resell the homes (but not the land under them) at lower prices than the house plus land would command. The land is held in trust to keep the housing prices low and is sometimes subject to a recorded covenant requiring owner-occupancy of the house and limiting either the price (usually the purchase price plus a small percentage of appreciation) at which the house can be sold or requiring that the home be sold only to households below a certain AMI. Among other things, this approach takes the home partly out of the speculative housing investment market, since there is no way to turn a quick profit by buying the old house and replacing it with a bigger and newer house to be sold to someone else.

While the work of community land trusts is invaluable and should be expanded, the speculative investment value of older and more affordable homes could also be removed by adopting an affordable housing zoning district or overlay district. Since many NOAH neighborhoods contain smaller older homes, those homes are often sold for the value and location of their lot rather than the house. After the purchase, the house is either demolished and replaced with a much bigger house (a scrape-off) or modified with a large addition or a second floor (a pop-top) in order make the property more valuable. Either way, the investment is often not made by a long-term resident (many of whom lack the funds or credit to do so). It is often made by a speculative investor interested in reselling the property or by someone with more financial resources who purchased the property to live in the neighborhood. Either way, the community has not gained any new housing units, but it lost a NOAH unit and gained a less affordable house. Note that this is not necessarily bad for the community. It gained a house that better meets the space and design desires of today's households and will probably last a lot longer than the old house. But if the community's goal is to protect affordable housing, then this was a missed opportunity.

Preserving Naturally Occurring Affordable Housing

An affordable housing zoning district or overlay district could reduce the speculative pressure to replace NOAH by limiting the amount by which the house can be expanded over a defined period of time (e.g., every five years). If the NOAH district stated that the floor area of existing homes below a certain size (or below a certain assessed value per square foot of floor area) cannot be expanded by more than 20 or 25 percent during any five-year period, buyers interested in financing a scrape-off or pop-top that would result in a much less affordable home would be encouraged to buy elsewhere. A small, old house is not necessarily an affordable house, but limits on the ability to expand the size of the existing NOAH would tend to focus attention on the value of the home rather than the lot and would slow down the rate at which the affordability of the neighborhood erodes.[22]

Although I am not aware of any community that has adopted this type of building regulation explicitly to preserve affordability, it is important to remember that we already do something similar in historic residential districts. Because of the importance of those districts to our shared urban heritage or the uniqueness of the homes in historic districts, we often place significant restrictions on the rights of property owners to replace or significantly modify or expand existing contributing historic structures. When you buy a home in one of these districts, you know doing what you want with the property will require approval from the historic preservation commission, and that commission will want to confirm that your proposed change will not significantly undermine the public purpose behind the district. And that is true even if your proposed change, expansion, or replacement would result in a more valuable property for you and higher property tax revenues for the city. The community has made a decision, following the requirements of due process and consistent with constitutional protections of private property rights, that in these cases the community benefits of restricting the type and scale of investments in historic properties outweigh the rights of property owners to maximize the value of their properties. If that can be done based on the aesthetic and cultural benefits of preserving the historic structures, it can also be done to preserve the affordability of homes.

As with all housing affordability zoning strategies, however, this one has weaknesses. Perhaps most importantly, it may prevent long-term homeowners from realizing the speculative market value of their homes if they were purchased for their lot—rather than home—value. Every neighborhood has a mix of residents and property owners. Some property owners are recent purchasers interested only in improving and reselling the property, and others are recent homebuyers who hope to improve the property and then live in it. But others have owned their homes in the neighborhood for a long time and may have waited for the day when they were ready to move or their property value rose to their hoped-for selling price. Removing the speculative value of expanding or replacing the existing home would be opposed by all three groups, and although housing affordability advocates may not care about the impacts on speculative investors, or even the impact of buyers who want to make the house less affordable but then live in it, many would care about the impact on long-term property owners, particularly when they have watched some of their neighbors sell their homes for more money.

The new ordinance could, of course, be drafted to apply only to recent buyers, but experience shows those types of zoning distinctions are hard to administer and may lead to avoidance strategies. When the ability to develop property in the way you want applies only to recent purchasers, prospective buyers may decide to lease the property with an option to buy after the construction of their new or expanded home, which no longer needs to be expanded after purchase because it has become the home the buyer wanted.

There are many alternative strategies for preserving the affordability of existing housing. Establishing a system of rent controls, giving local governments or housing authorities rights of first refusal to purchase affordable properties, or requiring contributions to an affordable housing fund when NOAH properties are redeveloped into larger and more expensive homes all fall into this category. In addition, the community could just offer some form of compensation to long-term property owners harmed by the restrictions in the new zoning district. These and other strategies are not discussed here because they are not implemented through zoning regulations.

4.2. Improving Equity

The second key focus of this book is how to make zoning more equitable to historically disadvantaged communities. Let's start with the basic fact that equity is not the same as equality. More specifically, it is not the same as equality of opportunity (everyone has the same chance to win) and not the same as equality of outcome (everyone wins the same amount). In the context of zoning, equity requires looking at the disproportionately negative zoning outcomes that have been experienced over decades by some parts of the US population, asking whether our zoning rules have perpetuated those outcomes, and taking steps to stop perpetuating them. Again, Richard Rothstein's book *The Color of Law* does a great job of demonstrating how unfavorable zoning outcomes are not just a chance byproduct our economy; they are the predictable outcome of the rules we have written. Equity requires that we strive to undo the damage created by those rules.

Those who have historically borne the brunt of unfair and unhealthy zoning outcomes include groups protected against discrimination by the Fair Housing Act of 1968 and the Fair Housing Amendments Act of 1988. I will refer to those acts jointly as the Fair Housing Act. For a refresher, those federal acts (often reflected in parallel acts adopted at the state level) make it illegal for anyone—including local governments—to "make unavailable" housing on the basis of the race, color, national origin, religion, sex, familial status, or limited physical or mental abilities of the person seeking housing. Some states have added prohibitions against discrimination based on age, sexual orientation, or other personal characteristics. The federal act goes further to encourage the courts to interpret the provisions of the act broadly in order to achieve their intended purpose, and the courts have done so. In fact, based on the act's strong language about fairness, courts have generally interpreted the phrase "make unavailable" to mean "make unavailable on the same terms that housing is available to the rest of the population." In other words, local governments are to regulate housing so that they are available on equal terms regardless of race, color, national origin, religion, sex, whether the residents have children in the household, or whether any of the residents are experiencing limited physical or mental ability.

Incidentally, any local government that accepts federal funds for housing purposes (and that includes almost every local government of any size) is required as a condition of accepting the money to agree that it will "affirmatively further fair housing." That means taking steps to remove existing regulations or government practices that result in unequal access to housing for any of the groups protected by the Fair Housing Act. This requires that local governments evaluate whether their own practices or rules are contributing to unequal access. In practice, this requirement has not been enforced very strictly. Some presidential administrations have required HUD and the Department of Justice to enforce the duty to affirmatively further fair housing more seriously, but others have not.

Finally, any action to change zoning rules to promote equity should be considered only in close collaboration with the renters and property owners who will be affected by the change. Equity can be improved only *with* those disadvantaged, not *for* them. Stakeholders and interest groups can and should be welcome to participate, but many solutions that sound good in the abstract can further harm those already disadvantaged in a particular neighborhood. So the voices of those most disadvantaged by the current rules and most directly affected by the proposed change matter most. This point is so important that I will repeat it again several times.

4.2.1. The Role of Income in Equity

Income is not one of the factors addressed by the Fair Housing Act. This very strong piece of federal legislation does not require that people with less income be treated the same as those with more income. In our economy, the market is the primary determinant of housing rents and prices. Not everyone can afford to live in the housing they want in the location they want, and the Fair Housing Act has nothing to say about that. Instead, the federal government and state governments have addressed perceived unfairness or negative impacts of unaffordable housing through grants, loans, and other support programs. They have viewed housing affordability as a public policy challenge because of its direct and indirect impacts on public health, education, and the economy but not as a prohibited form of discrimination.

But there is a problem with a legal framework that ignores income. The problem is that expensive housing disproportionately impacts several of the groups whose right to nondiscriminatory treatment is protected by the Fair Housing Act. As of 2023, households headed by Black people earned approximately $0.63 for every $1.00 earned by households headed by White non-Hispanic people.[23] Their median household assets were about 25 percent as large as those of households headed by non-Hispanic Whites.[24] Households headed by women earned approximately $0.75 for every $1.00 earned by households headed by men,[25] and their median household wealth was only about 55 percent as high as that of male-headed households.[26] The same disparities exist for several of the other groups whose rights to nondiscriminatory housing are protected by the Fair Housing Act.

That means that zoning rules that increase the rents or sales prices of housing disproportionately disqualify households headed by women or Black people from occupancy of those units. Although fewer studies are available, the same disproportionate disqualifications are probably true for households headed by Latinos or Latinas, other ethnic minorities, and people experiencing physical or mental disabilities.

In short, many of the disproportionate negative impacts on housing availability for those protected by the Fair Housing Act actually occur through the mechanism of affordability. As a corollary, local government zoning changes that reduce the costs of housing or slow the rise of housing costs likely have a disproportionately positive impact in allowing households headed by historically disadvantaged racial and ethnic groups, women, and people experiencing disabilities to find good, affordable housing. So although federal and state fair housing legislation does not address disproportionate impacts created by housing prices, local governments that want to improve zoning equity need to pay careful attention to how their own zoning systems may limit housing choice for the very groups that federal and state policies call out for special protection.

Although most discussions of zoning equity focus on how current regulations affect fair access to housing, zoning can also harm the historically disadvantaged by making it harder to form and operate businesses in certain locations (or from their homes). Zoning can also affect the ability of these communities to access good public services and schools. And it can significantly affect their exposure to pollutants and conditions that affect their health and shorten their life expectancy. This section will address each of those topics in turn.

In addition, zoning can make it harder for members of historically disadvantaged communities to engage with or influence the procedures by which zoning controls are drafted, changed, or applied to their properties or the properties they occupy as renters. That topic is addressed in Chapter 5.

The key principle of avoiding overcomplex zoning, and many other potential zoning changes addressed in this chapter, are consistent with the American Planning Association's 2022 *Equity in Zoning Policy Guide*. That document is an excellent resource for those interested in more detail, and more ideas, about this topic.

4.2.2. Improving Equity in Housing Opportunities

As discussed above, many of the limits on historically disadvantaged communities' opportunities to occupy good housing are created through zoning's impact on housing affordability. Ways in which zoning can avoid increasing housing costs are covered in Section 4.1, and I will not repeat that discussion here. Remember, though, that zoning to lower housing costs and preserve existing NOAH is probably one of the most powerful and direct ways in which zoning can promote housing equity. To avoid repetition, this section addresses other zoning rule changes that can promote housing equity.

Protect the Most Historically Disadvantaged Households

One key way zoning can improve housing equity is by targeting zoning changes to increase the variety of housing opportunities in areas where those opportunities are most limited and the surrounding population is not vulnerable to displacement through the introduction of new and more profitable types of housing. The second part of that sentence is important, because the same zoning change that would open up housing opportunities for excluded populations if applied in a wealthier neighborhood could lead to displacement of vulnerable populations if applied in poorer neighborhoods. For too long, zoning rules have been drafted as if the household incomes and economics of the areas where the rules are applied did not matter. But that is clearly not true. Allowing triplexes in wealthier zoning districts currently limited to single-household homes could well open up new opportunities for populations who need smaller homes or smaller yards and want to live in that neighborhood. The same change applied to a low-income neighborhood could result in investors buying up single-household rental homes and replacing them with triplexes that are much less affordable and that result in the involuntary displacement of current renters.

Targeting the availability of new types of housing in this way takes advantage of the "neutrality" of the Fair Housing Act on issues of affordability and income. While proponents of more affordable housing may bemoan the fact that the act does not explicitly protect low-income households, it also does not prohibit local zoning rules that try to address inequities experienced by low-income households. It would clearly be illegal to say, "These new zoning rules can be used only if the occupants of the new housing will be women, or immigrants, or ethnic minorities," because the Fair Housing Act prohibits discrimination based on those characteristics. It would also "make unavailable" housing for other protected groups on the same basis that it is available for those three.

To be clear, not only does the Fair Housing Act prohibit housing rules that discriminate against populations with the characteristics listed in the act, but it also prohibits discrimination in favor of those groups, with one exception. Interestingly, that one exception does not relate to race, color, ethnicity, or religion; it relates to familial status. In the rare cases where Fair Housing Act challenges involve alleged discrimination based on familial status, some courts have reviewed the legislative history of the act and concluded that it prohibits discrimination against families with children but does not prohibit discrimination in favor of families with children. Except in this one case, the Fair Housing Act prohibits both discrimination and reverse discrimination based on the personal characteristics listed in the act.[27]

In contrast to the examples above, it would not violate the act to say, "These new zoning rules can be applied only in neighborhoods where the average household income, as reported by the most recent US census, is greater than 120 percent of the area median income," because the act does not prohibit discrimination based on income. Zoning rules can be written so that opportunities for new types of housing are not available in neighborhoods where that new housing is likely to be occupied by households with significantly more wealth and income than current residents. Remember: Zoning is good at excluding things.

The economic targeting of new housing opportunities described above could be achieved in at least three ways. This section addresses potential changes to the text of the housing regulations themselves, such as a change to the permitted use table adding "triplex" to the list of available housing types in census tracts where the AMI is at least 120 percent of the citywide AMI. The second way is to change the criteria for approval of rezoning applications so that applications for rezonings to increase the density or variety of housing types are to be approved only in neighborhoods with AMIs above 120 percent of the citywide AMI. This approach is discussed in more detail in Chapter 5. The third way is to change the map so that areas with incomes below 120 percent of the citywide AMI are in zoning districts that allow fewer varieties of housing or less housing density. This approach is discussed in more detail in Chapter 6.

Note, however, that any zoning change that restricts housing development opportunities in some areas or allows more housing variety only in other areas is likely to reduce overall housing production. That is important, because in the long run increased production is perhaps the most powerful engine to promote housing affordability (and indirectly housing equity). This and other tensions between the various possible zoning changes discussed earlier are addressed in more detail in Chapter 7.

Before we move on, however, it is worth talking about whether housing equity can be improved by mitigating the impacts of involuntary dislocations rather than tailoring zoning to avoid that dislocation. For example, instead of prohibiting some market-loosening housing changes in disadvantaged and vulnerable neighborhoods, we could just require the developer to compensate any dislocated residents for the cost of moving to different housing. Or perhaps we could require the developer to offer current residents a right to occupy some of the new units after they are built and maybe subsidize their higher rent for a period of time. Both of those options sound reasonable and allow the builder to monetize the costs of involuntary dislocations rather than preventing the construction of new housing units that the community needs.

The short answer to the question of whether mitigating the impacts of dislocation improves equity is "yes." But the more accurate answer is "not really," or at least "not very much." The yes answer simply acknowledges that any form of mitigation is better than no mitigation at all. Being dislocated without getting a check is worse than being dislocated and getting a check. At least the latter reflects the fact that, in this case, the zoning rules adopted for the public good have harmed a lower-income household that the local government did not want to harm.

The more accurate answer is that cash payments or rights to occupy seldom work very well. They seldom place the dislocated household in anywhere near the economic position they were in when they lived in their previous housing and neighborhood, for several reasons. As discussed in connection with protections for manufactured home communities and affordable housing buyouts above, while well intentioned, the levels of payments required are almost always far below even the economic cost (let alone the social cost) of dislocations. This gap can be dramatically seen in the difference between what the federal government requires under the Uniform Relocation Act (which applies when federally funded projects dislocate existing residents) and what state and local governments require developers to pay dislocated residents. The former can require large cash payments to those being relocated, plus assistance in finding new housing, plus rent or cost subsidies in the new location for a period of two years.[28] It is expensive. In contrast, many state and local regulations require only a one-time cash payment in a fraction of that amount, limited assistance in finding new housing, and no continuing housing subsidies.[29]

In addition, these mitigation approaches ignore the likely nonhousing impacts of dislocation. Studies from around the world show that many relocated residents either lose their existing employment or face longer and more difficult commutes to get to that employment. The benefits of replacement housing—even affordable replacement housing—are significantly compromised if your new location puts your ability to pay for that housing at greater risk than it was before.

The frequent need for relocated residents to find new jobs closer to their new housing is one reason why giving current residents a right to occupy the new housing in their former neighborhood usually does not work very well. It often takes one or two years to construct the new housing, and by that time the dislocated household has usually (with or without compensation) found replacement housing and possibly new employment, so that returning to their old neighborhood would create as much disruption as the original displacement. In addition, even when rents on dwelling units are set at the "affordable" rates generally used by the community for other affordable housing programs, they often exceed the former residents' ability to pay. As a result, few residents who are awarded a right to occupy the new housing development successfully exercise that option.[30] Very importantly, the lower the skill level of the person displaced, the more a job in hand is worth far more than a possible job in a new neighborhood, even if the new neighborhood has more and better jobs available than your old neighborhood. Similar uncompensated impacts include the need to find new schools or childcare.

Finally, mitigation requirements usually apply only to the residents directly displaced by a new development, not those indirectly dislocated nearby as landlords look at the new development and decide that the neighborhood is now "better" and their rents should go up. Granted, it is very hard to identify who those indirect dislocates are (as opposed to those who voluntarily moved for other reasons after the new construction). But that does not make the impacts of economic displacement any less real for those households. The dislocation impacts of a new housing development in a disadvantaged neighborhood can flow far beyond the boundaries of the property where construction occurs.

While it is tempting to say that these impacts are just the unavoidable result of living in a capitalist economy or that dislocation of the poor when more wealthy households want to move into a neighborhood is just a fact of life, that is really not the case. The engine of these impacts is a combination of real estate economics and zoning, and while local government cannot control the former it can clearly control the latter. Zoning sends messages to the real estate market, and those messages can say that the need for new housing is always more important than the impacts on existing residents, or it can say that in some cases protection of disadvantaged and vulnerable residents is more important than the marginal increases in the housing supply that would occur in their neighborhoods. Economic targeting of new housing opportunities through the zoning text itself helps the community send the second message.

Remember the Elderly and Those Experiencing Limited Abilities

Equity in zoning for housing also means seriously addressing the different needs of the elderly and those experiencing limited abilities. As we all know, America is rapidly aging. But perhaps less known is the fact that the percentage of elderly living in poverty is growing, and the percentage of elderly women living in poverty is about twice that for men.[31]

Let's also avoid the mistake of discussing housing for those experiencing disabilities as if we are talking about someone else. While some disabilities are long-standing, others come and go. People get injured, and then they heal. They get diagnosed with a mental health condition, and then they receive treatment and recover from that condition. About 46 percent of Americans will meet the criteria for a diagnosable mental health condition sometime in their lives. And about the same percentage will experience a physical injury or disability that affects their ability to live normally at some point in their lives. This is not about someone else. About half of us will experience at least temporary disability sometime in our lives.

While planners sometimes think that the needs of these populations have already been taken care of through the Fair Housing Act and the Americans with Disabilities Act, that is only partially true. Both of those acts were groundbreaking pieces of legislation that address many of the special needs of the aged and those experiencing limited abilities, but much more can be done at the local level to expand the limited housing supply for these people. More seriously, federal law—and even state laws that parallel the federal acts—is enforced only through court action, which is time-consuming and expensive. But in spite of these hurdles, most of the litigation surrounding enforcement of the Fair Housing Act is not about discrimination based on race or color or nationality; it is about housing for people experiencing limited abilities. More specifically, it involves efforts to locate group homes for people with physical or mental "handicaps" (the term used in the act) in low-density residential neighborhoods. In contrast to this stream of expensive litigation, local zoning regulations can often be changed to open up new housing opportunities and then enforced administratively much more quickly and at lower expense.

To make a long story short, complying with the intent of the Fair Housing Act means that small group homes (let's say up to eight occupants) should be treated exactly as single-household homes are treated for zoning purposes. It also means that larger group homes should be treated exactly the same way that apartment or condominium buildings are treated for zoning purposes. That means no special permits, no spacing requirements from one another, no additional fencing or landscaping requirements, and no additional parking requirements. Additional parking requirements often make no sense at all, since many residents of group homes do not have cars and the few support staff living in the home may well use fewer parking spaces than a typical single-household in the neighborhood (particularly one with driving-age children living at home). Spacing requirements are also legally suspect, since the few studies that have documented any negative impacts from concentrations of group homes emphasize that those impacts occur only when several are located very close together (typically on the same block).[32] I am not aware of any studies documenting negative impacts of group homes on the health or safety of children in nearby schools or users of public parks, but many older codes still include those types of spacing requirements. If a household where no one has limited abilities is a permitted use, then a group home of the same general size should be a permitted use subject to the same conditions.

It is important to remember the purposes of the Fair Housing Act. The intent is to allow people with limited mental or physical abilities, or people with a history of those limited abilities, or those considered by the community to have those limited abilities (whether or not there has been a formal diagnosis or documentation of those limits) to have the same opportunities for housing as the general population that is not currently experiencing disability. In this case, people experiencing those limitations may often need supporting services (caregivers or monitors to live in the same house, or counseling services, or support with daily living), and those should be treated as part of the household. By analogy, parents often provide these and similar services to their children—or their live-in parents—in the household next door. They monitor their safety, they advise, they remind them to take their medication, and they help the young and old in their families get on with their lives. In fact, many states require that interpretation. Support services, even those for which fees are paid directly or indirectly, are deemed to be part of the residential use and cannot be excluded because they are commercial activities that would not be allowed as freestanding uses in the same zoning district. I think Oregon is one of the few states that has gotten this right. Group homes for those covered by the act are treated exactly the same as similarly sized residential buildings occupied by the general public. The result may be politically difficult to adopt, but it is simple to administer and easy to understand.[33]

The same approach should be taken for elderly people who are not in group homes. Remember that the Fair Housing Act does not explicitly prohibit discrimination against the elderly, although the fact that they may have limited physical abilities or declining cognitive abilities means they may be protected on that basis. Two key zoning changes can help improve equity for the elderly population. First, since many of the elderly living in single-household homes want to age in place, each neighborhood should offer housing opportunities usable by the elderly when they are no longer able to maintain that home. That often means allowing small apartment or condominium or cooperative housing buildings in close proximity to where they currently live. In many American communities zoning regulations would prevent that.

As noted earlier, 50 to 70 percent of many cities is zoned for single-household uses and would prohibit this important form of missing middle housing. Smaller multihousehold uses do not need to be allowed in every part of a low-density neighborhood, but they should be allowed in areas adequate to serve the need for aging in place. That could mean making them permitted uses along the edges where low-density residential areas abut collector or arterial highways. Or it could mean allowing them as permitted uses on property formerly used as schools, religious institutions, or other institutions (which zoning already recognized as non–residential uses acceptable in the area). While this proposal often faces vocal opposition from single-household homeowners in the area, planners find it ironic that the debate often takes place in neighborhoods that often already contain those types of institutional uses and where nobody has complained about their impacts for years.

Another way to improve opportunities to age in place is to require that some percentage of new single-household, duplex, and other low-density residential structures that are not covered by the Americans with Disabilities Act meet the principles of universal design. Simply put, those principles often require that at least one entry to the home be at grade (no steps), that doors to key parts of the home be wide enough to accommodate a wheelchair, that bathrooms be built to include or accommodate assist rails, and that a few similar minor design changes be incorporated. Universal design is sometimes thought of as "ADA light," because its requirements can generally be achieved at lower cost than full compliance with building and site design requirements for multihousehold structures under the Americans with Disabilities Act. But if more homes were built with these design changes, more of our elderly would be able to move into one of them as they age.

A third key change is to allow supportive services needed by the elderly to occur close to where they live. If the elderly can age in place in low-density residential neighborhoods, then those supportive services should be allowed in or near those neighborhoods. That is equally important even if missing middle housing is not allowed in the neighborhood, because then the elderly may be living in single-family homes individually or in small groups where their need for delivery of outside services is even greater. Support facilities can be limited in size to match the scale of the neighborhood, but they should be permitted nearby.

And as the population continues to age, we will need more types of supportive services in more places. These include small health clinics, meals on wheels distribution centers, visiting nurse support centers, and adult day care centers. Again, these uses do not need to be permitted everywhere in the neighborhood. The key question is whether there are enough of them located close enough to the growing elderly population so they can access these services without needing to drive there. If that is not the case, then find more locations where they can be permitted.

4.2.3. Improving Equity in Employment Opportunities

As important as it is to improve America's exclusionary housing patterns, it is also important to address inequities in the opportunities for members of historically disadvantaged communities to make a living. Many older zoning regulations contain unnecessary restrictions on the ability to create new businesses or employment—unnecessary because they have nothing to do with public health or safety and very little to do with public welfare or the achievement of planning goals. Looking at them carefully reveals that they are another way in which the DNA of exclusion produces negative impacts on the very populations that most need better employment opportunities to thrive in America.

While addressing this form of inequity is important for all disadvantaged and low-income populations, its impact on immigrants has been documented. In *Arrival City*, Douglas Saunders studied twelve cities across the world (including the United States) to answer the question, "What policies can cities adopt to best allow immigrants to succeed economically?"[34] The answer was simple. First, allow them to buy and own property, particularly real estate, and the United States does that pretty well. Second, allow them to create a business. That is where zoning comes in, because we often make it too hard.

Let's be clear though. Not all barriers to forming a business are bad or unnecessary. Health codes based on documented health risks are necessary, and periodic inspections of restaurants that provide food service to the public, are necessary. Building codes to ensure public safety, and periodic inspections to ensure they are being followed, are necessary. Requirements for safe access to public streets and safe access to the property by emergency service vehicles are necessary. This section focuses on zoning regulations that make it more difficult to create businesses in ways that are not grounded in fact-based risks to public health and safety. Many of those barriers also have disproportionate impacts on disadvantaged and vulnerable populations that are directly at odds with the community's stated planning goals.

Focus on People, Not Stereotypes

The first and most obvious step in improving commercial zoning equity is to review the table of permitted and conditional commercial and industrial uses in each zoning district, as well as the conditions attached to each use, and ask the "why not?" questions. Why is this use not allowed here when we allow it elsewhere? Why do we require a public hearing before approving this use in this location? And why did we put these size, scale, location, screening, or spacing requirements on this use? And in each case, is that reason closely related to public health and safety or to the achievement of an important planning goal? In going through this exercise with my clients, I often find that no one can remember why the use was excluded or limited as it was.

In some cases, limits on commercial activities are based on documented health or safety concerns. For example, many communities restrict the ability to create a new gas station in the heart of downtown or in high-density residential districts because of number of people in the area and fears that an accident involving flammable fuels could injure those people. While accidents involving fuel are extremely rare, there is indeed a factual correlation between the number of people living and working in an area and the likelihood they would be injured by nearby activities involving dangerous substances.

In other cases exclusions are based on stereotypes about the nature or appearance of the business. Examples include common exclusions or limitations on pawn shops, hair salons, nail salons, check cashing facilities, and day labor halls. None of these pose a significant risk to public health or safety, but the restrictions are sometimes based on assumptions about the income levels, race, color, or behavior of the owners or patrons. In other cases, these businesses are just considered inconsistent with the intended character of the commercial areas. Many codes also limit locations for used tire repair and recapping shops, which handle a product whose improper disposal can have negative environmental impacts. But those impacts could be addressed through standards governing the operation of the business without prohibiting it. A final example is used car sales businesses, which function very much like new car sales businesses, but many zoning codes subject them to stricter limitations or geographic prohibitions. The primary reason given is the poor appearance of the business, but that could also be addressed through fairly simple site design controls without prohibiting the use itself.

A secondary reason sometimes offered is that the named uses generate lower sales or property tax revenue than the businesses the community would like to encourage. But a careful reading of the zoning regulations often shows that many other low-tax-producing uses are permitted. What all these businesses have in common is that they have relatively low barriers to entry. Compared with other activities, these businesses often cost less to create and are therefore more often formed by people with fewer financial assets at their disposal.

Additional examples of commercial exclusion involve blood plasma centers and outpatient clinics for treatment of drug and alcohol addiction. Many communities single out and restrict much-needed methadone centers and opioid treatment centers more than they do other types of medical clinics, despite the fact that their operations are very similar. Whether you are going for methadone or for a tetanus shot, you arrive, you are seen by a professional, you receive medication, and you leave. The difference is in the perceived clientele of the facility and perceptions about what it may do to the character of the area or nearby property values. If we were really concerned about public health and safety, we would be finding ways to encourage, not discourage, methadone and opioid treatment centers. Although studies show that some forms of drug use are equally distributed across income levels, wealthier people often have more options for treating their addiction (e.g., expensive residential treatment facilities), while lower-income populations rely more heavily on these types of neighborhood facilities.

As with other zoning regulations that have disproportionate negative impacts on historically disadvantaged populations, the key is to ensure that exclusion of commercial activities from specific areas is based on data-driven public health and safety impacts rather than stereotypes and that any conditions attached to the formation and operation of the business address those impacts. If there is data showing that allowing a specific use will lower nearby property values, it is important to ask whether those impacts are more important to the community as a whole, given the disproportionate impact that excluding the use may have on low-income populations and those that particularly need the services being excluded. The serious problem of letting possible property tax impacts drive zoning policy for the community are addressed in more detail in Section 3.3.4.

Protect Unique Established Business Communities

In some cases, the economic viability of a commercial area is due to the concentration of businesses formed by members of, or intended to provide services of particular value to, historically disadvantaged populations. The most visible example is concentrations of restaurants or grocery stores located conveniently to populations that particularly value access to those types of foods. A less common example is concentrations of retail stores that sell goods in little demand by the general public but considered necessary for participation in specific cultural or religious events (e.g., a specific type of clothing commonly worn or gifts commonly given at a festival). Mixed in with these types of uses may be personal service businesses that repair items, such as cell phones and computers or printers, which are more often replaced rather than repaired in wealthier neighborhoods. Although these commercial concentrations may sometimes serve concentrations of households of a particular race, color, national origin, or religion, other communities also have commercial concentrations that serve a similar purpose for the LGBTQ+ community.

These are examples of agglomeration economies. The success of each business is tied to the presence of other similar businesses or of businesses patronized by the same population. More people come because they can buy more than one thing or accomplish more than one task related to a specific culture or lifestyle or because they may run into others who share the same culture, background, and values. Outsiders sometimes come because of the perceived unique character or culture of the area, and the total business activity can be more than the sum of the parts if they were more scattered geographically.

Business areas that serve historically disadvantaged populations may be at risk of incompatible new investments in the area, particularly if the new investor can pay higher prices for real estate than the existing businesses. We know how to protect areas with unique historical value through historic preservation districts or overlay districts, and we discussed earlier the potential to use the same overlay zoning district tool to protect areas with NOAH. We can use the same approach to protect the integrity of culturally unique business areas.

Although the Fair Housing Act does not apply to nonresidential commercial activities, its principles should inform this discussion. Just as we have decided, nationally, to prohibit housing discrimination based on race, color, religion, or national origin, we should ask whether particular commercial areas have special importance for disadvantaged people in these groups for cultural or religious reasons, or whether public awareness of the concentration of these types of businesses and services contributes significantly to their economic viability. Close collaboration with those businesses (not just the property owners renting to those businesses) is essential. In some cases, the community may want to protect the established mix of uses, but in other cases it may prefer new investment that raises property values and creates new job opportunities.

Zoning regulations to protect the ability of these concentrations to serve historically disadvantaged populations should not be based on the race, color, religion, or national origin of the owner or employees of the business, of course. Although the Fair Housing Act does not address nonresidential commercial activities, those types of discrimination are prohibited by other provisions of the Civil Rights Act of 1964. New and inconsistent investment can also be discouraged in other ways. One way is to limit the size or scale of new buildings and building expansions. Where the commercial fabric of an area is made up of small lots and small buildings, zoning can prohibit the assembly of those lots to accommodate bigger buildings. And just as zoning can limit the size of a new house to promote affordability, it can limit the size of new buildings on a single lot to reinforce the built fabric of an area. A commercial area protection zoning district could also prohibit the creation of additional parking spaces on existing lots.

These days, many forms of investment in commercial real estate are driven by corporate franchising formulas that require businesses of at least a minimum size and with at least a stated minimum amount of parking. Dimensional and parking restrictions to match the established character of the area can be effective in limiting the types of nationally driven retailing and services that would undermine the agglomeration economy. In addition, limitations on the creation of new parking can help preserve commercial areas that currently serve populations within walking distance or a short bus ride away. While economic forces seem to push toward more community- and region-serving scales of commercial businesses (think of the money behind Home Depot and the large areas it needs to serve to be successful), a commercial protection overlay zoning district can push back.

Note that, unlike the previous discussion, the paragraphs above do not focus on public health and safety. The desire to protect unique concentrations of businesses serving a historically disadvantaged population is usually grounded in considerations of public welfare. While I stand by my earlier statements that equity would be improved if zoning regulations were firmly grounded in data-driven considerations of public health and safety, this is an exception. The discussion of whether to draft zoning protections for these areas acknowledges that they probably have only a weak connection to public health and safety but may make a significant contribution to the economic and social viability of a population that has suffered disproportionately negative impacts from past zoning practices. Again, this must begin with discussions with the area businesses about the potential positive and negative consequences of protection and their clear indication that they want to limit outside investment in the area. That does not require unanimity, but there should be a clear preponderance of businesses that want those protections.

Limiting investment means limiting potential new property and sales taxes that could occur without those limits. And while the discussion above focused on business owners and operators, there may well be a difference between the desires of those businesses owners (many of whom could be renting their commercial spaces) and an owner of the property who would welcome new investment regardless of the current unique character of the area. In fact, all of the caveats listed above for an affordable housing overlay zoning district apply here as well.

But just as residential zoning is moving from a historic focus on and involvement of only property owners to one that includes renters, the same should be true of commercial zoning. Of course the property owners are involved, but they should be treated as a key stakeholder, not the key decision maker. For too long, zoning has been based on the assumption that only the interests of the property owner matter, and this false assumption has been an important driver of inequity for disadvantaged communities. Always favoring the owner in owner versus tenant disputes about what is best for a disadvantaged community perpetuates the current disparities.

Get flexible About Home Occupations

The preceding discussion assumes that we are talking about a separate building or space in which a commercial business operates. But it is equally important to consider economic activities that can help disadvantaged populations thrive but that cannot support the costs of buying or renting a business location outside the home of the business operator. That means rethinking our approach to home occupations, which is a trend already well under way.

Long before zoning inequity became a hot topic, many cities were revising their home occupation regulations. Older zoning codes tried to list each of the (few) economic activities that residents could perform in their homes, but newer codes focus on controlling the impacts of home business activities without listing them. Permitted home occupations listed in typical older zoning codes include hairdressers, dressmakers, music and dance lessons, tutoring, and sometimes accounting and bookkeeping. Although very dated, these names provide an insight into the purposes of home occupation regulations. Even in the prewar era elected officials were willing to allow limited commercial activities in residential areas, and those activities were largely those performed by women who (the elected officials who adopted zoning may have assumed) should not or could not leave home because they had to care for children or the elderly.

Not only were old approaches to home occupations based on unfair and outdated assumptions about gender roles and the nuclear family, but they illustrate the futility of trying to affirmatively name all the things you could do in a home without creating politically unacceptable impacts on your neighbors. As zoning has moved away from trying to list each specific primary use available in a zoning district in favor of fewer, broader zoning categories, it has moved in the same direction for accessory uses, particularly for home occupations. That trend grew with the emergence of the digital economy, which produced a previously unimaginable number of ways to earn money through the internet without leaving your home. And the COVID-19 pandemic further accelerated this trend by showing that many types of home activities that we thought might create unacceptable neighborhood impacts clearly did not.

When I do not get my work done at the office between 9:00 a.m. and 5:00 p.m., I bring it home to complete after my children go to bed. At what point does that constitute conducting a consulting business from my home? What if I do it every day instead of just occasionally? Who can tell when my niece is using her computer to teach English to children in Guatemala, and at what point does that constitute running a school from her home? What if she does it so much that she teaches more students than an English school operating out of its own office? Rather than trying to answer these questions, newer codes take a different approach.

To start with, all office uses or internet-based activities that do not involve customer visits or deliveries to the home are permitted. In a reversal of the earlier approach, some newer zoning codes also list the activities that are prohibited as home occupations. That (short) list of prohibitions often includes activities with a fairly clear impact on the peace and quiet of surrounding properties, such as outdoor car and equipment repair, and those with a perceived impact on public safety, such as gun sales.

While focusing on the impacts of home occupations is almost certainly the right approach, they tend to be very difficult to quantify, monitor, enforce, or distinguish from the nonbusiness impacts of homes that are not conducting home businesses. Attempts to address such impacts through zoning include limits on the size of the area used to conduct the home business, the number of nonresident employees, the number of additional parking spaces provided for employees and customers (beyond any minimum required for a home), the size and type of permitted signage, the amount of permitted outdoor storage (if any) of goods related to the business, the number of deliveries per day or week, the number of outside customer visits per day or week, and the permitted hours of operation. A number of current codes also limit the conduct of the home occupation to the inside of the primary residential home and prohibit both conduct of the business and storage of goods for the business in accessory buildings such as sheds or garages, even though many households without home businesses store lots of goods and engage in their hobbies and recreation activities in those types of accessory structures.

The first challenge is that each of these is very labor intensive and intrusive to monitor and enforce. It is very difficult for a neighbor to know how much of a home is being used to conduct a business or for a zoning inspector to distinguish between areas clearly used for household activities, those used for business activities, and shared areas (e.g., a home office or storage room) used for both.

The more serious issue is that in each case we can envision a household without a home occupation creating more of the impact than one with a home occupation. Households that do a lot of online purchasing can receive more deliveries in a week than a home-based business. Households that receive daily visits from caregivers for elderly parents may receive more visits in a week than a home-based business. Households with multiple drivers may easily have more cars parked in and around the property, and coming and going from those parking spaces, than a nearby home business. Some households have more equipment (e.g., boats) and materials (e.g., firewood) stored in their backyards than home businesses.

Our traditional answer to these inconsistencies is that it matters whether the listed item is used for household purposes or commercial purposes. But of course the impacts on the neighbors are the same either way. Improving equity often means opening up new opportunities for historically disadvantaged populations to use their homes to make the additional income needed to thrive in America, and that may require rethinking what types of activities actually do create unacceptable impacts in a residential neighborhood.

Because working from home is particularly valuable to people who cannot afford to work elsewhere, the general trend toward more flexibility for home occupations is an important step toward zoning equity. But much more can be done, particularly for the economic activities most easily available to households with lower levels of education, limited saleable skills, or limited abilities to travel outside the home.

For many people, this may mean cooking food for other people or repairing household or office goods. But home occupation regulations often do not allow either of those activities, although they allow inviting the neighborhood to a communal dinner or repairing things for the neighbors. Focusing on their impacts might mean allowing both activities to occur as home occupations. Where businesses with low entry barriers create potential risks to public health (e.g., food preparation), that availability can be conditioned on the same types of health and safety regulations applicable to the same activities conducted in separate premises. And if a freestanding business is required to have a business or sales tax license, it is fair to require that their home-based competitors do the same. The goal is to allow households to engage in these types of activities from their homes, not to give home occupations a free pass on health and safety issues.

One place to start is by asking local business and community organizations what types of home businesses their clients would like to create if not for zoning restrictions, and then exploring whether there is a way to allow those activities with community-supported conditions to mitigate documented land use impacts. As mentioned in the discussion of commercial protection overlay zones earlier, it is essential that the discussions of how to accommodate more types of home-based economic activities occur in close consultation with residents who would be affected by the change. While some neighborhoods with high concentrations of historically disadvantaged populations may welcome these types of changes, others may feel that there are already too many impacts from (presumably unpermitted) home occupations. This is another case where changes must be discussed and negotiated *with*, not *for*, the neighborhood.

4.2.4. Improving Equity in Access to Quality Public Services

A third form of inequity created or reinforced by many zoning codes concerns access to high-quality public services. Historically disadvantaged communities generally have less access to good schools, health care facilities, recreation centers, community meeting facilities, and child or elder care centers than wealthier neighborhoods.[35] I did not include police and fire stations in that list because most communities distribute these as needed to meet state or regional laws, insurance requirements, or fire and police response times, which tends to reduce the shortage of these key facilities in disadvantaged neighborhoods. The other uses listed above tend to be located further away, to have lower-quality facilities, or to provide a lower level of service in disadvantaged neighborhoods.

In most cases, this is not primarily because of zoning regulations. It is the result of decades of underinvestment by the elected officials in some areas of the community, and zoning cannot fix that. But zoning can do two things to help improve equity. It can make each type of needed public facility a permitted use in most or all zoning districts (except park and open space districts). And if the location of a large education or health care facility would harm the neighborhood fabric, it can limit the permitted size and scale of the facility to match the scale of the neighborhood. In my experience, most zoning codes already do this, although a few still require a discretionary rezoning action for each facility. Unfortunately, I know of one city that requires the creation and mapping of a new "one use only" zoning district for each new public facility.

Although older codes often distinguish between publicly owned and privately owned facilities, that distinction is disappearing. Public service agencies sometimes lease private properties from which they conduct their operations, and cities sometimes allow private providers to lease their publicly owned properties to provide these services. At a minimum, the code should allow neighborhood-serving facilities that are either publicly owned *or* publicly operated. But it may be worth asking whether the public or private nature of the service provider matters. If a historically disadvantaged or vulnerable community does not have conveniently located health care or childcare facilities and the local government cannot or will not fund the construction and operation of those facilities, perhaps private facilities can fill that gap. And if so, zoning should not get in the way.

While debates about the merits of private versus public health care facilities, schools, and recreation centers will no doubt continue, it is clear that zoning should not be used to reinforce current patterns of poor access to public services. The question is not whether the local government should increase health and education investments in underserved areas; the question is whether zoning should be used to limit the availability of these community services in areas that want and need them. For all these reasons, newer zoning ordinances often do not distinguish between public and private or ownership or operation. They define what types of services are provided, attach any conditions needed to mitigate impacts on the surrounding neighborhoods, and widen the range of zoning districts in which they are permitted. This is an area where zoning generally needs to get out of the way, because public health and safety are promoted when they can be located where they need to be located to serve the public.

The second way zoning may be able to help improve equitable access to these types of services is to incentivize them in historically disadvantaged neighborhoods, but this is subject to the same challenges and limitations that apply to other incentives. Most importantly, it is difficult to draft them so that they work economically while avoiding unwanted consequences. For example, in recent years some communities have adopted zoning amendments offering increased density in return for the inclusion of affordable housing, but they also include a provision allowing developers to include space for childcare facilities, community meeting spaces, or other supportive amenities in lieu of one or more of the affordable housing units necessary to earn the incentive.[36] This means that the rents and sales prices of the market-rate housing units, or the value of the incentive, needs to offset the below-market (and probably below-construction-cost) rents that will collected from the operators of these spaces. And there is an inherent tradeoff involved: Requiring or allowing space for neighborhood-serving uses often means one or two fewer affordable housing units.

To make things more difficult, the benefits of space for community services and events are hard to quantify, so it is hard to know what the local government should trade in return for including them. Not only is it difficult to establish how much space should be required, but it is also not clear whether the builder will be able to find a childcare provider or community meeting space manager, or whether the builder should be obligated to find or subsidize those providers for a period of time as a condition of receiving the incentive. There is also a question of whether the incentive should be offered to nonresidential builders, although the currently shrinking demand for office space in the post-COVID era and for retail space in light of online shopping trends may make this a moot question. Probably because of these challenges in quantifying benefits, I know of very few communities that have used an incentive approach to encourage these types of community service spaces, and I think few of the incentives for these types of spaces have been used.

4.2.5. Improving Equity in Exposure to Public Health Risks

A final important way that zoning rules can improve equity for historically disadvantaged communities is to reduce their generally higher exposure to air, water, soil, and noise pollution and other public health risks. The higher levels of exposure to these risks experienced by Black, Brown, and low-income population have been well documented.[37] In addition, these neighborhoods often have less tree cover and landscaping to mitigate the impacts of urban heat islands. As a result, they sometimes experience summer temperatures up to 10 degrees Fahrenheit warmer than in areas with more vegetative cover. And continued exposure to high temperatures can by itself increase the risk of heatstroke, heart attacks, and other health problems.[38] Each of these impacts is particularly serious for older adults and those with preexisting health conditions. And higher levels of preexisting health conditions have also been documented in Black, Brown, and low-income populations.

In many communities, zoning directs multihousehold developments to areas along major highways (not just arterial and collector streets) where larger utility lines are already present and where they can act as a noise, odor, dust, and particulate buffer for lower-density residential neighborhoods farther from the road. But the residents of those apartment and condominium projects are often those who cannot afford to buy or rent the single-household home that gets the benefit of the buffering, and they are the ones who are exposed to those air quality and noise impacts. Correcting these disproportionate impacts is the heart of the environmental justice movement. And since protecting the health and safety of all community residents should be at the heart of any zoning code, they should be at the heart of this discussion.

Zoning has clearly contributed to this inequity, but it is not the only reason. The causes are complex. Obviously, when zoning limits the ability to locate or operate a polluting industry outside disadvantaged or vulnerable neighborhoods, zoning is a big cause of these health impacts. But decisions by elected officials to locate or expand or extend the life of public facilities such as sewer treatment plants, transit and public service vehicle repair yards, recycling transfer stations, or public waste processing facilities are also a major cause. A more complex cause is income levels themselves, because people vote with their feet.

The types of facilities listed above are sometimes called locally unwanted land uses (LULUs). When a LULU locates in a neighborhood, people with higher incomes have more ability to move away from the LULU. This is true regardless of whether it was the result of zoning restrictions, a market decision unrestricted by zoning (zoning would have allowed them to locate in several neighborhoods, and they chose the one that worked best for the operator), or a local government decision regarding a construction of a public facility.

Zoning changes and public facility decisions are both guilty of concentrating LULUs in historically disadvantaged neighborhoods, and both can be changed. In theory (although politically unlikely) they could even change the rules to allow future LULUs only in medium- and higher-income neighborhoods in order to even things out. But zoning cannot prevent those with enough income from moving away from the LULUs if they want to, and over time the homes they leave will tend to be occupied by households with fewer choices about where to live. That is why it is so hard to achieve environmental justice through zoning alone, but it is not a reason why zoning should not be changed to minimize its contribution to these public health disparities.

Zoning to Avoid Concentrations of Environmental Risk

At one level, the required zoning change is technically simple, even if it is politically difficult, at least for new LULUs: Either broaden the range of districts and neighborhoods where LULUs are permitted, require that they be located far from each other (to reduce the concentrations of contributing sources of pollution), require that all or most of the activities be conducted indoors, require much more intense buffering and mitigation of impacts, or do all of those things. But the challenge turns out to be more difficult than that. One common issue is that a new LULU often represents new jobs, and disadvantaged communities are often short of jobs. When a new LULU is proposed, there is almost always a debate about whether the advantages of new jobs outweigh the disadvantages of continuing to concentrate these uses in areas where fewer residents have the ability to move away from them. That debate can be resolved only on a neighborhood-by-neighborhood level after listening to the voices of those most affected.

However, zoning has a much greater ability to protect public health and safety (through the steps listed above) than to preserve the jobs created by the new facility, because zoning cannot prevent the new LULU from going out of business or reducing staffing over time. The difference between the fairly certain benefits of reducing concentrations of potential health risks and the uncertain long-term job benefits of a new neighborhood employer should be part of the discussion.

Amortization of Existing Risks

The more serious challenge is that most LULUs are not new—they already exist, often in historically disadvantaged neighborhoods. Because of the federal Clean Air Act, the Clean Water Act, the National Environmental

Policy Act, the Resource Conservation and Recovery Act (which designates Superfund sites for cleanup), and a host of other federal, state, and local legislation, even unpopular uses generally have much lower environmental impacts than older LULUs created fifty or seventy-five years ago. And new LULUs just do not happen that often. Because it is so politically difficult to locate LULUs, it is usually easier for a private company or government to expand the capacity of an existing facility than to find a good location for a replacement facility. That means that LULUs often stay around for a very long time. If the facility is subject to environmental permitting or licensing, then the need to renew that license or permit may offer a periodic opportunity to raise environmental standards to something closer to what would be required of new facilities. But the cost of these improvements and the difficulty of retrofitting older structures for newer technology means that even these improvements tend to happen slowly. And some existing LULUs, such as a municipal equipment repair yard, may not be subject to licensing or permitting requirements.

Of course, local governments faced with the continued operation of existing uses that create environmental risks for historically disadvantaged or vulnerable communities could simply purchase those uses to stop the activities. In many cases, the public health and safety benefits would justify the use of eminent domain even over the objections of the existing operators. However, purchasing those uses takes money, money is almost always in short supply, and the use of eminent domain is always unpopular. More importantly, eminent domain is not a zoning tool, and so it falls outside the focus of this book.

However, there is one zoning tool that can sometimes produce a similar result. In some states, local governments have the power to "amortize" the existing use. In most cases, that means allowing a use of property that creates negative impacts on the surrounding area to continue for a period of years and treating the revenue earned by the owner in those years as the local government's payment for shutting down the property.[39]

The use of amortization is easiest to understand in the context of impacts that could be considered nuisances under common law. When an activity that is not prohibited by zoning or other laws nevertheless produces impacts that disturb the health, safety, or ability of nearby property owners to use their properties as intended, the local government usually has the power to sue them for creating a nuisance. If the suit is successful and the judge agrees that the activity creates a nuisance, the court can then order the owner to stop the activity. The owner can then either find a way to continue operations without creating the nuisance impacts (e.g., by installing additional technology or equipment to reduce emissions) or give up the operation completely. Court decisions have confirmed that if the only possible use of a property creates a public nuisance that could be prohibited under common law, then the government can prohibit that use without compensating the owner.[40]

This happens because the common law of nuisance exists alongside zoning powers. While zoning to prohibit an activity is one way to codify what the local government thinks will create unacceptable impacts, it is not the only way. Enforcing nuisance law is the other way. Stated bluntly, if a judge agrees that your actions create a public nuisance, you do not have a right to continue doing it, and the government does not need to pay you to stop.

Using zoning to force the amortization of an existing health risk is an extension of this logic. In essence, the local government is saying that although it had not considered the impacts of the use to be unacceptable before, it does now, because the full health impacts of the use have become clearer or because their disproportionate impacts on vulnerable communities have become clearer. As an alternative to a lawsuit that could force the use to stop operations today without compensation, the city will allow the use to continue for *x* years so that the owner receives some compensation for stopping the activity. Amortization reflects a middle ground between the use of eminent domain (which provides for full compensation for the fair market value of the use) and a successful nuisance suit (which might allow for no compensation).

The main problem with using amortization to remove preexisting health and safety impacts is that not all states allow its use in this way. Some states have prohibited the use of this tool outright, including Illinois, Missouri, and Pennsylvania. Others have prohibited it for certain purposes, such as the removal of billboards or other types of signs, while not addressing the legality of amortization for other purposes. And a number of states have upheld the use of this tool provided that the amortization period is long enough to allow "fair" compensation to the owner. Nevertheless, because health and safety remain close to the heart of what zoning is intended to protect, if amortization is legal in your state, it remains a potentially important tool to end disproportionate impacts of environmental risks to the health of disadvantaged neighborhoods.

4.3. Improving Sustainability and Resilience

The third way to improve zoning outcomes is to take the need for sustainability more seriously and integrate those protections into our base zoning regulations rather than creating add-ons. This is an important point. In the few cases where my clients have urged me to have a separate chapter of zoning regulations on sustainability, they have invariably changed their minds and instead asked me to integrate those regulations with the form, use, and development standards already in the code. The reason is simple. Every topic that needs to be addressed in order to improve sustainability and resilience is already there in the table of contents of a zoning code; we just haven't taken the trouble to revise them with the long-term consequences of climate change in mind. A separate chapter on sustainable development regulations would find itself tripping over similar regulations in other chapters of the code, which confuses everyone.

Instead of adding a chapter of new regulations, improving the sustainability and resilience of our communities requires addressing the weaknesses identified in Section 1.4. To recap, those key mistakes reflected in many current zoning ordinances are

- Not allowing enough mixed use;
- Missing connections;
- Limiting renewable energy;
- Limiting local food production;
- Failing to reflect rising climate risks; and
- Not adequately valuing the existing built environment.

Unfortunately, efforts to reform zoning to increase sustainability are often undermined by focusing solely on new development. It is not too hard to think through improvements in sustainability in areas where we have a blank slate to think creatively, use new technology, and not have to work around too many existing constraints from prior investments and development. Real progress happens when reforms are based on realities of the communities that we have already created rather than idealized greenfield scenarios.

4.3.1. Avoiding Climate Risk Areas

While many—perhaps most—new community comprehensive plans now address the need for future development to avoid areas where climate change will threaten public safety, it is still rare for zoning ordinances to do so. But as the very real impacts of climate change become more apparent, that is changing. In Norfolk, Virginia, and Miami, Florida, for example, debates about the causes of climate change have been largely replaced with discussions about what to do about the water flowing in the streets during monthly high tide events. The three most obvious geographies at risk from global warming are (1) lands abutting rivers and streams that are likely to see more frequent and intense storm events, (2) ocean shorelines likely to be affected by sea level rise, and (3) the wildland–urban interface (WUI), where more frequent and intense wildfire events are likely to occur. Let's take each of these challenges in turn and discuss how zoning can change to better protect public health and safety.

One key fact to keep in mind is that the challenges of avoiding climate risk areas are much greater if the land has already been subdivided into lots and parcels and those development sites have been sold off to individual landowners. Some of those challenges are discussed in more detail in Section 5.1. But reducing the risks to human life and property in already subdivided areas is not impossible. The Sonoran Institute has published a useful monograph titled *Arrested Development* that presents several examples of how existing subdivision plats have been modified to address these types of challenges.[41]

Increased Stream and River Flooding

Lands adjacent to streams and rivers are sometimes subject to flooding, and the frequency, intensity, and unpredictability of storm events that cause flooding are all expected to increase in the future. However, the United States already has in place a system designed to reduce property damage and risks to public safety in these areas. That is the National Flood Insurance Program (NFIP) administered by the Federal Emergency Management Agency (FEMA), and most local zoning ordinances directly or implicitly recognize that system. At its core, the NFIP includes a process by which the probable boundaries of various flood events are mapped and another by which those boundaries can be changed when conditions change. Residents of communities that restrict or prohibit development within those boundaries are eligible for lower flood insurance rates if they can find a policy that covers flood losses.

Unfortunately, many homeowner and renter insurance policies do not cover flood losses and would not benefit from those lower rates.

Generally, NFIP maps include the boundaries for 1 percent storm events, or the largest storm event that has a 1 percent chance of occurring each year. These have come to be called 100-year storm events, since a storm that has a 1 percent chance of occurring each year (theoretically) has a 100 percent chance of occurring once in the next 100 years. As FEMA will quickly remind you, however, this is very misleading. The fact that a 1 percent storm occurred this year does not mean that it will not occur in the next ninety-nine years. Because each 1 percent probability is based on modeling (not knowledge of the future) and because each 1 percent probability is independent of all other 1 percent probabilities, there could be another 1 percent storm next year, and one could occur the year after that.

Because of the tens of thousands of miles of river and stream frontage covered by the NFIP program, it is difficult to keep the ways updated to reflect the actions of property owners upstream and downstream that may affect flood risks. And because of the increasing unpredictability and potential intensity of storm events, it is difficult to keep NFIP maps updated to reflect likely increases in risk due to storm events. In fact, I have never worked in a community that thought its NFIP flood boundary maps were accurate, and the process of getting those maps amended to reflect changing conditions is lengthy and complex, but in most communities those are the only maps of flood risk available. Or, more accurately, since compliance with the NFIP maps is required to reduce flood insurance rates, most communities have decided not to invest the time and money to complete the complex rainfall and drainage modeling needed to create an alternative set of flood risk maps.

NFIP flood protection regulations are often overseen by state-level agencies that sometimes tailor those regulations to better reflect local conditions and flood risks. Some of those state agencies periodically update their regulations and either encourage or require local governments to use those revised regulations. But the issuance of permits confirming that applicants have complied with flood protection regulations is almost always handled by a local "floodplain administrator" (the term used by FEMA), who is often the local planning director, zoning administrator, or town engineer. In many cases, approval comes in the form of a floodplain development permit issued before, during, or after other zoning and development approvals. If compliance with flood protection regulations is fundamental to the viability of the project, a floodplain development permit may be required earlier in the process. If compliance is just a matter of minor changes to site engineering, it may be required after other approvals but before construction on the site.

In many communities, NFIP regulations exist outside the zoning ordinance but are implicitly recognized by requiring that lands within NFIP 100-year floodplains comply with NFIP flood risk prevention regulations before the city will approve or issue permits for a proposed development. However, because NFIP maps and related regulations operate much like a zoning overlay district, they are increasingly included as a new overlay district when codes are updated. More specifically, the NFIP 100-year floodplain maps are cross-referenced and entered as a new layer in the community geographic information system maps like the boundaries of other zoning districts. Not only does this help property owners understand whether all or part of their property is located within the NFIP boundaries, but it helps the local government coordinate the timing and sequencing of floodplain development permit applications with other zoning, subdivision, and development approval procedures.

Because there is an existing federal regulatory system and because the availability of less expensive flood insurance acts as an incentive to comply and coordinate with that system, few newer zoning ordinances include separate regulations to address the impacts of climate change on stream and river flooding. Instead, communities concerned about protecting the public from these impacts usually lobby FEMA to revise and update the NFIP maps. In addition, because studies of damage from Hurricane Katrina in New Orleans in 2005 and from Superstorm Sandy in New York City in 2012 show that requiring building foundations to be elevated higher would have significantly reduced property damage,[42] some communities are modifying their local versions of NFIP regulations to do that. They are modifying traditional requirements that building foundations be raised 1 foot above base flood elevation (BFE) to require that they be located 2 or 3 feet above BFE. In some communities, this is viewed as a permanent change to reduce storm damage, and in others it is enacted as a stopgap standard that will be revised when FEMA updates the floodplain boundary maps or when the relevant state agency recommends a different approach. While a few communities have gone further to adopt stricter-than-NFIP stream and river flood protections or to integrate floodplain regulations with other sensitive land controls,[43] most have not strayed far from the FEMA maps and regulations.

Increased Risk from Sea Level Rise

The second major way in which zoning regulations could better protect public health and safety from the impacts of climate change is by reducing development potential in areas subject to rising sea levels. As noted earlier, Miami and Norfolk are two of the US cities most affected by early impacts of consistently higher tides. In both cities, flooding of city streets during high tides is increasingly common. While water levels in those two cities have risen gradually, the damage from Hurricane Katrina in New Orleans and Superstorm Sandy in New York vividly demonstrate how the impacts or rising seas are compounded when storm events occur.

While the human suffering caused by those two major storm events was broadcast nationwide by the media, the human costs to residents and businesses in low-lying areas of cities like Miami and Norfolk are no less real, and they often fall on those least able to relocate to safer land or to absorb the financial blows of damage to uninsured property. Beyond those human costs, however, are the huge economic costs of mitigating coastal flooding risks and rebuilding after storm events occur. All four of these cities play important roles in the US economy: Miami is a financial gateway and travel hub to Latin America, New Orleans is a major shipping port, Norfolk is home port of the US Navy Fleet Forces Command, and New York is perhaps the most important single node in the global financial system. When sea level rise interrupts those activities, the financial consequences ripple across the country.

Responses to sea level rise tend to fall into three categories: (1) hardening coastlines (sometimes called coastal armoring), (2) retreating from coastlines, or (3) combinations of the two. As their names suggest, hardening strategies focus on investments that can help keep sea water away from people and development, and retreat strategies focus on gradually moving people and development away from the sea.

There is no right answer, of course. The strategy that works best in each community will vary based on the seriousness of anticipated flooding, the coastal terrain, the level of existing investment along the coast, the number of people (particularly vulnerable people) who live there, the availability of funding for different strategies, and the personalities and preferences of the elected officials who need to balance those competing factors.

Unfortunately, most hardening strategies are very expensive, because they cannot be implemented in a piecemeal fashion. Constructing sea walls along a short portion of a coastline just means the water will flow onto other properties that are not protected by the sea wall (or around the ends of the wall onto the very properties they were installed to protect). To be effective, hardening strategies often need to be implemented along all or almost all of the coastlines abutting significant residential populations or expensive business facilities. Zoning regulations cannot force these massive investments to occur; those are capital investment decisions outside the realm of land use controls.

In theory, zoning could require that each property owner engaged in redevelopment along the coastline "harden" their property by building some sort of structure, but that approach has two problems. First, zoning operates when property owners want to change the use or development of their properties. If no applications are filed, the local government generally does not have an opportunity to require private construction of sea walls, and no sea walls will be built. Decades may pass before any properties are protected against sea level rise. Second, building coastal hardening structures on individual properties would generally just force water to move around those structures and compound flooding on nearby properties that have not yet built theirs, which may actually increase damage and risks to life and health. For all these reasons, this book will focus on the role of zoning regulations as an element of retreat strategies.

Retreat from sea level rise comes in two forms: horizontal and vertical. Horizontal strategies generally limit the amount of new investment that can occur in areas where increased flooding is likely or require reduced occupancy and use of structures in those areas. Vertical strategies generally require that portions of new development or redevelopment most vulnerable to flood damage (e.g., key electric and plumbing equipment necessary for safe occupancy of the building during a storm event) be located higher above sea level than they were in the past. Vertical strategies often include a combination of changes to flood protection regulations and changes to building codes. Potential revisions to flood protection regulations were discussed in Section 4.3.1 and will not be repeated here, and changes to building codes are beyond the scope of this book, so we will focus on the role of zoning in horizontal retreat strategies.

The most obvious zoning change that could reduce risks from sea level rise is to increase required building setbacks from anticipated high tides. Hawaii County, Hawaii, has been a leader in using statistical models of anticipated sea level rise and coastal erosion to establish larger building setbacks.[44] Although the process of adopting those setbacks was lengthy, they have rarely been challenged. Now that the science of modeling climate change impacts has evolved, however, the county is planning to use a different modeling method to revise the required setbacks. In addition, although the original setbacks were based on an anticipated building life of forty or fifty years (i.e., the setback must be adequate to protect the building throughout its anticipated lifespan), the new model anticipates a building life of seventy years. While complex, these types of modeling efforts provide a strong statistical basis for establishing new zoning regulations, and the regulations themselves can be simple. We have been drafting building setback regulations for over 100 years. Few would argue against using the best and most accurate data available to establish zoning regulations, but one unanticipated consequence of this update is that some buildings constructed in compliance with the first-generation setbacks may be nonconforming under the new ones.

A second zoning approach to sea level rise is demonstrated in Norfolk, Virginia's 2018 Building a Better Norfolk Zoning Ordinance.[45] Norfolk uses a point system to require that all new development and significant redevelopment take some action to improve the resilience of the city to sea level rise. Points can be earned for a wide variety of actions, but applicants must earn a minimum number of points to gain development approval. More accurately, most types of development (and redevelopment that is valued at more than 50 percent of appraised value or that increases floor area by more than 50 percent) can choose between (1) obtaining approval of a site plan that is subject to significantly stricter requirements for building elevation, stormwater management, and energy resilience or (2) earning points through a Resilience Quotient system in which bigger developments have to earn more points. Scores of actions are listed in the Resilience Quotient tables, with more expensive actions generally earning more points toward the required minimum.

The Norfolk ordinance also establishes a Coastal Resilience Overlay (CRO) zone and an Upland Resilience Overlay (URO) zone. New development in the CRO is required to earn even more Resilience Quotient points and is subject to higher building elevation and open space and infiltration area standards. In contrast, projects in the safer URO can earn significant Resilience Quotient points by purchasing development rights from properties in the CRO. Land from which development rights are purchased must then be owned by a land trust or nonprofit and used for open space purposes under terms that allow the city to make investments in the property to increase its ability to infiltrate surface water. In other words, the system allows owners of less environmentally risky land to voluntarily buy out the development rights on more environmentally risky land through a market transaction.

Increased Risk from Wildfires

The third major climate risk that zoning regulations can address effectively is wildfire. In the center of the country—and particularly the arid Western states—this is of much greater concern than sea level rise. But just like the experience in coastal areas, the frequency, severity, and unpredictability of major wildfires seem to increase almost every year. In 2021, when the Marshall fire burned over 1,000 homes in Boulder County, Colorado, in a single afternoon, we thought we might have seen the worst that nature can do. But only four years later, the wildfires surrounding Los Angeles burned over 10,000 homes over a nine-day period. And the damage is not limited to the fires themselves, because hillsides ravaged by those fires cannot hold the soil in place as well, which increases erosion into nearby valleys, streams, and rivers and can increase flood risks in those areas.

Fortunately, improved zoning regulations can significantly reduce the risks to human life and property from wildfire. The most effective approach would be to take existing wildfire risk maps seriously and to restrict or prohibit new development in areas where wildfire risks are high. Where land has not yet been subdivided and remains in single ownership, this approach is sometimes workable. Subdivision regulations can be revised to require that new development lots avoid high-risk areas and instead be clustered on parts of the property where risks are lower. Clustering strategies are already in common use to protect wetlands, wildlife habitat, ridgelines, and several other geographic features. This assumes, of course, that there are some areas of the property owned by the same person where development would be safer. If that is not true, then a more complex system of transferable development rights between owners or land areas may need to be created.

In addition, subdivision regulations can be revised to require roads wide enough and with gentle enough grades to accommodate the types of fire trucks needed to fight wildland fires. Additional entry and exit points can be required to give residents more ways to flee a fire, and evaluations of the capacity of evacuation routes can be required during the subdivision process. Where needed water and sewer services are controlled by the city, it could also refuse to allow the expansion of those services into high–fire risk areas.

But protecting the public from the risks of wildfire gets much more challenging if the land has already been subdivided and some or all of the lots are in mapped high fire risk areas. In theory, elected officials should not have let this happen, but lots may have been platted decades ago before the wildfire risks were known or mapped. Regardless of how it happened, once a lot has been platted and is available for development, the local government generally cannot prohibit all development on the lot, because each owner must be left with at least one "economically reasonable use" of the property (see Section 5.1). In many communities, the lowest-intensity use allowed on a platted lot is a single-family house, so zoning allows that use on each existing platted residential lot regardless of the fire risks involved.

An in-between case arises if the lots and roads have been platted but all of the land is still in a single ownership, which is sometimes called a paper plat. Although these are rare (most owners who subdivide land start selling platted lots as soon as they are legally permitted to do so), an existing paper plat with lots in a high–fire risk area can be replatted to avoid that layout before lots are sold to individual owners for development. To encourage that result, the city or county can offer incentives, such as the ability to include even more developable lots if they are located in safer areas. Once individual platted lots have been sold to different owners, and some of those owners have built on their lots, the problem gets significantly trickier, because it is very hard to get a group of differently motivated owners to agree to a replat.

Let's assume for the moment that lots have been platted and sold and that the local government is unwilling or unable to prohibit development of a single-family dwelling on an existing platted residential lot. Then the discussion sometimes shifts to what kind and size of house needs to be permitted. Some communities faced with the need to discourage significant development of legally platted lots have instead limited the maximum size of the house that can be constructed. Construction of an 800-square-foot cabin represents a much lower level of investment to put at wildfire risk than a 3,000-square-foot home. And a small cabin is much less likely to be occupied full time, which means that if a fire occurs, the chance of the owners being at personal risk is lower. Pitkin County, Colorado, limits the size of homes built on old mining claims in "Rural and Remote" areas of the county in order to discourage significant investment and occupancy of those areas.[46] Hawaii County, Hawaii, recently considered a similar strategy to reduce public safety risks on legally platted lots located in predicted lava flow routes from the Kilauea volcano.[47]

The most difficult situation, of course, is when platted lots have been sold to individual property owners who have already built homes on those lots. In that case, roads that may not meet fire access standards have already been designed and built, lots may have already been located in high–fire risk areas, and buildings have been built that may not meet modern fire retardance standards. Zoning ordinances can nevertheless be revised to require the creation of "defensible space" around each existing home. Although there are exceptions, defensible space standards generally require that trees and fire-susceptible vegetation be cleared for a distance of about 30 feet around each structure. They often add that firewood and flammable materials may not be stored within that area.

The difficulty, of course, is enforcing defensible space regulations over time, since few local governments have the resources to proactively monitor whether property owners are actually complying with the new rules. Some local governments try to fill this gap by enlisting the help of homeowners' associations to monitor and remind property owners of their duties, because failure to do so not only risks their own home but enables the faster spread of fires to neighboring homes. In addition, some cities and counties offer assistance by providing public works vehicles to take away and dispose of brush and flammable materials cut by property owners as they maintain defensible space.

Zoning regulations can also be revised to require that when home or building owners apply to expand or modify those buildings, they are required to take additional actions to improve fire safety. Among those sometimes required are the installation of fire-resistant roofing, improved screens over roof vents (since flying embers blown inside roof structures are a common vector for spreading fires), and disconnection of decks and fences from the primary house structure (since flammable decks and fences are common routes by which fire spreads to homes). Revised regulations can also require that new fire-retardant materials be used whenever a building permit is issued to replace an aging roof. And some local governments are considering requirements that single-family homes include interior sprinkler systems like those we require for commercial and institutional buildings.

4.3.2. Allowing More Mixed Use

The next several sections of this book focus on the ways in which zoning can promote sustainability by reducing greenhouse gas (GHG) emissions. Fortunately, this is one area where zoning can make a big difference. The two most significant sources of GHGs are emissions related to (1) heating, cooling, lighting, and operating buildings and (2) moving people from place to place in fossil fuel–powered vehicles.[48] And basic changes to zoning regulations can reduce emissions from both sources.

The most important change is to increase opportunities for mixed-use development. Allowing more residential uses in zoning districts currently reserved for commercial development opens up new opportunities for people to live closer to where they work, or study, or recreate and to reduce the time spent commuting or transporting family members from one to the other. Every mile of driving avoided by allowing shorter distances between our frequent destinations is a mile of GHG emissions avoided.

In recent decades, this is one of the most common changes my clients have made, for several reasons. The first is concern about climate change, and the second is the desire to reduce traffic congestion. But another reason is that the rise of e-tailing and the work-from-home impacts of the COVID-19 pandemic have resulted in many vacant or almost-vacant buildings previously zoned for only commercial forms or uses. In some cases, the vacant buildings can be converted to housing uses, but even when they cannot, allowing residential redevelopment of that land by right can remove the time, expense, and uncertainty of a rezoning or conditional use process before constructing a new residential structure. The point is not that everyone wants to live near their workplace or their children's schools or their gym but that some of them do, and zoning should not stand in their way unless there are serious public safety or environmental reasons to do so.

Unfortunately, on any given day market conditions may favor one of the uses allowed in a mixed use zoning district more than the others, which can lead to fears that all available properties will be developed for that preferred use. In recent years this fear has come up most frequently when multihousehold uses are added to commercial districts. Because of the serious housing shortages in many communities, elected officials fear that allowing multihousehold uses will result in a neighborhood with only housing uses rather than a healthy mix that offers residents working and living options. That outcome would defeat the intent of a mixed-use district but could potentially also reduce tax revenues from lost sales taxes or lower tax rates applied to residential development.

This is a very valid concern, and there are ways to prevent that outcome, but they require careful thought about where the benefits of mixed-use development come from. Hint: They do not come from having a mix of uses in each building or on each property. Horizontal mixed use provides almost exactly the same benefits to the environment and affordability and choice as vertical mixed use. So any zoning tool designed to prevent an entire mixed-use area from being redeveloped with only residential uses needs to address the overall mix in a defined area rather than the mix on any given lot or in any given building. That requires one of two solutions.

First, the planners can take a closer look at where, geographically, current commercial-only zoning districts should be changed to allow completely residential uses without trying to get mixed-use everywhere, and then map them that way. Careful thinking about where mixed-use neighborhoods are successful will show that many of them have purely residential buildings in some areas. The point is not that everyone has options to live right next door to the commercial and support services they use frequently, but that those who want to can find those services and facilities within a short walking or biking distance of their home. Unfortunately, we do not seem to have learned that lesson, because many newer zoning codes zone far more land into mandatory mixed-use districts than the market can support. Think carefully about how much land is really needed for commercial, sales, or employment uses and then allow other lands to help meet the huge unmet demand for housing without requiring mixed use (even on the ground floors).

Second, the zoning ordinance can make the availability of the most desired use contingent on the existence of other (generally supporting) uses within a defined distance of the subject property. As an example, I helped one community revise commercial-only business park zoning to allow multihousehold uses, but only after at least 80 percent of the land in the business park had been developed with nonresidential uses. Similarly, some newer codes require that before mixed-use zoning is applied to any property larger than a single lot, the property owners submit a plan for where different uses will occur within that defined area. The plan can be approved administratively and can be amended administratively when property owners or market conditions change, but it cannot be changed to allow more than a stated maximum amount of the use that elected officials fear will take over the entire area.

Both these responses act as brakes on mixed use, of course. And if the fear is that residential development will use up all the land, and limits are applied to prevent that, they also act as brakes on much-needed residential development. So these types of restrictions are not recommended unless there is a real and substantial worry that market forces will defeat the intent of mixed-use development, and then only after careful thinking about whether there is an oversupply of commercially zoned land that should simply be rezoned for residential use.

4.3.3. Improving Connectivity

Another key zoning change to improve sustainability and resilience is to require improved connectivity through both new development and redevelopment parcels. In many cities, the historic layouts of lots and blocks were developed with an eye to maximizing lot values (before World War II) or auto accessibility (after World War II) but not with much concern for the convenience of pedestrians. Exceptionally walkable downtown Portland, Oregon, is divided into blocks 264 feet on a side (twenty streets to a mile), which is smaller than in many cities. In contrast, central Denver, Colorado, has blocks that tend to be 330 feet by 660 feet (sixteen streets to the east–west mile and eight to the north–south mile). Manhattan is an anomaly, with blocks of 264 by 900 feet and no intervening alleys (twenty streets to the north–south mile and only six to the east–west mile).

While these differences may not matter much to those driving a car or truck, they should, because the more direct the route to your destination is, the shorter the time needed for the trip. And, of course, more direct routes also reduce emissions. Just as importantly, however, these kinds of differences do matter to pedestrians, bicyclists, and people using wheelchairs, walkers, or canes to get where they want to go. For them, a longer block and a less direct route can discourage them from making the trip at all. Or it may lead them to drive a car when they would have preferred to walk or ride. Connectivity is one area where the design of our communities often contributes directly to the amount of GHGs being added to the atmosphere.

For major developments and redevelopment areas, one of the common counterarguments to designs with smaller, better-connected blocks is their cost. Streets cost a lot of money to build and even more to maintain over time, and some developers would like to construct only those necessary to maximize the value of the lots within each block. And higher infrastructure costs can mean higher prices for each resulting lot unless those costs can be offset in one of two ways. The first is to allow the construction of smaller, less expensive streets and accept dedication of those streets for public maintenance in the future. Revising street design and engineering standards will require close partnerships between planning and transportation staff and usually a willingness to impose lower speed limits on the resulting smaller streets.

But these types of changes to permitted street design are in fact happening. The second way to offset the costs of more fine-grained street systems is to allow higher development densities or broader mixes of uses on the resulting lots, which is clearly within the control of local zoning regulations.

In recent years some communities have met the challenge of increased mobility in larger development and redevelopment projects by using a connectivity index.[49] They require that the applicant count the number of nodes and links in their proposed design and then meet a minimum ratio between the two. Nodes are street intersections (either within the development or along the edges where those streets connect to an existing street network on the edges of the project). Links are the street segments between those nodes. If a minimum ratio of nodes to links is required, auto trip lengths can be reduced and walking and bicycling can be encouraged. An applicant whose initial design does not meet the connectivity matrix standards will need to rethink the pattern of lots, blocks, and points of entry to or through the development to include more connections. That in turn usually means more options for shorter and more direct routes to where residents of the new development, as well as residents in the surrounding area, want to go.

As noted throughout this book, however, most zoning actions actually involve small-scale redevelopment of one or a few lots that does not involve the design or construction of new streets. In this context, the key to increased mobility and reduced emissions is often the addition of connectivity standards requiring pedestrian and bicycling connections to supplement an existing street system. These can take the form of a midblock connection requirement allowing pedestrians (and sometimes bicyclists) to pass from one street to the next without walking or riding to the end of the block. As with requirements for additional streets, the costs of midblock connections can be offset by allowing additional development intensity or by allowing offsets against other development fees imposed to fund transportation improvements.

4.3.4. Facilitating More Renewable Energy

Although America's move to replace fossil fuel–powered generating plants with solar, wind, geothermal, and biofuel plants is well under way, many zoning ordinances are stuck in the distant past. Updating zoning regulations to allow and encourage renewable energy generation, distribution, and use can accelerate our move away from one of our major sources of GHG emissions. More specifically, zoning ordinances can be revised to (1) allow a wider range of renewable energy production in more locations, (2) facilitate the conversion of existing gasoline and diesel filling stations to accommodate other types of fuel, and (3) allow accessory renewable energy fueling stations in more locations. Because an increasing number of states are moving in this direction, each of these changes should be aligned to complement and not to conflict with any applicable state requirements or incentives.

Most older zoning ordinances list and define only one type of "electric power plant" or include that use in a broader defined use of "major utilities." Because historically this meant a large regional-scale fossil fuel–fired facility, which was often heavily regulated by a public utilities commission or other state body, most codes included very few standards addressing the size, scale, or impacts of these plants on the community. Instead, they were allowed only in the heaviest industrial district. Attempts to mitigate any impacts were limited to large building setbacks and required landscaping along the edges of the property.

The most serious problem with this approach is that it assumes electric power is generated only in large regional-scale facilities that produce lots of impacts on their neighbors, when this is increasingly not the case. We began to see smaller-scale biofuel, trash-to-energy, and cogeneration facilities decades ago. In most cases those facilities served a single, large industrial complex or a single institutional campus, and the negative impacts (if any) of the activity were felt mostly by that complex or campus. While a few zoning ordinances were revised to list these types of new generating facilities as permitted uses in industrial and institutional zones, most communities simply interpreted the generating plant as an accessory use to the primary industrial or institutional activities and did not bother to update their codes to reflect that change.

More recently, however, the pace of change has accelerated. In addition to campus-specific and area-specific generating plants that burn alternative fuels, we have seen the rapid proliferation of wind, solar, and in some cases geothermal energy-generating facilities. Importantly, these new uses can occur at several different scales, and newer zoning ordinances need to address most or all of them. More specifically, renewable energy production can occur in industrial or community-wide facilities, neighborhood-scale facilities, and single-property facilities, and each of them requires a different zoning approach.

Because state or interstate power generation and transmission regulations may affect each of these, local zoning must align with those regulations.

In some cases, state-level regulations may impose additional permitting requirements, and in other cases they may provide that state-level authorities may override local decisions to prohibit or limit the location of generating facilities. The discussion that follows will focus on ways to encourage broader use of renewable energy through zoning reforms assuming that there are no conflicting state requirements.

Small Accessory Facilities

Since most land use activity is small-scale redevelopment, I will start there. Because the growing use of solar power is a recent phenomenon, many city and county zoning ordinances do not list solar energy collectors as a permitted accessory use of land in any zoning district. Newer codes address this oversight, generally by permitting rooftop solar collectors in all or almost all zoning districts by right, subject to compliance with all building and electrical codes. One common partial exception is to require approval of the historic preservation commission when these are located in designated historic districts. Newer codes also generally permit ground-mounted solar collectors in backyards and sideyards, subject to minimum setbacks from neighboring properties and in some cases maximum height limits.

To encourage installation of rooftop collectors without the need for a variance, some newer codes allow them to encroach some distance (often 18 inches) into the height limit that would otherwise apply. Installation of accessory solar collectors in front yards is often limited to industrial or heavy commercial districts. In some cases, newer codes also allow administrative adjustment of backyard and sideyard landscaping and screening requirements when those would interfere with the operation of the solar collectors.

Accessory and smaller-scale wind facilities are a bit trickier. While the internet is full of drawings and illustrations of roof-mounted wind generating facilities, it is rare to see them built and operating. The major reason is that wind generating facilities often need 30 feet or more of "clear air" to ensure the predictable airflow needed to generate a meaningful amount of electric power. That is hard to come by in urban areas unless wind generators are allowed to be about 30 feet taller than the buildings that surround them, and most zoning codes (even newer ones) allow that only in industrial and heavy commercial districts. In most other zoning districts newer city codes allow accessory wind generation in backyards and sideyards (not front yards) but limit them to the same height limits (or maybe a few feet more) applicable to other buildings in the district. County zoning regulations are generally more flexible and may allow accessory wind installations 30 feet taller than other buildings in rural residential and agricultural districts. This compromise allows those who want to demonstrate their support for wind power, or who want to generate a small and variable amount of power to offset part of their electricity bill, to do so. But it generally does not generate significant amounts of electricity, even for the single property where it is located. It also demonstrates the continued high level of concern over permitted maximum heights of all types of structures, even in communities that have endorsed sustainability and more flexible approaches to mixed-use.

As an aside, in areas of the country that have significant sources of geothermal energy, many newer codes allow accessory geothermal facilities by right with few restrictions except compliance with building and electrical codes. Since these facilities are underground, they are almost invisible after installation, and there is little reason to restrict them.

Community-Scale Facilities

Community-scale renewable energy generation is an in-between case where trends are harder to generalize. This category includes all nonaccessory facilities (i.e., those located on a lot or parcel without a different primary use of the land) that are too small to be regulated as public utilities. Those can include parcels in a residential, mixed-use, or nonresidential zoning district that the owner wants to use to generate solar or wind energy, either to serve a particular area or development or to sell the electricity to a larger public utility.

In order to distinguish these uses from larger and more intensive generating facilities, some codes define this scale as generating no more than 10 megawatts of power and occupying no more than 10 acres of land. Although a few newer codes allow community-scale solar or wind power generation as a primary use of land in residential and mixed-use districts, most do not. Instead, the few codes that address this new scale of power generation generally limit them to heavier commercial and industrial districts where a wider range of visual impacts from development is expected anyway. Where community-scale facilities are allowed in other zoning districts, they often require a conditional use approval rather than being available by right, and they are often subject to maximum height limits lower than those that would apply to industrial-scale facilities.

This is an area that is ripe for zoning reform, since the variety of ways in which medium-scale power can be generated is increasing rapidly, and most codes do not address them at all. Zoning ordinances should be revised to define and allow this use, with its relatively moderate impacts on neighboring properties, in a wider range of locations than industrial-scale facilities. That could include light industrial areas, business parks, and many industrial- and commercial-oriented mixed-use districts. Because there is no separate primary use on these parcels, the solar collectors or wind generators can be located nearer the center of the lot, and side and rear yard buffering and screening can be required without significantly compromising the power-generating potential of the facility.

Even communities that are not ready to permit community-scale wind and solar generation as a primary use of land (or those willing to allow it in only a few zoning districts) may want to consider allowing them as interim or temporary uses of land, particularly where little permanent development has taken place. Hundreds of thousands of lots and immense areas of unplatted land are currently zoned for residential use in rural areas of the country. In many cases little or no development has occurred on those lands (i.e., they are paper plats). They were zoned in anticipation of development that may take decades to be supported by the market. Communities in this situation should consider allowing wind and solar power generation as interim uses of land under a renewable permit for a period of ten or more years. Permits could be renewable, but they could also be subject to removal agreements or requirements to post a bond ensuring removal when the permit expires.

Industrial-Scale Facilities

At the large end of the spectrum are industrial-scale wind and solar farms, facilities that often require large areas of land to be efficient and are therefore generally located on unincorporated rural county lands. Because these are usually developed and owned by large utilities and serve as significant sources of power that is distributed over a wide electric grid (which may involve other providers and other states), they are often subject to significant regulation by state public utility commissions or federal bodies.[50] Those regulatory bodies may or may not require that proposed solar and wind farms be located in areas where they are permitted by local zoning. Even where consistency with local zoning is required, however, there are often provisions in state or federal law allowing higher-level regulatory bodies to override a local government prohibition, denial, or imposition of conditions that make the facility impractical to develop.

Because these larger facilities are almost always located in unincorporated rural areas, they generally need to be addressed in county (rather than city) zoning regulations. Unfortunately, many county codes do not list industrial-scale wind or solar power generation as a permitted use or include them in a broader definition of a medium or heavy industrial use. In newer codes, they are often specifically listed and, like other types of power plants, are often subject to a conditional use approval process. They are often subject to significant conditions regarding screening and setbacks from property lines, and in some cases requirements for removal of the facilities when they are no longer in operation (either because the equipment has become less efficient or because technology has evolved to make other energy sources more efficient). Another common provision is for the operator to reimburse the county for any damage done to county roads in the process of moving heavy equipment, generators, and collectors to the site for installation. In many cases, these types of facilities are also subject to a discretionary conditional use approval process.

4.3.5. Encouraging Local Food Production

Yet another way that zoning can improve local sustainability and resilience is by allowing and encouraging more local food production. In addition to providing the well-documented health benefits of eating more fresh produce and fewer processed foods,[51] increasing local food production also helps reduce GHG emissions. Recent data suggest that the operation of the food supply chain is responsible for 16 percent of GHG emissions. That figure includes 4 percent for food processing, 6 percent for transport, 5 percent for packaging, and 3 percent for retail sales operations.[52] And because poor access to fresh food disproportionately affects poor and historically disadvantaged communities, improvements in local food access will provide disproportionately positive benefits to exactly those Americans.

Local food production can occur as a small accessory use to another primary use or as medium-scale community garden-type uses that are the primary use of a lot or parcel of land. Of course, it can also occur in full-sized farms covering hundreds or even thousands of acres, but these uses are generally already addressed and permitted in county zoning ordinances. In contrast, small- and medium-scale food production can occur in both urban and rural settings and is not addressed (or not addressed well) in many current zoning ordinances.

Small Accessory Uses

Although almost all communities treat backyard gardening as a permitted use of residential land, it is often not mentioned in their zoning ordinances. I think that is because it was always assumed to be part of residential occupancy, like parking a car in a driveway. If they were ever asked about this omission from the zoning code, local officials would say, "Of course you can grow vegetables on your own property. We all do that." But this answer leaves many secondary questions unanswered. The better practice is to list accessory agriculture in as many zone districts as possible. A growing number of newer zoning codes explicitly allow accessory gardening by right, not only in residential zones but also in mixed-use zones and sometimes even in commercial and industrial zones. Many limit accessory gardening to backyards and sideyards, but others allow it in front yards as well. Newer codes also answer three follow-on questions.

1. Can I build a structure (generally a greenhouse, hoop house, coldframe, or raised bed) to protect the plants? Many newer codes say "yes" but require small setbacks from neighboring properties and limit the amount of the backyard area that can be covered by these structures to 25 or 50 percent.
2. Can I sell the food I grow to others from a stand on the property? Again, a growing number of zoning ordinances say "yes" but limit the maximum size of the sales stand. A few go further to require that the stand not be located in the front yard. And a few go further to require that you get a business license like all other businesses operating in the community.
3. Can I process some of the vegetables into secondary products, such as tomato sauce or applesauce, and sell that from the property? Most newer codes do not permit this, primarily because of worries that it will result in residential properties looking more like businesses and because of worries about public health risks from improperly processed food. A few newer codes do allow small-scale processing, however, while imposing limits on the size of the processing facility and sometimes requiring business licenses and periodic health inspections as they would for other food-producing facilities. Since the impacts of small-scale processing can be addressed through size limits and operating controls, and since this is an economic activity that could be entered into by many people in historically

disadvantaged communities, we should be moving toward allowing this in more locations.

A fourth and somewhat related question often needs to be answered: Can I raise chickens and other animals that produce food on the property? This topic is often referred to by planners as the "chicken wars" because emotions can run high, and outcomes vary a lot. Nevertheless, three trends appear clear.

First, a growing number of cities and counties are allowing hens (but not roosters) to be raised in backyards. The maximum number of chickens permitted often depends on the size of the lot on where they are kept, and some communities go further to establish minimum standards for coops. Second, many of the worrisome what-if scenarios that caused vigorous debate when the issue was first raised do not occur. Noise and nuisance issues tend to be few and far between. As that becomes clear over time, communities sometimes revisit and simplify their original regulations to make life easier for both residents and enforcement staff.

The third trend is that many communities decide that these regulations belong in their animal control regulations rather than zoning ordinances. Although the reasons vary, the most common is that when complaints or concerns are raised, animal control staff are often better qualified than zoning inspectors to evaluate the health risks and identify what needs to be done to protect the health of both animals and humans. Zoning enforcement staff are rarely trained on those topics. Treating chicken regulations as animal control rules also allows better coordination with regulations for other types of pets and permitted animals.

A few cities allow the raising of other food-producing animals such as goats, sheep, and rabbits as accessory uses, but those that do almost invariably integrate them with other animal control regulations outside the zoning ordinance. Those types of regulations are beyond the scope of this book.

Medium-Scale Community Garden Uses

Medium-scale community garden food production is another example of an in-between land use where best practices are still evolving. Part of the challenge is that these are primary uses of land; they do not occur on land with another primary use where the owner of the property lives on the property and can be quickly contacted for zoning compliance. Part of the challenge is that this scale of use can occur in many different ways. It can be a community garden organized by a group of neighbors on an informal basis (with no single entity responsible for managing or maintaining the facility) or by an incorporated nonprofit that can be held responsible for management and compliance. Or it can occur when the owner of a lot or parcel of land does not need to use it for any other use at the present time and thinks food production would be a good interim use of the land. Or it can occur as a medium-scale enclosed hydroponic or aquaculture facility owned and operated by a nonprofit or for-profit company.

Note that food production at this scale is almost inherently an interim use. Just because you planted vegetables on your vacant lot last year does not mean that you have to plant them again this year. Because medium-scale agriculture is usually just one of several uses allowed in the zoning district, you could decide to put the property to one of those other allowed uses next year. Strong advocates of local food production sometimes argue for the creation of a separate zoning district (or more than one) that would allow *only* medium-scale food production, but very few zoning ordinances take this approach.

The main reason is that in many locations where this use is likely to take place, agriculture is not the most valuable use of the land. It happens because of the personal preference of the property owners despite the fact that the land may be more economically valuable in a different use. Many property owners who are happy to make that decision for a period of time are unwilling to commit to only medium-scale food production for the long term, and most elected officials are unwilling to force them to do so over their objections. While it is unlikely that a farmer in a rural area zoned for farming will simply decide to stop farming as long as that use is economically viable, the same is not true for growers who are acting voluntarily. The community garden may decide to disband next year due to lack of interest or membership, or the property owners could decide to leave the parcel unused, both of which mean no local food will be produced until they change their minds again.

As zoning ordinances are revised to allow medium-scale food production, they face the same three secondary questions that occur for backyard gardening—but the answers are often slightly different.

Can we build a structure to protect the plants? The general answer is still "yes," but some communities go further to require that any tools and equipment be stored in a closed structure when not in use. The difference is that most communities do not want to monitor storage of tools on properties where people live or work (and can generally be counted on to take care of their tools) unless failure to do that creates a nuisance. But the same assumption is weaker when no single person or entity lives on the property, and unattended tools and supplies on unoccupied properties invite theft.

Can we sell the food we grow to others? Again, the answer is generally "yes," with the same types of limitations applicable to backyard gardening, including limits on the size of the sales stand. Some communities require that any sales facility that is not dismantled and stored at the end of the sale period be secured to prevent theft or vandalism.

Can we process some of the food we grow into secondary products? In this case, the usual answer is "no" unless the garden is located in a zoning district where freestanding food processing is allowed anyway. Again, the general worry is that construction of a production facility will change the appearance of the area from a residential or mixed-use area to something more commercial and industrial.

Unlike the case for accessory backyard gardening, most newer codes do not permit the raising of chickens or other animals as part of this medium-scale food production use. The primary reason is concern for the health of the animals and the public health risks that arise if the animals are not treated properly. It is one thing to assume that backyard chickens can be raised without significant risks, because their owners live on the same property and can be easily contacted and held accountable for failure to do so. It is another thing to monitor and enforce the same types of regulations when no one lives on the property.

There is one additional challenge to local food production at this middle scale, particularly in urbanized areas. In many cases, the soil must be tested to ensure that dangerous pollutants are not present. At the accessory backyard gardening level, this issue is usually ignored, because the amounts of food being produced are small and the amounts of that food being sold to the public are also small. In addition, much of the land used for accessory gardening has always been in residential use, so the probability that harmful chemicals have been disposed of in or on the soil is low. And, of course, requiring every homeowner to prove that their soil is safe for growing vegetables would be both burdensome and unpopular.

In contrast, as the range of uses producing food at the community garden scale has increased, the amounts of food being grown have increased, and the amount of that food that enters the public food system is also likely to increase. And unlike backyard gardening, the land used for medium-scale food production may have previously been used for commercial or institutional or industrial uses, each of which may have generated pollutants that are still in the soil. For all these reasons, a growing number of cities require that owners of land whose primary use will be to grow food demonstrate that the soil is safe for that purpose. As zoning ordinances are revised to recognize and list medium-scale food production as a primary use of land, they often require or perform a background check to see whether the land has ever been used for a nonresidential purpose. If the answer is no, either the food production use is approved or only a simple soil test for the presence of lead is required.

The reason for the latter approach is that for decades it was common to use lead-based paint for both residential and nonresidential buildings. When those buildings are removed, some of that lead may wind up in the soil and can be absorbed by the roots of plants grown in that soil. Since ingesting even small amounts of lead can produce serious health impacts, and since testing for the presence of lead is inexpensive, newer codes sometimes require testing as a condition of all medium-scale food production on previously developed land. If the land fails this test (i.e., if significant concentrations of lead are found), the use may still be approved but with a condition that plants be grown only in raised beds filled with clean soil brought to the site.

If zoning records show that the lot or parcel proposed for food production was previously used for nonresidential uses, a growing number of newer codes require more extensive testing for other pollutants, particularly heavy metals that could have serious health impacts if they entered the public food system. Requirements sometimes include testing for the presence of arsenic, cadmium, mercury, molybdenum, nickel, selenium, and zinc, using methods approved by the US Environmental Protection Agency.[53] While some of these metals are used only in rare and specialized heavy industrial production activities, others are present in some automobile catalytic converters and could be found in sites previously used for motor vehicle servicing and repairs.

If any of the listed metals are present, food may be grown on the site only if their concentrations are below the residential screening levels established for safe direct contact by the state health agency or if plants are grown in raised beds containing clean soil brought to the site. Although testing for these heavy metals can be significantly more expensive than testing for the presence of lead, it is necessary to ensure that local responses to one public health challenge (the absence of fresh produce without high processing, packaging, and transportation costs) does not create another public health problem (direct contact with or ingestion of dangerous chemicals).

Unfortunately, both the challenge of increasing the supply of fresh local produce and the challenge of avoiding contaminated soil have an equity component. Not only do historically disadvantaged neighborhoods often have low availability of fresh locally produced food, they often have higher than average concentrations of polluted sites that may not be safe for food production. That is because residential land near formerly or currently polluting land activities is often less expensive and is therefore occupied by those without the financial resources to move further away. In order to effectively promote local food production in these neighborhoods, it may be necessary to provide assistance to bring in clean soil and build the raised beds necessary to grow food safely.

4.4. Restrictive Covenants Are Not the Answer

As mentioned in the introduction to this chapter, I clearly agree that current zoning practices are counterproductive and unfair, but I do not agree that zoning is so broken that it should be replaced by reliance on restrictive covenants. The three previous sections list just some of the many ways that we can fix zoning to get the more affordable, equitable, and sustainable communities we want.

There are four problems with relying on restrictive covenants as a primary approach to land use regulation. The first is that they tend to be even more restrictive and exclusive than the land use controls that also apply in the same areas. Restrictive covenants usually embody a "ratchet-up" effect toward exclusion. As acknowledged in Chapter 2, zoning rules are almost inherently restrictive, but most private residential covenants tend to exclude even more uses and structures than zoning. In most cases that was deliberate. They were drafted and recorded by the developer before residential development began so that properties subject to the covenants could be marketed as better or higher quality or safer investments than those in the surrounding areas without covenants. The developer hoped that the covenants would help the lots command higher sales prices, and higher prices tend to exclude some potential residents.

The second challenge is that the process of drafting restrictive covenants—deciding what to exclude or require—is generally done privately (usually between a landowner and a lawyer), while drafting zoning controls usually takes place through a public process with required public meetings and hearings. This is one reason why covenants tend to be more restrictive than zoning. The zoning controls reflect judgments about what is in the public interest and what is "too restrictive," made by appointed and elected officials operating in public. Privately drafted covenants can include levels of control that would not be approved in a public process, either because they are too complex or subjective or because they seem explicitly designed to exclude poorer households or disfavored populations.

One example of the different outcomes of public and private systems of land use controls comes from the discussion of small group homes for people experiencing physical or mental disabilities discussed in Section 4.2. Since 1968, the federal Fair Housing Amendments Act has prohibited local governments from "making unavailable" housing based on whether their occupants are experiencing limited physical or mental abilities.[54] And the broad language of the act has led the Civil Rights Division of the US Department of Justice to interpret this requirement to mean that local governments need to allow housing for these people on the same basis as they do facilities for those without disabilities.[55] Most state fair housing acts and related court decisions have similar language, both because there are advantages to aligning with federal law and because there is often broad support for this fair housing goal at a statewide level.

To achieve that goal, many group homes for people experiencing these limitations often need to be in low-density residential neighborhoods, and that is sometimes unpopular with the residents of those neighborhoods. Most local zoning codes try to get beyond that unpopularity and come into compliance with federal and state acts by allowing small group homes in at least some of their low-density residential districts. Over the decades that I have been drafting zoning controls, many communities have adopted codes with fewer restrictions on these types of small group homes; none of my clients has publicly adopted a code that is more restrictive. But many restrictive covenants—even new ones—prohibit all commercial activities in residential areas or explicitly prohibit group homes for those experiencing disabilities. That happens despite the fact that several court decisions have refused to enforce similar covenants. More specifically, several court decisions have held that small group homes for those protected by federal and state legislation need to be allowed in zones where single-household homes are allowed and may not be treated as commercial activities despite the fact that the group home is receiving or charging money to provide housing. Broad public acceptance of fair housing goals at broader levels of government continues to be undermined by covenants at the neighborhood level, both because the neighborhood perspective is often narrower and because the drafting and recording of covenants did not require public review.

The third challenge of relying on a covenant-based system is that it would be very difficult to design a covenant approach that covered an entire community—or even all the residential and mixed-use neighborhoods in a community. In mature cities and counties, some neighborhoods are subject to covenants and others are not. Universal or almost-universal covenant coverage is found only in newer suburbs, usually those on the wealthier sides of the cities that serve as employment centers for their residents. Imposing restrictive covenants on a neighborhood after development has occurred and multiple property owners are involved is very difficult.

Property owner attitudes toward contracts that restrict their use of property are more likely to align at the time when lots are first purchased and what your neighbor might do with their property is less certain. As time passes and property ownership changes, some new property owners may value the additional restrictions on their neighbors, while others wish they could use their property in different or less restrictive ways than the covenants allow. This split of opinion becomes clear when individual property owners ask for exceptions or changes to the covenants. Usually some of their neighbors will agree and others will oppose the application. The difficulty of changing or approving exceptions to already-imposed covenants is just a shadow of the opposition likely to emerge if a city tries to impose a covenant system after the fact. In addition to the usual split of opinion between those who want more or fewer restrictions, additional opposition will come from those who deliberately bought property in the area because it did not have the second level of land use controls embodied in covenants.

As a practical matter, moving from a system of zoning controls to a covenant-based system of controls without zoning would be extremely challenging. It might have even been challenging in Houston, which is famous (at least among planners) for not having zoning controls. But even that city twice adopted zoning controls, and the voters have twice reversed that approval. Both of those votes occurred before the adopted zoning system had been implemented and when the city's alternative system of covenant controls was still in effect. Houston makes its land use system work, but its citizens were never faced with the choice to replace an up-and-operating system of zoning controls with a covenant-based system. They voted to keep what they had.

The final problem with relying on restrictive covenants as a primary tool of land use controls is that enforcement of covenants tends to be selective and, in many cases, unpredictable. Enforcement of covenants tends to be through the courts, and that takes time and costs money. And courts are often backed up for months. In some neighborhoods (particularly residential areas and master-planned communities), enforcement of covenants is rigorous and consistent, and the residents and property owners expect that and are willing to pay for it. In other neighborhoods, enforcement can be sporadic, unpredictable, or based on the popularity of the property owner who is violating or wants an exception to the covenant. It can also depend on whether the property owners' association charged with enforcing the covenants is active or passive, is knowledgeable (or not) about the covenants, or has funds available to file an enforcement lawsuit. When covenants have been selectively or seldom enforced, courts may refuse to enforce them. And, in general, wealthier neighborhoods with more active property owners' associations have greater ability to enforce covenants than less wealthy neighborhoods. At worst, covenants remain in the title records while being ignored by property owners because knowledge of them or willingness to enforce them has been lost in the mists of time.

Imagining a cure for the selective enforcement problem requires us to imagine that a local government could replace zoning controls with a covenant system that has equally broad coverage and that the local government would get involved in the enforcement of those covenants. While city or county enforcement of a wide variety of covenants covering most of the community might in theory be more consistent and principled than private enforcement, it would also be time-consuming and expensive. Covenant enforcement almost always requires a court action, while zoning enforcement (especially in newer codes) often includes administrative enforcement mechanisms that are quicker and cheaper than court actions. In many communities, zoning violations are treated more like parking tickets. You can decide whether to pay the parking ticket or dispute it, but disputes are often managed by an administrative official or parking magistrate at much less time and expense than going to court. There is one key difference, however. Most communities view zoning enforcement as a system to bring the property back into compliance with the code, not as a way to collect fines and fees. They offer time, and sometimes help, to bring the property into compliance before imposing fines on those who ignore those opportunities.

So to imagine a community-wide covenant-based land use control system with enforcement time, expense, and consistency similar to zoning enforcement, we need to imagine the creation of a new system of administrative enforcement to replace court actions. Or we have to live with the current system of unpredictable private enforcement. In addition, because covenants currently in effect cover a very wide range of topics, we also have to design a system that can distinguish between which current covenants are in the public interests (and worth enforcing) and which are just exclusionary, do not serve a public purpose, or have disproportionate impacts on historically disadvantaged residents (and probably should not be enforced). For all these reasons, I think replacement of zoning controls with a covenant-based system of land use controls is both unlikely and unwise, particularly if we want the result to be more sustainable, affordable, and equitable.

The better approach is to fix zoning, not try to replace it. It can be revised to achieve the goals of this book, and those changes will be adopted through public processes that involve more than just the narrow range of property owners or potential buyers involved in drafting or agreeing to be bound by covenants.

CHAPTER 5

Fixing the Procedures

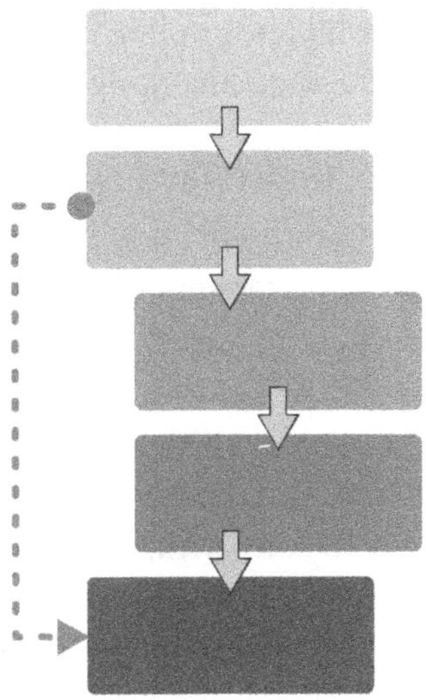

Many Americans think of zoning as the long set of rules that tell property owners what they can and cannot do with their properties, but zoning is also about the procedures we use to draft, apply, change, and enforce those rules. In some cases, those procedures can be more important than the rules themselves. Zoning procedures determine how much time it will take to review and approve a proposed investment, who will be invited to participate in the review and decision, whether the decision will be based on objective or subjective criteria, and how much the approval process will add to the cost of the project. They also determine who will get notice about a proposed change, whether the notice will be in plain language they can understand, and whether and how they may be able to influence the outcome of that decision.

Zoning procedures can be a significant barrier to achieving all three of the key challenges addressed in this book. The time and expense of confrontational public hearings, and the uncertainty of the outcomes of those hearings, can significantly increase the costs of housing projects. Zoning procedures can prevent vulnerable groups from influencing development in their neighborhoods while enabling more privileged residents to thwart zoning changes that would increase equity and affordability in their neighborhoods. And environmental review procedures can be misaligned or inconsistent with zoning controls, leading builders to avoid sustainable development projects that require those additional reviews.

Several years ago I interviewed affordable housing builders in Denver, Colorado, about what the city could do to increase the production of affordable housing. I gave them a choice of the "usual suspects" considered when municipalities want to increase housing supply: more height? more density? less parking? more lot coverage? fewer design restrictions? shorter approval processes? Without exception, they said, "If you could design an approval process that would avoid public hearings on affordable housing, you could forget all of the other zoning adjustments you just mentioned. They would be nice, of course, but as long as we face expensive and unpredictable discretionary approval procedures, height and density, parking, lot coverage, and design controls will always be secondary concerns."

5.1. Understanding the Legal Framework

Zoning operates within a framework of federal and state constitutional law that places important limits on how local governments can use this tool. That legal framework was explained in detail in *A Better Way to Zone*,[1] and that full discussion will not be repeated here. Instead, I will focus on the key legal opportunities and constraints that may limit how zoning procedures can be revised to improve affordability, equity, and sustainability.

To start with, there are no federal laws on zoning. All zoning laws are created by state or local governments, but they must still comply with state and federal constitutional requirements and state statutes. All fifty states have their own laws on zoning, subdivision, and land and environmental regulation, and those highly varied rules are often further tweaked by local governments using discretion granted to them by the state legislature. So it is impossible for a book like this to accurately summarize what law applies to a given site in a given location in a given state. Instead, I will focus on generally applicable federal constitutional principles that apply everywhere. But remember that these principles are often modified or expanded by state laws, as discussed in Section 5.1.5. And—no surprise—none of the content here is intended to provide legal advice to anyone.

5.1.1. Due Process

The Fifth Amendment to the US Constitution states that "no person shall be deprived of life, liberty, or property without due process of law," and the Fourteenth Amendment makes that provision applicable to all fifty states. What "due process" requires differs widely for different types of government action, but in general the requirements are sometimes lower for government actions that affect property rather than life or liberty. In general, "due process" means that government actions to change the rules regarding the use or development of property must be done with notice to those affected and with an opportunity for those affected to voice their opinions about the proposed change.

Zoning decisions that affect many people or many properties, or all or a large area of the community, are often called "legislative" decisions and are made by elected officials. They are often based on judgments about what is wisest for the entire community and do not depend on a careful analysis of the impact of the proposed change on specific properties. In contrast, zoning decisions that affect only one or a few properties or property owners are often called "quasijudicial" because they depend more on specific facts related to the affected properties. In these cases the decision maker is acting more like a judge to determine how the proposed changes will affect specific properties, and the decision maker is sometimes an appointed individual (such as a hearing officer) or body (such as a planning commission), rather than an elected body.

In general, quasijudicial decisions are entitled to more due process than legislative decisions. This is because the opportunities to treat individual property owners unfairly, either by favoring one or discriminating against another, are greater when only a few property owners are involved. As a result, quasijudicial due process often requires notice to those property owners, gives them an opportunity to comment in writing or in person about the proposed change, and sometimes requires that those offering comments be given a chance to rebut claims about the property or the impacts of the change that they think are inaccurate.

Notice must always be given to the affected property owners, and it is often required be given to nearby property owners, but it is rarely required to be published in a newspaper or provided to everyone in the community. The types of notice given (i.e., mailed, posted, published, or electronic) and who is entitled to receive notice vary greatly both by state and community. Due process also generally requires that the decision be made on the record (i.e., based on facts stated in the application or in writing or in person during the approval process and documented so that a judge can review the decision later if it is challenged).

In contrast, due process for legislative changes often requires that the decision be made after a public hearing, that notice of the public be hearing be published in advance, and that the public be allowed to testify about the proposed change. It often does not require that the decision be on the record because all actions of the elected officials are documented. In addition, legislative due process generally does not require that those testifying have a chance to rebut statements that they think are inaccurate. If testimony about the impacts of the proposed change differ, the elected officials are expected to make decisions based on that testimony without having to referee a debate between those testifying.

In the context of this book, it is important to remember what constitutional principles of due process do *not* require. They do not require that every decision about the development or redevelopment of an individual property be made after a public hearing. Most zoning decisions do not involve creating new zoning districts, modifying the text of a zoning district, or reclassifying properties from one zoning district to another (all of which would generally require a public hearing). They involve determinations as to whether a proposed change to the use of property or a proposal to develop or redevelop property complies with the applicable standards and criteria in the zoning ordinance. Although smaller communities sometimes send these decisions to appointed or elected bodies, most treat these as administrative decisions that can be made by staff without a public hearing but can be appealed if someone thinks that staff applied those standards and criteria incorrectly. In some communities two or three times as many planners are involved in these administrative development review decisions as are involved in legislative or quasijudicial matters that require public hearings.

5.1.2. Equal Protection

Right after saying that no state shall deprive any person of life, liberty, or property, the Fourteenth Amendment goes on to say, "nor deny to any person within its jurisdiction the equal protection of the laws." Those unhappy with zoning decision sometimes think this means that they have a right to have their property (or their neighbor's property) zoned in a way that is "equal" to someone else's property. That is almost never the case.

To be blunt, this constitutional provision is almost never relevant to zoning, for two reasons. First, when this clause is invoked in disputes involving property (as opposed to fundamental rights such as life or liberty), federal courts have interpreted the clause to only require inquiry as to whether the law has a "rational relationship" to a legitimate government interest. Not only is the right to be zoned or not zoned—or to have your neighbor zoned or not zoned—in a particular way not a fundamental right or liberty under the US Constitution, but the "rational relationship" standard is a very low bar. If the court determines that there is any way that the regulation could promote a legitimate government interest, it passes the test, even if the court does not think it actually will achieve that result.

Equally important, zoning is a creature of state and not federal law, and federal law is silent on whether states can zone your property in a certain way—unless their actions violate another constitutional protection. But that also means that state law can expand equal protections to include requirements that similar properties be treated similarly, and many have. In fact, many state zoning enabling laws state that all buildings or development in a zoning district be subject to "uniform" standards. But even that language does not usually help someone challenging a zoning action on equal protection grounds, for the reason discussed below.

The second reason that equal protection challenges to zoning actions almost never succeed is that it is very hard to prove that two properties are "equal" and therefore have to be treated the same. There is always some factor that the local government can cite for why two similar properties that are zoned differently really are different. For example, one is closer to an environmental risk, or a road, or a sensitive facility such as a school, or has different soil or utility conditions. And zoning provisions that treat properties in a zoning district differently based on these types of factors are usually upheld because there is in fact a "rational relationship" explaining the different treatment. Although they do not treat everyone in the zoning district exactly the same, they treat everyone similarly situated with respect to those types of named factors the same way, and that is generally enough to pass the "uniform" standards test.

There is one important exception, however. If a property owner can show that their property has been singled out for zoning restrictions or that a zoning change drafted to sound like it applies to an entire group of properties and uses in fact only restricts their one property—courts sometimes agree that the equal protection clause has been violated.[2] This situation is sometimes referred to as a "class of one" challenge; it claims that only you (not you and a few others) have been singled out. Class of one challenges are rare, because local government zoning actions that penalize only one property owner are very rare. And in the rare cases where a local government adopts a change that inadvertently deprives only one property owner of a key zoning use or development opportunity, and that impact is brought to their attention, they often amend the ordinance, approve an exception or variance, or attempt to mitigate the unfairness in some other way.

The key principle to remember is that no one has a constitutional right to be zoned in a particular way unless state zoning enabling law says they do. But they probably have a right to not be singled out for restrictions that apply to no one else.

5.1.3. Regulatory Takings

The third constitutional principle relevant to zoning systems and decisions comes from the Fifth Amendment phrase "nor shall private property be taken for public use without just compensation." This is a complex area of law that is often misunderstood and that has been the subject of several significant US Supreme Court interpretations in recent years. We can only cover the basics here.

Although the clause quoted in the previous paragraph was originally intended to mean that "if the government wants to own your property, they have to pay you for it," that meaning was expanded by the US Supreme Court in the 1920s to mean something like "if the government adopts regulations on your property that limit its use so severely that you really have no viable use left, then they need to compensate you for the amount by which they reduced the value of your property."[3] This principle is referred to as regulatory takings, because although no one took your property (you still own it), the impact of their regulations is so severe that they should have probably bought the property from you. In making this change, the Court acknowledged that "government hardly could go on if, to some extent, values incident to property could not be diminished without paying for every such change in the general law." It went on to say that a regulation that "goes too far" can result in the government being required to pay compensation for the reduction in property value caused by that regulation. And for the past hundred years property owners, government officials, and the Court have been struggling with what "goes too far." While this discussion is still going on, six principles are important in the context of this book.

1. Focus on "what is left" to the property owner. The question of whether a property owner is entitled to compensation because of the impact of a zoning regulation on their property is almost always resolved by looking at what remaining uses of the property and types of development are still available to the owner, not by looking at what uses or types of development are no longer available due to the regulation.

2. The "whole parcel" rule. Unless state law requires otherwise, the question of whether compensation must be paid is generally resolved by looking at the impact of the regulation on all of the owner's contiguous property rather than just a part of it. Since every regulation can be described as taking away "all" of something (the right to develop in a setback, or the right to start an aircraft factory), courts have decided that the true impact on a property owner must consider the entire contiguous property.[4]
3. "Reasonable economic use" and "per se" takings. The regulation must leave the property owner with at least one reasonable economic use of the property. As a corollary, a zoning regulation that prevents every reasonable economic use of all of the property is a "per se" taking. The government must then pay compensation to the owner of the property, with almost no exceptions.[5] However, this almost never happens.
4. The "rational nexus" requirement. Regulations that obligate the property owner to give the government a piece of land, or to pay the government cash, must have a rational nexus between that requirement and an impact of the development that the government is trying to mitigate or offset and that the required land or cash can help offset. A zoning regulation cannot be used to exact land or money if that exaction cannot possibly mitigate an impact of the development that the government is authorized to regulate.[6]
5. The "rough proportionality" requirement. If the local government is requiring land or cash as a condition of approval, the amount of land or cash required must be roughly proportional to the impacts caused by the development.[7] By the way, the rational nexus and rough proportionality requirements apply regardless of whether the land or cash requirement is being negotiated individually for a specific proposed development or pursuant to a formula adopted by the government that is applicable to an entire class of development proposals (e.g., a formula stormwater mitigation fee based on the amount of impervious surfaces).[8] Based on the names of the Supreme Court cases that established the fourth and fifth principles, I will refer to these as the Nollan–Dolan–Sheetz requirements.
6. The "unconstitutional conditions" corollary. If a zoning regulation fails to meet the Nollan–Dolan–Sheetz requirements, and the landowner refuses to contribute the land or pay the money, the local government cannot simply deny the application.[9] In other words, an

attempt to apply unconstitutional exactions is illegal whether it leads to a condition on an approval or a denial of the application. This is a particularly difficult principle to understand, since the local government may not know that its requirement violates the Nollan–Dolan–Sheetz requirements until after they are challenged and overturned in court. Few local governments intend to adopt unconstitutional zoning standards. As a practical matter it means that governments should evaluate whether their requirements for dedication of land or contributions of money meet these key constitutional requirements before they discuss applying them to a particular proposed development or embedding them in a formula fee.

Together, these six principles establish significant protections for private landowners and significant restrictions on the types of zoning regulations that local governments can adopt. But they also leave local governments lots of room to change zoning regulations over time without needing to pay compensation. Very importantly, the Nollan–Dolan–Sheetz requirements are focused on required contributions of land or money, and most zoning regulations do not involve either of those. Common zoning regulations addressing permitted or conditional uses, maximum building heights, minimum building setbacks, maximum lot coverage, or building and site design and layout are not subject to the requirements of rational nexus or rough proportionality established by those cases. And cases where zoning regulations do not leave the property owner with at least one reasonable economic use are extremely rare. Many of the zoning changes to improve affordability, equity, and sustainability suggested in this book will in fact open up new and potentially more profitable forms of development rather than restricting them in ways that might trigger a regulatory takings claim. If it is not already clear from the earlier discussions, constitutional law on regulatory takings does not mean the city or county must pay compensation whenever a zoning change reduces someone's property value, denies them their preferred use of the property, or prevents them from undertaking a new development that they had in mind when they bought the property.

However, there is one additional restriction on zoning changes that needs to be respected, and that is the legal principle of estoppel. "Estoppel" just means that sometimes a local government cannot change its mind without compensating those who are hurt by the change. If the city government tells a property owner that a proposed development is permitted, they may be "estopped" from later saying it is not permitted unless they pay damages for the harm caused by that change. More specifically, if a local government official with authority to do so has advised a property owner that a proposed development is permitted or will be approved, the property owner moves ahead and makes substantial investments based on that advice, and the local government then changes the zoning regulations so that the development is not permitted, the government may have to pay damages to compensate the owner for the investments made. This basic principle of fairness had its origins in English common law and is also discussed in at least two other ways. The limitations on local government ability to change its mind about a proposed development is sometimes discussed as vested rights, but that term has its own complex legal history, often has a specific defined meaning in state law, and those meanings differ significantly between the fifty states. So a claim that zoning regulations violate vested rights is often treated by the courts as a factual question as to whether vested rights exist rather than whether a regulatory taking has occurred.

In the context of regulatory takings, the "you cannot always change your mind without paying" principle is also sometimes discussed as a requirement that the government respect "reasonable investment backed expectations."[10] But that phrase does not mean that the local government must allow the property owner to do whatever they reasonably expected to be able to do with their property. Most cases that use this phrase hold that compensation is due only if the property owner took steps to confirm with the local government that their expectations were correct and then made significant investments in reliance on those assurances.

The level of investment needed to claim reasonable investment-backed expectations usually means something beyond purchasing the land itself and incurring "soft costs" such as preliminary site design and engineering or architectural work. Both land purchase costs and soft costs are considered routine items that are sometimes lost if developments do not move forward for other reasons, and courts have generally decided that local governments should not be held responsible for those expenses even if they do change their minds. "Reasonable investment-backed expectations" often means moving forward with construction based on permits approved by the local government. Although the laws of estoppel, vested rights, and reasonable investment-backed expectations are different from each other, and differ depending on which state you are in, they are discussed together here because they stand for the principle that local governments that change their minds about how they will treat a specific development application sometimes have to pay compensation.

5.1.4. First Amendment Protections

One final set of constitutional constraints also affects zoning law. The protections of the First Amendment limit how local governments can regulate churches, mosques, synagogues, gurdwaras, and other religious institutions to ensure the free establishment and free practice of religion. However, those constraints have very little to do with the three challenges addressed in this book. To my knowledge, the close attention given to the regulation of religious land uses by the federal courts has not varied depending on the income, race, ethnicity, or national origin of those involved in the case. Those court decisions have not contributed to the nation's affordable housing shortage and have not materially contributed to the sustainability of current development. In addition, the federal Religious Land Use and Institutionalized Persons Act (RLUIPA)[11] has established a separate body of law that applies to most challenges to the establishment or operation of religious facilities, and a review of that law is beyond the scope of this book.

However, one key principle embedded in RLUIPA is relevant to America's affordable housing challenge. Local governments cannot limit religious land uses more strictly than they do similar secular uses of land. That applies not only to religious worship activities but also nonworship activities that religious institutions conduct to carry out their mission. But that may not include every activity that the institution says is necessary to the exercise of its religious. When challenged, the courts will evaluate how central or important the activity is to religious exercise, and zoning regulations that restrict community services and facilities have sometimes been upheld.

More specifically, use of church land to construct housing (affordable or not) has generally been held to be a general land use decision that zoning can regulate without violating RLUIPA. The fact that a housing project is owned or operated by a church, is located on its lands, or houses people related to the church or people that it cares about will not generally exempt it from zoning laws that regulate housing construction simply because the property owner is a church. However, as discussed in Section 4.1.1, some states and local governments have changed their zoning regulations to make it easier for churches to build housing on their properties with fewer zoning hurdles.

Importantly, RLUIPA does not stop local governments from restricting religious institutions *less* than similar secular facilities; it just prohibits them from being *more* restrictive. With that one exception, federal constitutional principles about freedom of religion do not significantly affect the menu of possible zoning improvements for sustainability, affordability, and equity and will not be discussed further in this book.

The First Amendment also limits how cities, counties, and townships can regulate signs, billboards, and adult entertainment, each of which has generated a long and complex string of court decisions that attempt to balance local governments' power to regulate land with the need to protect rights to free speech and expression. Again, however, these court decisions have had almost no impact on the affordability or sustainability. There may be a higher concentration of adult entertainment uses in disadvantaged communities, but it may be difficult to show that the location of those businesses has limited housing or employment opportunities for the residents of nearby neighborhoods.

The presence of more billboards or more adult entertainment uses may have an impact on surrounding property values, and that could affect the ability of neighborhood residents to generate wealth through property ownership. However, those impacts are minor compared with the much more direct forms of zoning inequity discussed in Chapter 3. The tools that could be used to address those impacts are the same as those discussed for environmental risk and locally unwanted land uses in Section 4.2.5, and that discussion will not be repeated here.

5.1.5. State Law

Sections 5.1.1 through 5.1.4 above focused on key aspects of federal constitutional law that limit general zoning authority, because those generally apply consistently throughout all fifty states. In addition, many states have adopted parallel or analogous constitutional provisions or legislation, because those types of rights and freedoms are valued as constraints on state government action even when the federal government is not involved. And because the power to zone land is often delegated to local governments, those principles also generally apply at the local level. The adoption of state law provisions that parallel federal protections often makes it possible to challenge the same zoning action under either state or federal law.

However, it is important to remember that each of the fifty states may have enacted laws that address these key rights and obligations (due process, equal protection, property rights, freedom of religion, and free speech) in different ways. In some cases, state constitutions or laws do not offer as much protection as the US Constitution, and in other cases state laws go further to add protections or extend them to additional situations. As an example, some states prohibit housing discrimination based on the sexual orientation of the resident even though the US Constitution does not. In other cases, state legislation or court decisions define a prohibited regulatory taking more broadly than the federal courts.

When state protections differ from those in federal law, it does not mean that the federal protections do not apply. They almost always apply if they involve the constitutional protections discussed earlier, if the federal government has adopted legislation on the topic (such as the Fair Housing Act), or if the project will involve the use of federal money. It just means that someone who objects to a local zoning action may have a legal claim in state court when they do not have one in federal court, or vice versa. For all these reasons, the general constitutional principles discussed in Sections 5.1.1 through 5.1.4 should always be understood and evaluated in light of state law related to those topics. You should never assume that the federal constitutional constraints summarized above either support or undermine a local zoning action until you also review state law on the same topic.

5.2. Clarifying the Role of the Public

Zoning exists, at least in theory, to serve the public good. It was created because we thought our communities would be better with it than without it. Those general desires were mixed in with less altruistic motives, including racism and classism, and one goal of this book is to help identify ways to reverse the impacts of those less-than-admirable intentions. But if zoning is to serve the public, then of course the public needs to have an important role in how it is designed and applied. In fact, one of the core aspirational principles of the American Institute of Certified Planners is to encourage equitable and informed public participation in planning and plan implementation. More specifically, that document states that those involved in planning should "facilitate the exchange of ideas and ensure that people have the opportunity for meaningful, timely, and informed participation in the development of plans and programs that may affect them."[12] The question is how to do that in a way that promotes affordable and sustainable development without the disproportionate negative impacts on historically disadvantaged communities than we have created in the past.

5.2.1. The Spectrum of Public Participation

It is helpful to view the various opportunities for public participation in zoning along a spectrum. Let's look at seven potential zoning actions and where they fall on that spectrum:

1. *Community-wide rules and incentives.* At the far left end is drafting a completely new zoning ordinance and map that will affect everyone.
2. *Neighborhood-wide rules and incentives.* Next to the right is drafting area- or neighborhood-specific changes to the zoning ordinance and map that will affect many properties in an entire area of the community, such as a new district to address transit-oriented development or a historic preservation overlay district.
3. *Topic-specific rules and incentives.* In the middle of this imaginary spectrum are topic-specific updates, such as a new section addressing accessory dwelling units or short-term rentals, which affect many properties that may be geographically scattered rather than neighborhood-specific.
4. *Large development approvals.* Further to the right is the approval of a large development or redevelopment project on a specific site covering one or more blocks of the community—something large enough to require judgments as to how streets, utilities, and open spaces should connect or complement those around the development.
5. *Site-specific rezoning decisions.* Next to the right is the rezoning of a single property or a handful of properties.
6. *Conditional use approvals.* Next is a site-specific zoning decision to approve a new use of an existing property that does not require rezoning or significant redevelopment of the current building or site.
7. *Site-specific project approvals.* At the far right end of the spectrum is the approval of a development project that does not require a rezoning (i.e., one that involves a permitted use and a building that meets the current zoning standards for the property).

This spectrum is illustrated in Table 5.1.

Type of Decision	Community-Wide Rules and Incentives	Neighborhood-Wide Rules and Incentives	Topic-Specific Rules and Incentives	Large Development Approvals	Site-Specific Rezoning Decisions	Conditional Use Approvals	Site-Specific Project Approvals
Need for Public Input	High	High	High	High	High	Mixed	Low
Risk of Self-Interest	Low	Low	Low	Medium	Medium	High	High

Table 5.1. The Spectrum of Public Participation

I believe that the public needs to be meaningfully educated and engaged in all these types of zoning decisions except the last two, which are discussed in Section 5.2.2.

Community-wide, neighborhood-wide, and topic-specific zoning decisions establish rules that everyone, or everyone engaged in a particular type of use or development, must follow. This is where public participation is most likely to have the broad interests of the community at heart and where the impacts of the decision will have the biggest impact on the community in the long run. These are also the cases where individual self-interest is least likely to undermine a decision that is broadly consistent with community goals for the future.

The fourth case—large development approvals—presents difficult questions about the connections between important public systems and investments (e.g., streets and parks), as well as potentially significant impacts on a fairly large area surrounding the proposed development. These are questions where we need to allow for significant public debate, because reasonable people with the best interests of the community at heart really can differ in their assessments of how the scale, intensity, and design of the project can maximize public benefits and minimize neighborhood impacts. Because they are site specific, individual self-interest (not only of a specific property owner but of the surrounding neighborhood residents) will play a bigger role, but robust public engagement is still needed because of the large numbers of people who may be affected by the development.

5.2.2. The Challenge of Narrow Self-Interest

Starting with the fifth case, the discussion gets a bit harder. In most states, state law requires that decisions to rezone individual parcels of land from one district to another be made after a public hearing to discuss the proposed change. Whenever public hearings are required, the public should be educated about the impacts of the change and equitably engaged in the decision-making process. This is an area where there is great room for improvement but also an area where the self-interest of a few neighbors or a small area near the property can and often does derail projects that are clearly consistent with the community's planning goals. In fact, these types of decisions are at the heart of our affordable housing challenge and the inequitable zoning outcomes embedded in our current system. When a comprehensive plan calls for more housing in a sustainable location without significant impacts on disadvantaged neighborhoods, and we refuse to rezone individual properties to accomplish that result, we deepen the affordable housing hole. And if Whiter and wealthier neighborhoods are better able to participate in hearings to object to those proposed rezonings, then we tend to perpetuate disproportionate zoning outcomes.

For those reasons, some communities have adopted site-specific rezoning criteria that place heavy emphasis on consistency with community and neighborhood plans and less emphasis on localized impacts such as parking and traffic. Others, such as Washington, DC, require that the public engagement and hearing occur before the appointed zoning commission (which is more focused on community-wide impacts) rather than an elected body (which may be more focused on the dissatisfaction of immediate neighbors).

The role of the public in the two remaining types of zoning decisions—conditional use hearings and site-specific development approvals that do not require a rezoning—are discussed in Section 5.3.2. But—spoiler alert—I'm not sure it is wise or necessary to involve the public in those types of minor site-specific zoning decisions.

5.3. Reducing Time, Expense, and Unpredictability

Now we can move on to talk about specific changes to zoning procedures that would promote more affordable, equitable, and sustainable redevelopment. Keep in mind that this section is about procedures, not the zoning rules covered in Chapter 4 or changes to the zoning map discussed in Chapter 6.

One of the key levers that zoning uses to change the future is its ability to make it easy for a property owner or developer to do what we want and harder to build or operate things that we do not want. Remember that every property owner probably has an idea of what they want to build or do or operate on their property, and zoning exists to prevent those things from happening when they are inconsistent with the goals the community has set for itself in the comprehensive plan. This is part of the DNA of exclusion discussed in Chapter 2.

When we are not sure whether a proposed redevelopment would be consistent with the community's goals, we often put the application through a review process with an appointed or elected body. That takes more time and money and makes it harder to achieve than it would be if it clearly aligned with the comprehensive plan goals and the zoning regulations for that site. When a zoning code does not allow a particular use or building or level of development quality, it creates a "no." When it lists the action as a conditional use or an alternative development standard, it creates a "maybe" and makes the establishment of that use or facility harder than if staff could review and approve the application (which would be a "yes").

One of the key roles of a zoning code is to clearly communicate to property owners and neighbors what is a no, what is a maybe, and what is a yes in each area of the community and to make sure that each category is aligned with the community's planning goals for the future. When it comes to procedures, one of the key goals is to reduce the number of maybes in the code, because maybes increase the time, expense, and unpredictability of redevelopment. A developer once told me, "I would like a yes, but I can accept a no. What I cannot afford is the need to wait for three months to know what that answer is." More time means more expense to the developer, and the very fact that the maybe process could result in a no at the end inserts uncertainty into the process. A zoning code that makes it take longer, cost more, and take a risk of denial to do what the community wants is fighting against itself. We know exactly how to draft a "yes" process: Complete the application, pay the fee, and staff approves it if it meets the objective code requirements. But those yeses are often very poorly aligned with the needs of more affordable, equitable, and sustainable development. I call time, expense, and unpredictability the "negative trifecta" of zoning, and it is a prize you do not want to win.

Remember two of the key facts discussed in Chapter 3: Most development is redevelopment, and infill is the only realistic alternative to sprawl. Redevelopment sites are almost always smaller than greenfield development opportunities and sometimes as small as a single urban lot. When a redevelopment project includes a half or a full city block, it is tempting to think that the applicant is a large corporation that can absorb the cost of a discretionary approval process, and that is sometimes the case.

But a discretionary approval process does not come for free. The added costs of holding land for more months before construction or completing additional studies of impacts has to be made up somewhere. At best, the corporation may have multiple projects in multiple cities, and it can offset the costs of those delays here with savings they found somewhere else. But at worst it results in higher rents or sales prices for the housing, business, or public facility described in the application. And smaller firms often do not have other projects against which they can average and offset the costs of delay.

In addition, the American Planning Association *Equity in Zoning Policy Guide*[13] concluded that conditional approval procedures tend to work to the advantage of wealthier residents who are more likely to speak fluent English, to understand how local government operates, to understand the zoning code, and to be able to attend public hearings, and make their wishes known. All those factors contribute to the long-standing problem of inequitable zoning outcomes. This key fact—that the time, expense, and uncertainty of zoning procedures are usually the enemy of getting what the community wants—underlies each of the recommendations below.

5.3.1. Reducing Individualized Study Requirements

One potentially costly and time-consuming element of many development review procedures is the need to conduct and submit individualized studies related to the proposed development. The topics to be addressed by these studies vary widely. The most common involve the traffic and parking impacts of the proposed development, but studies are sometimes required to document water supply requirements, sewer service capacity, environmental impacts, outdoor lighting impacts, or the health or equity impacts of the development. These types of studies are sometimes justified for major complex projects in areas that do not currently have significant roads or infrastructure in place, but they are rarely helpful or justified for smaller infill projects, for three reasons.

First, because infill and redevelopment projects tend to be smaller, these types of studies impose a greater proportionate cost on the project budget. While the impacts of a smaller project are probably smaller (and less costly to document), the study requirements almost always include comparison of those impacts with the existing capacity and performance in a defined area around the project site, and the costs of documenting conditions in the surrounding area do not decrease much with the size of the project. So the costs of required studies are often not proportionate to the size of the project; they stay high even if the project is small. As a corollary, the time needed to complete a study of system impacts around a small infill project also does not decrease with the size of the project, and a one- or two-month delay in waiting for a study to be completed has a much bigger impact on a smaller development budget than it does on a larger project budget. It also has a larger impact on small and disadvantaged businesses than on larger development companies.

Second, the street networks around many infill projects are usually fixed, and the same is often true of infrastructure capacities. These public mobility and service frameworks were often built long ago and cannot be easily expanded except at great cost. Once they are built, development tends to use up the capacity in those systems. As a result, study requirements often just document that already-known fact. Even small projects can be shown to exceed the remaining traffic or utility capacity, and that fact is often used to stop smaller redevelopment projects. Planners learned long ago that requiring documentation of incremental demands on existing road and infrastructure systems actually feeds sprawl, because there are almost always more ways to expand capacity at lower costs in raw land development areas.

As an example, in the 1970s and 1980s the State of Florida operated a statewide planning system that (1) said the state favored redevelopment over raw land greenfield development but then (2) required larger "Developments of Regional Impact" to complete a thorough analysis of their impacts on existing street and infrastructure systems. In practice, these two goals were in tension, and they made it almost impossible to approve larger redevelopment projects in urban areas, because the project impacts always exceeded the existing infrastructure and service capacity. So between 2015 and 2018 the state abandoned its requirements to document those types of systemic impacts.[14] Why incur the time and effort to do a complex analysis to confirm an answer that you already know?

Third, these types of studies implicitly assume that public behavior will not change as a result of the proposed development. But of course it does, both in response to individual projects and as a result of general growth in the community. When a new or wider road is opened, more people drive because driving is easier. When an existing street is closed for reconstruction, drivers find other routes or decide not to drive through the construction area. When on-street parking becomes scarce or public parking lots become crowded, people consider riding the bus or carpooling.

Many redevelopment projects involve the reuse of vacant or little-used buildings or sites, so of course the project will create more traffic, but it is not clear why we should assume that increased demands on streets and parking cannot be absorbed through changes in driving and parking behavior, as they almost always are in real life. It is also not clear why an individual property owner should be required to pay the cost and absorb the time delays needed to document the impacts of smaller projects on larger public systems.

The point is not that the impacts of individual projects on the surrounding area should be ignored (although sometimes it would be reasonable to do so). The point is that it is inefficient and counterproductive to place the costs of documenting those impacts on individual development projects, particularly small ones. The first solution is simply to exempt smaller projects from the study requirements. Exemptions could include projects on lots smaller than 10,000 square feet, those proposing to expand an existing building by less than 10,000 square feet, and those proposing to reuse a vacant building for a different use without expansion of the building. Measuring the incremental costs of small projects on large, looped systems is fraught with uncertainty and ignores the ability of human behavior to adjust to those minor impacts.

If street, parking, or infrastructure capacities are actually at or near capacity, the second solution is to conduct a single area-wide study to document those impacts so that the cost of the study is borne by the local government or assessment district that purports to want infill and redevelopment to happen and the results of the study are publicly available to everyone. The local government can then decide whether to fund needed expansions publicly in order to promote reinvestment or to impose the costs of the improvements on the benefitting area through a taxing or assessment district, or do some combination of those two things. But individual redevelopers will be spared the time and expense of preparing a study whose results are largely known in advance.

5.3.2. Reducing Public Hearing Requirements

As noted in Section 5.2, the public should be fully educated and engaged in many types of zoning decisions. But there are at least two types of decisions where public engagement should occur during the drafting of the standards and criteria for zoning decisions rather than during individual review of site-specific applications. The first is approval of (most) conditional uses, and the second is approval of site-specific development plans that do not require rezoning or use approvals.

Conditional uses are those that may or may not be acceptable in a given location depending on their size, scale, hours of operation, or the nature and sensitivity of surrounding land uses. In most zoning codes, conditional uses are specifically listed for each zoning district. Most codes require that decisions on conditional uses be made after a public hearing, but that is not always the case. Some development codes divide these into minor conditional uses that can be approved by staff based on objective standards and major conditional uses that require a public hearing. Allowing for administrative approval of most conditional use applications is one important way to increase the affordability, equity, and sustainability of these types of development.

To be clear, not all conditional use decisions should be administrative. There are proposed uses that can have a dramatic effect on the future growth direction and patterns of the city or that will affect large areas of the community, and those should remain subject to public hearing requirements. Examples include the locations of major new public facilities such as airports, landfills, sports stadiums, or transit or utility facilities. In many cases those decisions are not really local, because a state or regional department or commission is involved in their location. But when the decision is local, public hearings are valuable and needed so that the elected officials can thoughtfully consider whether a different location, or different conditions on operation, would better serve all of the residents of a community.

But many development codes do not limit conditional use approval requirements to those types of major decisions. They include things such as hotels in business park zones and child or elder care facilities in residential zoning districts. In fact, many codes list almost all neighborhood-serving facilities and a-bit-unusual commercial uses as conditional uses in zoning districts where those uses are needed. This often reflects an overly casual approach to code drafting where every use that is not clearly acceptable is listed as a conditional use and required to complete a public hearing. A more thoughtful approach would engage the public in identifying exactly what aspects of the proposed use result in a desire to call it a maybe rather than a yes or no, and then addressing each of those potential impacts in turn through objective development standards.

Keep in mind that conditional uses are, by their definition, uses that might be acceptable in that location. In most cases, the circumstances that would make it acceptable can be identified in advance so that they match the scale of the surrounding area and mitigate any unwanted impacts of the use.

Public engagement should be focused on identifying those circumstances and including them in the code through objective standards. If hours of operation are a concern, limit them. If visual impacts on the streets or neighboring properties are a concern, require additional landscaping, buffering, or design features to limit them. If outdoor storage of goods and materials would be inconsistent with other establishments in the neighborhood, limit or prohibit it. Engaging the public in a series of good discussions about possible impacts can almost always result in a list of potential impacts and requirements to avoid or mitigate them, and those standards can then be applied even-handedly to all applicants proposing that conditional use through an administrative approval process.

Once that has been done, there is little need for the added time, expense, or uncertainty of a public hearing to address real land use impacts. And requiring a public hearing runs a significant risk that opposition will be based on something other than the land use impacts of a given decision. In the worst case, opposition will be based on the popularity, political connections, ethnicity, race, religion, or sexual orientation of the applicant or those who are expected to patronize the conditional use. But zoning is not about rewarding or penalizing persons or personalities. It is about identifying, avoiding, or mitigating anticipated land use impacts. Making most conditional use decisions administrative for all but major, community-impacting land uses does that.

The second case where public engagement should be limited is in site-specific development approvals that do not require a rezoning. Here, again, public engagement through a public hearing at the project approval stage is not needed or helpful. Zoning ordinances should clearly communicate to property owners and neighbors the permitted uses, scale of development, project designs, and development quality that are acceptable in each zoning district. In other words, they should clearly communicate what types of applications are a yes within the zoning district. When an application meets those standards, it is a yes that can be approved by staff without a public hearing because there is really nothing to discuss. If a yes application results in unanticipated impacts, the answer is to change the zoning code to address that impact in the future.

Not only are site-specific development approvals the type of decisions where individual self-interest is strongest, they are also those where the unpredictability of a public hearing on a site plan or building design is most damaging to the property owner. This is the "ninth inning" of the development process, where time and money have already been spent and the property owner who designs the project to meet the code should be confident that yes means yes. Remember, most development is redevelopment, infill redevelopers tend to be smaller than greenfield developers, and property owners and developers from disadvantaged communities tend to be less well financed than others. As a result, those most disadvantaged by an unpredictable public hearing process for an individual project approval that does not require rezoning are the very developers who could best help us accomplish more affordable and sustainable development and those whose economic success could help generate additional wealth in disadvantaged communities.

But public hearings on site plans and building designs are common in many US communities. Projects that clearly promote community and neighborhood goals and meet the publicly debated standards for desired development in that zoning district are nevertheless denied, often because of very localized opposition based on local desires for things that the code does not require. The answer is to avoid public hearings on these types of zoning decisions.

In addition to taking very seriously the added time, expense, and uncertainty created by public hearing requirements, it is important to recognize their embedded biases, not just in the conduct of the required hearings but in discouraging those who would undertake the types of innovative and inclusive projects that we say we want. Public hearing requirements are particularly hard on small developers, less-well-financed builders, those facing discrimination in mortgage lending, those whose property is appraised at a low value because of its location in a disadvantaged area of the community, and startup companies without experience working their way through development review procedures. Those are the types of applicants we need to succeed. Public hearing requirements favor larger and more experienced firms for which another month of mortgage payments during the notice and hearing period is not too worrisome. They also favor applicants for bigger projects, because the time and expense of the hearing can be absorbed through a smaller incremental price increase on each unit developed. But the bigger a project is, the less likely it is to be an infill or redevelopment project.

5.3.3. Removing Vague and Subjective Review Criteria

Assuming that the community has already reduced the number of required hearings, as discussed in Section 5.3.2, the next most important procedural change needed to promote more affordable and equitable development is to ensure that the remaining public hearings are based on clear and objective criteria. The use of vague and subjective development criteria is one of the most important ways in which many current codes limit the expansion of the housing stock and impose disproportionately negative impacts on historically disadvantaged communities. The most damaging criteria are words such as "compatible," "harmonious," "attractive," "high quality," and "neighborhood character." Each of these is so vague that it can mean whatever project supporters, project opponents, planning commissions, and elected officials want it to mean. They are simply an invitation to argue about topics that have no right answer and to claim that they do. But arguing takes time, costs money, and creates uncertainty as to whether the project will get approved. And when these arguments are conducted in public hearings where some parts of the community have greater abilities to testify than others, the result is fairly predictable. These terms act as a significant brake on housing production, on the use of new and more sustainable types of development, and on decisions that would open up new housing and business opportunities for disadvantaged people. They are an important way in which well-intentioned communities say they want more affordable and inclusive development and then regularly deny applications to do that.

The answer is to take these words out of the development code and replace them with clear and objective criteria that reduce opportunities for debate and argument about what the terms mean. Remember that one of the key roles of a development code is to tell everyone what development is acceptable within each zoning district. And that should be done in language that will be understood the same way by each participant in the process. Too often, words such as "compatible" and "harmonious" are used as shortcuts to avoid careful thinking about what those words mean. Is the community concerned about building height, massing with respect to neighboring properties, massing with respect to the street, doors and windows on the street, the location of parking, building façade materials, building color, or architectural style? Just listing the elements of building and site design that the community cares about is an important step, because now everyone knows what is *not* on the list, and arguing about those elements during development review is unfair. If they were important, they would be listed in the code, and raising them as new concerns after someone has relied on the language of the development code is unfair. For all these reasons, the

State of Connecticut in 2021 prohibited certain zoning and development applications from being denied based solely on their impacts on neighborhood or community character. Denials in that state must be based on failure to meet at least one other (hopefully more objective) criterion listed in the development code.[15]

Even objective standards can perpetuate zoning that harms historically disadvantaged communities, however. Consider, for example, a zoning change to allow duplex housing units in a zoning district that formerly allowed only single-family detached homes. If that change was applied in a more affluent neighborhood, it could open up new opportunities for less wealthy households to move into a neighborhood where housing and schools are better than where they currently live. But when applied to a lower-income area with small bungalow homes, it could motivate investors to buy and replace them with more expensive housing that is not affordable to most neighborhood residents. In fact, since land and homes in the latter neighborhood cost less, the real impact of the change may be much more dramatic (as well as less affordable and less equitable) in the less affluent neighborhood.

For that reason alone, the clear and objective criteria used in public hearings should include criteria that address the economic vulnerability of the neighborhood. As discussed in Section 4.1, economic vulnerability can be addressed by changing the zoning rules, but it can also be addressed by changing the criteria used to make rezoning decisions. This can be done by including standard or criteria addressing the area median income (AMI) or the existing building stock in different neighborhoods.

In the above example, the text adding duplexes to the list of permitted uses could clarify that the duplex use is available only in neighborhoods where the AMI exceeds the areawide average. Or it could say that the new use is available only in neighborhoods where the average size of a single-household dwelling exceeds 2,000 square feet. Or the criteria for approving a zoning text change could state that any change that increases the types of residential development permitted by right in a zoning district may be approved only if they include protections against dislocation of the existing residents. The economic vulnerability of the neighborhood can also be addressed by implementing the change through an overlay zoning district that is applied only outside the historically disadvantaged or low-income neighborhoods, and those types of map changes are discussed in more detail in Chapter 6.

5.3.4. Allowing Administrative Adjustments

Another important way to improve zoning procedures is to allow planning staff a reasonable amount of discretion in applying the development code to unusual site conditions. This is important because land is not always level, utilities are not always located in logical or expected locations, mature trees worth protecting are sometimes located in inconvenient places, and some lots were created in unusual ways before subdivision regulations required better design. All of those inconvenient truths occur more frequently in older, mature areas where we want to encourage redevelopment and infill projects. With apologies to Thomas Friedman, the world is not flat.

The traditional zoning answer to unusual site conditions is to require the applicant to obtain a variance, which usually requires a public hearing in which the applicant provides evidence of "hardship." In fact, when the Standard Zoning Enabling Act was being drafted in the 1920s, a lot of the discussion focused not on how to draft the rules on permitted uses and lot sizes but on when and how to approve exceptions to those rules. Unfortunately, it is not always easy to get a variance even when the needed deviation from zoning standards is small and common sense would allow the redevelopment to move forward. As with other public hearing requirements, variance hearings impose additional time and expense on the applicant, and those impacts fall most heavily on disadvantaged people, on smaller projects where profit margins are thin, and on the smaller developers that undertake many infill and redevelopment projects.

Note that in this case I did not say that variance hearing requirements impose the same levels of uncertainty into the redevelopment process as other public hearing requirements, because they often do not. Some state laws make it almost impossible to prove hardship and obtain a variance, but most allow significant freedom for local governments to decide how and when to approve variances, and many communities approve them routinely. In fact, some cities have established rules in which a request for variance x is always recommended for approval as long as mitigation y is attached to the approval. Whenever a discretionary public hearing process becomes so routine that the outcome of a particular application is predictable in advance, it is time to reconsider whether the time and expense of the hearing are necessary.

That is especially true when the requested deviation from zoning standards is small, such as a 1-foot encroachment into a minimum 10-foot side setback. Yes, a public hearing does give a neighbor the opportunity to object about that 1 foot, but that raises the question of how much staff time and taxpayer money the local government should be spending on what is essentially an individual neighbor-to-neighbor disagreement that will make no meaningful difference to the future health, safety, and welfare of the community. Whether a minor variance is approved or denied, it is unlikely that anyone but the two property owners involved will notice the change and extremely unlikely that the next buyer of either property will know or care about the outcome of the variance request. Yes, due process probably does require that the neighbor have an opportunity to object that the deviation creates a unique and unusual hardship in their specific case, but cases in which a 1-foot encroachment really creates a hardship are rare, so the opportunity to raise that issue can occur during an appeal.

Most state laws require that local zoning ordinances contain a variance procedure, but most do not require that the variance be the only way that exceptions to zoning standards be granted. Some communities already take advantage of this flexibility by creating an administrative adjustment process, and others call it an administrative variance process. Regardless of the name, these procedures allow staff to vary specific development standards within certain limits if the applicant documents unusual site conditions without a public hearing.

As an example, the development code could provide that staff may allow a proposed building to encroach up to 2 feet into required side and rear setbacks if the site is subject to unusual site or environmental conditions and the adjustment would permit the property owner to construct buildings similar to those on neighboring sites that do not have those complicating conditions. Unusual site conditions can be defined to include the presence of mature trees that would need to be removed unless the location of the building can be shifted slightly away from the tree. Or it could allow a similar minor shift in the building location necessary to avoid a preexisting utility line or area of soil contamination.

The keys to drafting legal administrative adjustment provisions are to clearly define (1) which development standards may be adjusted, (2) by how much, and (3) in response to which complicating site conditions. As long as those parameters are clearly identified and included in the code, this type of provision constitutes just another type of instruction from the elected officials telling planning staff how to do their jobs. Instead of telling staff to enforce a 10-foot setback, the elected officials have instructed staff to enforce a 10-foot setback unless they document specific site factors, in which case they can reduce that number to 8 feet. While these types of small adjustments may seem unimportant, they can open up opportunities for redevelopment of smaller parcels and approval of innovative infill development.

Because humans make mistakes, the resulting adjustment should be subject to appeal. But that hearing can occur after the decision has been made, and experience shows that in most cases no appeal will be filed because the decision was reasonable. Whether or not an appeal is filed, the need to incur the time and expense of a predevelopment variance has been avoided, and the likelihood of a successful redevelopment project has been increased.

One important addition to this approach can significantly improve zoning equity for people experiencing disabilities or limited abilities. In addition to provisions discussed earlier, the Fair Housing Amendments Act (FHAA) provides that a person experiencing limited abilities can file with the local government a request for a "reasonable accommodation," which means an adjustment to or exception from the rules otherwise applicable to their property in order to allow them to use the property in the same ways other people in the same zoning district can use their properties. The most common example is a request that the local government "reasonably accommodate" the needs of someone who uses a wheelchair, scooter, or walker by allowing the construction of a ramp to access the house, even if the ramp encroaches on a required setback. The city needs to act reasonably in making a decision on that request, and those that involve only a minor change from what is otherwise allowed in the zoning district need to be approved.

Since the purpose of the FHAA is to allow those experiencing limited mental or physical abilities to occupy the same types of housing, in the same locations, and under the same conditions as other residents, it makes little sense to call attention to their limited abilities by requiring a public hearing before making a decision on a request for a reasonable accommodation. For that reason, a number of newer development codes include deviations from code standards necessary to allow "reasonable accommodations" in the list of administrative adjustments that staff can approve without a public hearing. Newer codes authorize staff to approve deviations from code development standards (but not permitted use standards) up to the minimum amount necessary to comply with the FHAA, as determined by the city or county attorney. In this case, the limit of what staff can approve is not stated as a number, and the limit is instead based on the requirements of federal law. To be clear, the FHAA requires that local governments make reasonable accommodations even if this type of deviation is not listed in a section on administrative amendments, but listing it makes local government operations more transparent.

Two final notes. First, administrative amendments should not be used to allow land uses that are not allowed in the underlying zone district. The uses allowed on the site (with or without the adjustment) are those listed as permitted or conditional uses in the zone district where the property is located. Second, administrative adjustment should apply to only a single lot, because they are intended to address lot-specific site conditions. If the application involves ten lots that all have the same complicating site condition, the impacts of an adjustment on neighboring property owners is greater, and the variance process should apply.

5.3.5. Reducing Appeals

Another way to improve zoning review and approval procedures is to limit the conditions under which zoning decisions can be appealed and revise how those appeals are handled. In addition to internal appeals to a hearing officer or board of adjustment, of course, there may be appeals to a state district court, but because those are outside the control of the local government, this section will focus on internal appeal procedures.

To be clear, due process and state law often require that zoning decisions be subject to appeal, and that is as it should be. Zoning administrators are human and they make mistakes, and appointed and elected officials sometimes lose sight of the criteria that should be guiding their decisions. So it is important to have a way to review those decisions and spot and correct the mistakes. In many communities, however, who gets to appeal a decision and how it is revisited has itself become a source of housing unaffordability, unsustainability, and inequity in the zoning process. At its worst, the appeal process is used as a way to delay developments that are clearly consistent with both the goals of the comprehensive plan and the letter of the zoning code in hopes that the applicant will run out of time or money or patience.

The needed fixes to the appeal process are clear but sometimes unpopular. First, the party appealing to a zoning administrator or appointed body should be required to state specifically what section or standard or criteria in the development code was not applied correctly. The purpose of an appeal is to find and correct mistakes, not to have a different body make the decision over again in hopes of getting a different outcome. It is not a "second bite at the apple." You cannot correct a mistake when the alleged mistake is not clearly identified in the appeal.

Second, appeals should be on the record, as they are in most court proceedings. That means the appeal should not be reviewed de novo (i.e., starting over again and considering the facts anew). They should be reviewed based on the text, standards, and criteria in the code, the application forms and information provided with the application, and any testimony or letters submitted that were submitted before the decision was made and that are relevant to the standards and criteria in the code. Again, the question is whether a mistake has been made, not whether submitting additional information that was not presented to the decision maker would have resulted in a different decision.

Third, the appeal should be to a decision maker trained to make decisions based on objective standards. In some cases that could be a hearing officer who acts like a judge in reviewing the evidence presented. Or it could be to an appointed body such as a board of adjustment or appeals that is trained to do the same thing. It should almost never be to elected officials, because it is often hard for them to focus on whether a mistake was made rather than the popularity or unpopularity of the decision. City council members and county commissioners are elected to represent the will of their voters by creating rules of law that reflect that will, not by providing a way around the rule of law when the result is unpopular. The fair response to an unpopular zoning decision is to reconsider whether the zoning text and map have the right standards and criteria and to fix them if they do not. It is not fair to penalize applicants who have complied with the text of the development code just because the result is unpopular, so any appeal of the decision should be to a person or body less likely to be influenced by that unpopularity.

All of these fixes work better when the code itself does not include vague and subjective standards such as "compatible" and "harmonious." When those terms guide the initial decision, it is not surprising that an appeals body might find it difficult to determine whether a mistake was made. More significantly, vague terms invite more appeals, because they raise the prospect of getting a second body to interpret the terms differently. Where development codes include objective, measurable standards or well-defined ranges in which site-specific decisions can be made, it is not only easier to determine whether a mistake was made, but also much less likely that an appeal will be filed in the first place.

CHAPTER 6

Fixing the Map

Zoning operates not just through the rules discussed in Chapter 4 and the procedures reviewed in Chapter 5 but through the map that applies zoning rules to land in the community. In fact, when most folks think about zoning, they do not think about the text and tables that make up zoning rules; they visualize the colored map that identifies which properties are in each zoning district. When property is rezoned, it shows up with a different color on the map.

It is important to remember that many changes that would improve the affordability, equity, and sustainability of zoning decisions can be done in at least two different ways. Let's take the example of a vacant infill property in the Residential Low–Medium Density zoning district, which allows only single-household and duplex homes. If the city wants to promote affordable housing by expanding the number of properties where triplex and fourplex housing is allowed, it can

1. Amend the text of the Residential Low–Medium Density district to list triplexes and fourplexes as permitted uses; or
2. Remap some properties from the Residential, Low–Medium Density to the Residential, Medium–High Density district, where triplexes and fourplexes are already permitted uses.

In many communities, the procedure used to make either change would be pretty similar. A text change that will affect many properties is usually a legislative action, and a map change that also affects many properties (as opposed to one that singles out only one or a handful of properties) is also generally a legislative action. Both are likely to require a public hearing and recommendation from the planning commission and then a second public hearing and decision by the elected governing body. I mention this because, for any desired change to the development code, it is often useful to discuss whether a text amendment or a map change is the better way to accomplish the change. And if one of these options is not available due to local politics or policy or state law, the other option may still be available.

6.1. Un-Redlining

Unfortunately, many current zoning maps in older communities were at some point influenced by residential investment risk maps produced by the US government's Home Owner's Loan Corporation in the 1930s and 1940s. Although the federal government has never operated a zoning system, it does operate a mortgage insurance program, and the federal maps were produced for that program. More specifically, in the late 1930s Washington acted to expand housing affordability to millions of Americans by promoting self-amortizing mortgages and agreeing to accept some of the risk of defaults on those loans as long as the mortgages met certain underwriting standards.[1] The assumption that banks would be willing to make more long-term housing loans if the federal government insured the repayment of those loans turned out to be correct. But to limit its financial exposure, the federal government produced maps ranking residential neighborhoods based on the government's perception of lending risk.

The result was so-called "redline" maps that graphically showed where the federal government did and did not want loans to be made if the bank was going to request federal mortgage insurance coverage. And banks got the message loud and clear. They made more loans on homes in higher-ranked neighborhoods and fewer loans in the redlined areas.[2] History shows that this approach institutionalized a new form of discrimination against disadvantaged and vulnerable communities. Among the factors considered in creating the federal lending maps was the predominant race, ethnicity, and nationality of neighborhood residents (Black or Brown populations were assumed to make loans riskier), the income of the residents (lower-income households were assumed to be riskier), and the then-current housing stock (areas with fewer detached single-household homes were assumed to make the area riskier).

As a result, lower-income and Black and Brown households did not benefit from the explosive growth in homeownership that followed the Housing Act of 1937 or the incredible accumulation of wealth that flowed from homeownership after the end of the World War II. It is important to realize that the redline maps were created over twenty-five years before the Fair Housing Act was passed by Congress. They are artifacts from a much earlier era in American history, but their influence lives on.

That is because many current zoning maps look similar to the redline maps—often shockingly so. A side-by-side comparison of residential areas on those two sets of maps often shows that areas labeled as low-risk neighborhoods in the 1930s have the most restrictive zoning and the higher property values today. And vice versa. Over the past twenty years, books, articles, and press coverage of these similarities have proliferated, and because maps are highly visual, even those who do not study zoning understand that our zoning maps continue to reflect some deeply discriminatory policies established over eighty years ago. In fact, for some advocates of zoning equity, these maps are the key problem, and their overarching desire is to un-redline the zoning maps. Saying that is simple, but doing it in a way that does not further harm the historically disadvantaged communities that have already been hurt by the redline maps is not simple, for the reasons outlined below.

6.1.1. The Challenge of Voting with Your Feet

As discussed in Section 4.2.5, one of the key challenges with any significant neighborhood-wide zoning change is that people can vote with their feet. They do not always stay in the neighborhoods where they lived and worked when you did your affordability and equity analysis. They can respond to perceived improvements in the quality of a neighborhood by buying or renting or opening a business there. And they can respond to perceived decreases in neighborhood quality or increased public health risks by moving away or relocating their businesses elsewhere. Actually, it would be more accurate to say the people who have enough income and are not subject to discrimination based on race, ethnicity, or nationality have more ability to vote with their feet. Others may not have the same option to move, but they may be forced to move if neighborhood rents rise and they can no longer afford to live or do business there.

This is important, because the long-term impact of redlining is that many areas that were not able to benefit from federally insured mortgages now have smaller houses and fewer amenities, and real estate rents and prices are often lower than those in neighborhoods where residents could borrow and spend more on larger and nicer houses. But if zoning is changed to make the redlined neighborhoods more attractive, there is no guarantee that those who benefit from the change will be those who have lived or worked in the neighborhood during the decades when zoning and lending practices discouraged investment. The zoning changes may instead benefit others who have decided, or who will decide in the future, to buy, rent, or invest in the neighborhood. And those people may have obtained the money to make the new investments because they spent decades living and working in areas where greater availability of obtaining good insured mortgages and where more restrictive zoning allowed them to accumulate wealth. The key point is that un-redlining zoning by itself cannot siphon money from the pockets of those who benefitted from redlining into the pockets of those who paid the price.

6.1.2. Leveling the Playing Field Is Not Enough

That is why leveling the playing field by applying the same zoning on both sides of a mapped redline may not be an effective way to address the inequities of redlining. In fact, changing zoning so that historically disadvantaged communities have the same (more restrictive) zoning that more privileged neighborhoods have may hurt the residents and business owners in redlined areas. To see why this is true, let's look at a simple example involving neighborhoods A-Brook and B-Woods, which are located on opposite sides of Bypass Avenue. A-Brook was historically redlined and generally has lower property values and is occupied by households with lower income. B-Woods is the opposite. To make things simpler, we will assume that both neighborhoods are almost all residential. Residents may operate home occupations or home-based businesses, but there are very few freestanding businesses in either neighborhood.

The analysis would be simpler if the residents of both neighborhoods were the same people, or descendants of the same people, who occupied their homes and operated their businesses when the original federal lending maps were created. But of course they are not. Since then, people have moved in and out of homes, and the current residents may have no ties to the people who either did or did not qualify for federal mortgage insurance when their homes were built. And they are not all homeowners, either. Both neighborhoods probably contain a mix of homeowners and renters, and those two groups will be affected differently by zoning changes.

By and large, asset owners are pleased when the value of their asset increases, so homeowners will often be happy if zoning changes increase their property values. But not always. If higher property values lead to higher taxes, they complain. While A-Brook is less affluent than B-Woods, both neighborhoods probably have residents who live on fixed incomes, or who can just barely make their rent or mortgage payments, and would object to higher property values. Despite complaints about taxes, most homeowners have generally supported policy changes that increase the values of their homes even if they have to pay higher taxes as a result.

Renters are often in a different position. When property values rise, buyers have to borrow more to buy into the neighborhood, and they often try to recoup those higher prices by charging higher rents. Renters who cannot afford the higher rents are sometimes involuntarily displaced. They have to move somewhere else. While it is tempting to think that all property renters are large corporations just trying to maximize profits, many are not. Some are individuals who own only one or two houses and rent one home to one of their children or to a family friend at a less-than-market rate. Over time, however, as homes are bought and sold and financed, rising property values tend to result in higher rents. So renters may not be happy with zoning changes that increase the value of the homes they rent, particularly if they can barely pay the current rents.

The point is that zoning changes that attempt to undo the impacts of redlining in ways that may increase property values in A-Brook to be closer to those in B-Woods will not be welcomed by all residents of A-Brook. However, since homeowners generally have higher incomes than renters, and since A-Brook has lower incomes, it is likely that it has a higher percentage of renters, and zoning changes that increase property values may be less attractive to more residents in A-Brook than in B-Woods.

Because homeownership is one of the most important sources of wealth accumulation in the United States,[3] redlining has been a major cause of the vast disparities in wealth between historically disadvantaged households. Affordable housing advocates who are focused on the wealth-generating aspects of housing may still advocate zoning changes to level the playing field because they could allow current property owners in A-Brook to begin accumulating wealth at rates closer to those in B-Woods.

And that may in fact improve zoning equity for historically disadvantaged residents, particularly those who have owned their properties for a long time or who inherited them from their parents, because the longer they have owned the property, the longer they have been penalized by unfair zoning and lending practices. But the current property owners in A-Brook may well not be members of historically disadvantaged communities. They may be residents of affluent communities who have not been disadvantaged because of their race, ethnicity, gender, or level of mental of physical ability who bought the property as an investment. Leveling the playing field through zoning changes would also benefit those owners and enable them to accumulate more wealth.

In fact, the mix of owners, renters, and investors in A-Brook and B-Woods, and the degree to which they have been penalized by the history of redlining, may be so complex that the equity impacts of zoning changes to level the playing field are unpredictable. Or rather, any zoning changes with that intent should be considered only after analysis of the demographics and ownership and rental patterns in the neighborhood and full discussion of the options for zoning changes with the residents (both property owners and renters) of A-Brook so that the impacts of the change are clearly supported by members of that community.

Note that the outlines of these equity impacts remain generally true if we make the example slightly more complex by saying that the current zoning allows some types of multihousehold dwellings or commercial businesses in A-Brook but not in B-Woods. That could be true either because those businesses were already there in A-Brook when zoning was adopted or because the residents of B-Woods were successful in modifying zoning to keep businesses out. Leveling the playing field by changing zoning to remove commercial uses from A-Woods creates its own inequities, because the existing businesses are now nonconforming. They can continue to operate, even if the businesses sold or leased to other operators, but nonconforming land uses often have a harder time obtaining the business loans they need to improve the property or stay in businesses. That is true regardless of whether the business owns or rents its building.

In this revised example, the impacts of changes to permitted commercial and multihousehold uses need to be evaluated separately. To start with, leveling the playing field by remapping B-Woods into the A-Woods zoning districts to allow additional commercial uses in B-Woods (which could be a very difficult political fight) might not improve equity either. The higher property values in B-Woods mean that fewer businesses will be able to afford to locate there, and business owners and operators who have the financial means to do so are unlikely to be those owned and operated by may not be members of historically disadvantaged communities or those previously hurt by redlining practices.

The situation for housing is different and could improve both affordability and equity. If the A-Brook zoning were applied to B-Woods, the new allowance for apartments or condominiums would increase the variety of housing available, and some of those could be occupied by members of communities harmed by redlining. And the newly available apartments and condominiums may cost less than the single-family homes that were previously the only type of housing permitted. So leveling the playing field by allowing the broader A-Brook mix of housing into B-Woods is probably a net gain for both affordability and equity.

As an aside, the fact that A-Brook and B-Woods are separated by Bypass Avenue is probably irrelevant to the equity analysis. Examples of US cities that made highway location decisions to separate neighborhoods based on race, ethnicity, or income make for dramatic aerial photographs. And those images imply that removal of the highway would improve equity. Sometimes it would, because it would remove a highly visual reminder of a dividing line between the two communities. Over time, the removal would weaken the memory that the government had instigated or been complicit in the desire to separate and distinguish the two neighborhoods.

Assuming that Bypass Avenue could be narrowed to be less of a barrier, however, that action would not change the disparities in the existing building stock on either side of the avenue, in property values, in ability to access property improvement loans, or in the zoning rules themselves. The most significant financial, wealth, and housing quality impacts of redlining would not be erased by erasing or narrowing the structure that makes such a vivid picture of the government's role in this form of inequity. Although the optics of the dividing line are not unimportant, it is the difference in the zoning rules applied on either side of the line that makes the most difference.

The flow of potential equity benefits from neighborhood-wide map changes could be made more predictable, of course, if the zoning changes can be tailored to apply to only specific groups of residents. Tailoring residential zoning based on the race, ethnicity, color, national origin, sex, family status, or physical or mental abilities is illegal under the Fair Housing Act. But that still leaves the possibility of tailoring zoning changes so they apply only to rental properties or only to long-term owners and renters. But zoning has historically not been tailored in these ways, and in some states tailoring based on those categories would be illegal. Where it is legal, some communities (particularly resort communities) have tailored zoning to distinguish owner-occupied from renter-occupied properties, and some of those distinctions have been upheld in court.[4]

However, this distinction requires a significant investment in monitoring and enforcement that is beyond the administrative staffing levels of many communities. The city would need to know whenever an owner-occupied property is rented, or a rental unit becomes occupied by the property owner, which takes time and money. Similar attempts to regulate the use of accessory dwelling units (ADUs) for short-term rentals provide a useful lesson on the difficulty of administration, monitoring, and enforcement. Enforcing is hard, and it often works only when property rental companies or platforms are made to share information. For all these reasons, many communities interested in erasing the impacts of redlined lending maps on zoning have decided that leveling the playing field by equalizing zoning on both sides of a redline boundary may not be a good strategy to redress the harms of redlining.

6.1.3. Tailoring Exclusion to Protect the Vulnerable

At the beginning of this book we acknowledged that the DNA of zoning is based on exclusion. Zoning is very good at excluding uses or buildings from areas where we don't want them, but it cannot force uses to happen where we want them unless they are supported by market forces (plus any incentives we can offer to make them happen). So one way to un-redline disadvantaged neighborhoods may be to aim that exclusionary power in a different direction. Building on our earlier example, instead of trying to level the playing field by adopting similar zoning in A-Brook and B-Woods, we can tailor those changes as discussed below.

More specifically, we can use zoning to protect vulnerable neighborhoods from market forces of gentrification when they are likely to lead to increased rents and dislocation of low-income residents. And we can erase some of the zoning exclusions that currently protect wealthier neighborhoods from their fair share of the growth and change needed to provide housing and business opportunities for all of our residents. Let's discuss each of these in turn.

Some of the inequitable results of our current zoning system arise from the fact that the power to exclude has been used to protect wealthier neighborhoods from new or different uses while not doing the same for disadvantaged areas. But that can be changed. In areas of A-Brook where naturally occurring affordable housing (NOAH) is threatened by demolition and replacement by new buildings that the current residents will not be able to afford, zoning can be used to exclude the larger homes or multihousehold buildings or the new commercial buildings that it now allows. Yes, preventing the replacement of existing homes and apartments with more new housing is in tension with the desire to increase housing supply, and possible ways to resolve that tension are discussed in Chapter 7. But the point is simple: The power to exclude uses that will have perceived negative impacts on the neighborhood that has long been applied to wealthier neighborhoods can also be tailored to protect vulnerable neighborhoods.

In addition, the exclusion of new and different types of housing from the 50 to 70 percent of urban lands often zoned to allow only single-household uses can be weakened. In neighborhoods like B-Woods, those exclusions directly affect those with lower incomes and less wealth than the current neighborhood residents. And although we do not like to talk about it, the households excluded are disproportionately those where the primary income earners are non-White, nonmale, or experiencing physical or mental disabilities. They disproportionately exclude the very people that we tell ourselves America does not want to exclude. So some of those zoning exclusions can be removed. As discussed above, remapping B-Woods to allow the same mix of housing as in A-Brook could improve both equity and affordability.

A growing number of US cities are now removing long-standing exclusions of ADUs from most or all of their single-household neighborhoods. Minneapolis and Rochester, Minnesota; Portland, Oregon; Bloomington, Indiana, and other cities decided to allow duplexes, triplexes, and fourplexes in (at least some of the) neighborhoods where they were previously excluded. Because the expected occupancy of each new housing unit in America is significantly lower than what it was in the 1960s, in many cases the addition of new types of housing is not expected to increase neighborhood populations any higher than it was twenty or thirty years ago.

Whether those changes were motivated by changed thinking about housing affordability or equity does not matter; the results are the same, because increasing housing variety and affordability opens up new opportunities for residents of disadvantaged neighborhoods. As they looked beyond testimony about the "parade of horribles" that often accompanies any proposal for significant residential zoning change, the elected officials who approved these changes clearly did not think the changes would erode the quality of life in the existing neighborhoods. In short, our past elected officials wrote the exclusions that created disproportionate negative impacts on disadvantaged and vulnerable neighborhoods, and our current elected officials can erase them when that is needed to reduce or remove those impacts.

6.2. Overlays May Not Be Necessary or Helpful

Some barriers to more affordable, equitable, and sustainable development are found in overlay zoning districts, and proliferation of overlay districts in general can contribute to these challenges. Over a forty-year career partnering with local government to update their development regulations, I was continually surprised at how often and how fast the discussion of a potential zoning change turns to "maybe we need an overlay zoning district." Sometimes that is what is needed, but often it is not. Overlay zoning districts are useful when a different zoning rule or incentives really needs to apply to only one or a few geographic areas. For example, as discussed in Section 4.1.3, an overlay district may be helpful to prevent new investment that is likely to dislocate residents in a geographically defined neighborhood with a historically disadvantaged population or an area with low household incomes and few other housing choices.

But often the focus on overlay zoning districts distracts the community from a serious discussion of whether the permitted uses and standards in the base zoning districts need to be changed. Overlay districts are an add-on to more base zoning district regulations, but the more serious drivers of housing costs, unsustainable development, and unfair zoning outcomes are often embedded in the base zones. Instead of a discussion of overlay zoning controls, a careful review of permitted uses, dimensional standards, and development standards, particularly those applicable to single-household dwelling districts, would be more productive. This has become a routine part of most development code rewrites, and it can yield important equity improvements.

When rewriting a development code, it is important to carefully review the table of permitted uses, what types of approval are needed for those uses, and the limiting conditions (including building size, minimum lot size, setbacks, and minimum parking and open space requirements) and ask two important questions. To paraphrase the discussion in Section 4.2.3, first ask, "Why was this use not allowed or limited in this zoning district, and does that rationale still apply?" It is surprising how often the answer is "No one remembers" or "No, that reasoning is inconsistent with our planning goals."

Then ask, "If we decide to keep those restrictions in place, who will be hurt by that decision, and have those people or areas been historically disadvantaged or vulnerable?" If the answer is yes, then those people need to be involved in the discussion. For far too long discussions about possible changes have focused only on who will benefit from the change. And since over half of the land in many communities is zoned to exclude most uses except single-unit dwellings, regulations that keep those restrictions in place are assumed to benefit the many people who live in those districts. We often do *not* look at who will bear the impacts of exclusionary zoning, and that needs to stop.

When we exclude more affordable types of housing from half of the land in our communities, the need to accommodate those types of housing falls on other areas of the community. And by concentrating those types of housing in areas where they are already permitted, we tend to perpetuate and exacerbate the very differences in wealth and opportunity that the comprehensive plan says we want to reduce. In most cases, the revisions needed to make zoning less exclusionary involve changes to base zoning districts and not the creation of new overlay districts.

In addition, most overlay districts include additional forms of exclusion (e.g., they exclude projects that do not meet additional design standards or buildings that would block a loved view of a mountain). Each time an overlay district is added, it represents another layer of "and not that," and they sometimes overlap with other overlay districts. Because many of the barriers to fairer zoning outcomes involve overuse of zoning's power to exclude, the proliferation of additional types of "no" is itself a concern. At a minimum, their cumulative impacts with other layers of zoning and regulation should be evaluated carefully. Even when they do not compound zoning inequities, they often represent an end run around the changes to base zoning districts that would produce broader benefits in a way that is easier to understand and administer.

6.3. Different Kinds of Tools Will Probably Be Necessary

This book is organized to discuss zoning maps last, after discussing changes to zoning rules and procedures, for a reason. Because maps are visual and changes to zoning text and procedures are not, many people assume that the problem must involve redrawing the map. In many cases that is not accurate. Zoning maps simply apply the zoning rules to the face of the earth, and the inequities in our current zoning system are buried deep in the zoning rules and procedures. If those rules and standards and procedures are changed as discussed in Chapters 4 and 5, the maps will automatically apply those fairer and more inclusionary rules without the need to change the map. Discrete changes to the boundaries of base or overlay zoning districts should only be considered after more fundamental changes to the building blocks of zoning have been discussed, and they should generally be made only if those changes to text and procedures will not achieve the improved zoning equity that we want.

For the reasons discussed in this chapter, removing the historic impacts of redlining may also require the use of nonzoning tools. In many cases, those nonzoning tools will be more effective at protecting vulnerable populations than anything that can be efficiently administered through zoning. Examples of nonzoning tools that may be needed include

1. Stronger tenant protections for low-income populations;
2. Relocation assistance for those dislocated by redevelopment of NOAH or manufactured housing communities;
3. Publicly funded or insured grant or loan programs tailored to neighborhoods where property maintenance and expansion loans are less available because of the lingering impacts of redlining;
4. Financial assistance tailored to benefit long-term residents and property and business owners in disadvantaged neighborhoods;
5. Higher levels of public investment in neighborhood amenities to make up for past underinvestments;
6. Requiring or incentivizing Community Benefits Agreements that condition some types of development on providing specific types of negotiated benefits to the neighborhood where the development occurs; or
7. Creating a reparation fund to promote homeownership in disadvantaged communities.[5]

Many communities have already created these and similar programs, either at their own initiative or because some federal Community Development Block Grants and housing-related grants and loans must be focused on less advantaged areas of our communities. In addition, many banks and financial institutions have created programs that try to increase lending in disadvantaged and vulnerable neighborhoods in order to comply with the Community Reinvestment Act. But much more can be done. Importantly, many of these nonzoning tools can be better targeted to benefit those harmed by past redlining practices than changes to the zoning map. However, because they are not grounded in zoning, we will not be exploring them further in this book.

CHAPTER 7

Resolving the Tensions

Chapters 4, 5, and 6 listed some of the steps local governments can take to improve the affordability of housing, the equity of zoning outcomes, and the sustainability of the built environment. None of the steps are easy. Many are likely to provoke significant opposition because they threaten the status quo. They also weaken the exclusionary tendencies embedded in the DNA of zoning and undermine longstanding rules that favor outcomes preferred by wealthier neighborhoods. But rules do change over time when the impacts of those rules are no longer acceptable to voters and elected officials, and movement in many of the directions outlined in previous chapters is already happening in some US communities.

A more vexing challenge is that the recommended zoning changes outlined in this book are often in tension with one another. Actions that could increase environmental sustainability sometimes undermine the goal of affordability. Actions that could increase the supply of affordable housing sometimes come at the expense of equity when they cause displacement in vulnerable neighborhoods. Actions to protect the supply of naturally occurring affordable housing can weaken efforts at sustainability, since those older homes may well be less energy efficient than the new homes that would have replaced them. Unfortunately, such tensions between multiple public goals are often a reason for inaction in zoning reform. There is a perception that since there is no action that can be taken to achieve one important goal without compromising another important goal, nothing can or should be done. I think that reflects lazy thinking.

Planning, and zoning that implements that planning, is always involved in balancing competing public values that cannot all be achieved in each development. In planning documents we often solve that tension by using vague terms and phrases that each reader can read as favoring their preferred list of things that should happen. Zoning does not have that luxury. An effective rule of law requires that zoning clearly state what is or is not possible on a parcel of land and what process must be used to change those rules. To be fair to the public and to developers, zoning needs to talk in terms of "shalls" and "shall nots" rather than "shoulds." And when we have to decide what can and cannot be done on a parcel of land, the difficulty with choosing "yes" or "no" often leads to inaction and delay. Since there is no painless choice that will make everyone happy, we delay the decision or put the topic on hold to resolve in the future. My goal is to help staff and decision makers move beyond that stalemate.

The fact that there is no perfect solution does not mean that we cannot achieve better outcomes, and the three key challenges of affordability, equity, and sustainability deserve deeper and more careful thought about how to maximize the community benefits of zoning changes. Because these zoning goals are so important, this chapter dives deeper into the tensions and tradeoffs involved in pursuing zoning changes to achieve them. But there are two important caveats. First, the best resolution of these competing desires will vary between neighborhoods, because the patterns of less sustainable buildings, less affordable housing, and unfair zoning outcomes differ. So this chapter cannot provide a single right answer that will work in each neighborhood. Instead it suggests key principles to guide public efforts to think through and select the locally optimal mix of zoning changes.

The second caveat is to remember that disadvantaged and vulnerable communities have historically not fared well in the outcomes of these types of public discussions. Far too often the desire of the entire community to achieve an important planning goal becomes the rationale for imposing the costs of that change on poorer and more vulnerable neighborhoods. If impacts on disadvantaged neighborhood are not taken much more seriously than they have been in the past, it is likely that we will choose zoning changes that will improve sustainability and affordability in ways that—once again—disproportionately hurt disadvantaged neighborhoods. So this chapter emphasizes the importance of focusing discussions about potential changes around the question of who should bear any anticipated negative impacts of the change and ensuring that it is not the neighborhoods and communities that have disproportionately done so in the past.

7.1. Identifying the Tensions

To start the discussion, let's list the possible changes to zoning rules discussed in the previous three chapters to identify some areas of potential tension. Table 7.1 identifies potential tensions between the changes discussed above and rates the likelihood of those tensions. It also summarizes sources of the tension.

"High" indicates that there may well be an important tradeoff between achieving two or more of the changes discussed above. Changing zoning to achieve one of them will probably make it more difficult to achieve others, and the tension may affect large areas of the community. "Medium" indicates that the amount of land involved is probably lower, or the likelihood of conflicting impacts is lower. Making one of the recommended changes to achieve one goal may compromise the ability to achieve a second goal, but the compromise may be smaller and other lands may be available where the second zoning change could be applied and zoning outcomes could be improved in a different way. "Low" indicates that conflicts with other recommended zoning changes will be rare, and the amounts of land involved will probably be small.

The text that follows focuses on the recommended zoning changes that have a high or medium likelihood of being in tension with each other. It does not address those where the likelihood is low because the stakes are lower, and a reasonable approach or compromise can probably be worked out locally. Make no mistake, however: Even the changes marked "low" require changes to the status quo and may well generate public opposition.

In general, the potential tensions listed as medium or high in Table 7.1 can be grouped into four categories: (1) those that reduce land available for housing, (2) those that directly increase the costs of housing development, (3) those that create or increase the risk that disadvantaged or vulnerable populations will be involuntarily displaced through rent or price increases, and (4) those that perpetuate disproportionately high health and environmental risks in disadvantaged and vulnerable communities.

Choosing the right resolution for a specific neighborhood will depend on the existing quality of the built environment, the existing levels of unaffordability, the existing levels of inequity in specific neighborhoods, and the desires of community renters and property and business owners. In recent years I have often told zoning steering committees, only half in jest, that we will be looking for the "least bad" solution. That usually means the one that achieves more planning goals with fewer undesired consequences, because almost every zoning intervention into the real estate markets will have at least a few consequences that we would have preferred to avoid. Sections 7.2 through 7.7 list six principles that can help citizens, planners, and decision makers think through the best ways to balance and resolve tensions for zoning in a specific neighborhood.

Section	Potential Zoning Rule Change	Likelihood of Conflict with Other Changes	Description of the Potential Conflict
Improving Affordability			
4.1.1	Allowing more missing middle housing in low-density residential zones	High	Allowing new missing middle housing could result in displacement of vulnerable populations in current low-density districts.
4.1.1	Allowing more medium-scale housing in commercial zoning districts	Medium	New housing in commercial districts serving vulnerable populations could result in displacement of needed commercial services.
4.1.1	Allowing medium-density housing on institutional properties	Low	
4.1.1	Removing unnecessary density limits	Medium	Removing density limits could result in increased development that results in displacement of vulnerable populations in current low- and medium-density districts.
4.1.2	Offering affordability incentives	Low	
4.1.2	Tailoring affordability mandates	Medium	Affordability mandates could reduce the economic viability of housing construction and slow the expansion of housing supply.
4.1.3	Preserving naturally occurring affordable housing	High	Preservation of existing housing could keep energy inefficient housing in use longer and may slow the replacement of such housing with greater numbers of new housing units.

Improving Equity			
4.2.2	Improving equity in housing opportunities	High	Antidisplacement measures could reduce opportunities for redevelopment and the supply of new energy-efficient housing.
4.2.3	Improving equity in employment opportunities	Medium	Protection of existing business communities could reduce opportunities for redevelopment that could increase housing supply.
4.2.4	Improving equity in access to high-quality public services	Low	
4.2.5	Improving equity in exposure to public health risks	Low	
Improving Sustainability and Resilience			
4.3.1	Avoiding climate risk areas	Medium	Risk avoidance regulations could limit land supply to increase housing production or could further isolate neighborhoods particularly vulnerable to climate change.
4.3.2	Allowing more mixed use	High	Nonresidential uses could absorb land needed to increase housing supply.
4.3.3	Improving connectivity	Medium	Requiring smaller blocks could reduce design efficiency of new multihousehold buildings that could have been bigger at lower cost per unit.
4.3.4	Facilitating more renewable energy	Low	
4.3.5	Encouraging local food production	Low	

Table 7.1. Tensions Between Key Zoning Changes

7.2. Involve Everyone but Focus on the Most Vulnerable

Fundamental fairness requires that those who will be affected by a zoning text or map change be able to participate in discussions about the possible impacts of that change, and that requirement is often codified in state laws. It is also embedded in the aspirational principles of the American Institute of Certified Planners. Most communities have long aspired to do that. But state law requirements and our outreach and engagement efforts often focus on those owning property living in the zoning districts that will be directly affected by the change. They do not focus on residents of other areas that will be indirectly affected by exclusion, limitations, or increased development quality standards in a different part of the community. That second group needs to be involved, particularly if they have been historically disadvantaged, and the impacts on those communities need to be taken seriously. That will require new engagement techniques and more time and effort than we have invested in the past.

The bad news is that the answer is probably not to use a web-based engagement platform, because those we need to engage are often on the other side of the digital divide or do not have the time, availability, or language skills to engage in the ways we have asked them to in the past. It will probably take greater levels of in-person interactions to meet the residents and business owners in historically disadvantaged communities where they are, engage them in their first languages, and be willing to educate and translate zoning rules and standards into plain language. We will need to make a commitment not to adopt zoning changes until we are confident that the indirect impacts on disadvantaged communities are understood and their preferences valued.

7.3. Evaluate Market Responses at the Neighborhood Level

A book like this has to discuss potential zoning changes in general terms, but the impacts of zoning changes play out at the neighborhood level. That means that we need to evaluate the applicability and potential unintended or unknown consequences of the changes recommended in this book at that level. Both the neighborhoods that have been protected from needed growth and change by current zoning practices and those that have not been protected are unique. A zoning change that will promote housing affordability at the expense of equity in one low-density residential neighborhood could have the opposite impact on another one.

In addition to evaluating impacts on the current residents and business operators in each neighborhood, we need to evaluate the potential investment that will occur as a result of the change and where that is most likely to occur. This is one of the key weaknesses of our current zoning practice. We are very good at modeling and describing how proposed zoning changes will benefit the areas they are intended to benefit. But we are consistently poor at thinking through the market reactions to those changes in other neighborhoods where the proposed zoning will not apply. Anything that makes it harder or more expensive or more time consuming to respond to market demands in one neighborhood will push the market to try to satisfy those demands in other neighborhoods. Those indirect consequences are what we often fail to consider or explain. Or maybe we are just pretending not to know that they happen because that simplifies our zoning decisions.

7.4. Ensure that No One Is Exempt from the Needed Changes

Between 2002 and 2019, Denver used a comprehensive planning approach that distinguished between Areas of Change and Areas of Stability, and so did some other communities. That approach was very successful. In Denver's case it resulted in over ten times as much new development occurring where the city said it wanted growth to occur than in other areas of the city. Those preferred Areas of Change were mostly near transit, although they also turned out to be predominantly low-income and low-middle-income areas of the city. But it also had another unintended impact. It led residents of Areas of Stability to believe that no change would happen in their neighborhoods. But stability is not the same as no change. All communities are constantly changing: Old buildings are constantly being expanded or replaced, and permitted uses turn over. No part of the community, not even historic districts, should be exempt from the changes needed to allow more affordable, equitable, and sustainable development.

To avoid the impression that some areas are exempt from zoning changes or from new development, in 2019 Denver changed its approach to estimate the percentage of residential growth and employment growth that is expected to occur in each of six different types of neighborhoods. And no neighborhood type was assigned zero percent change. Perhaps surprisingly, there was not much opposition to that change in approach. Despite personal preferences for little change in the neighborhoods where they live, many Denver residents were able to accept the need for everyone to be part of the needed changes.

This is only fair because we know in our hearts that change is inevitable. And that is particularly true if we want our cities and counties to be more affordable, equitable, and sustainable. But, as discussed in Section 4.1, far too often we have protected some of our neighborhoods from change and tried not to think about how that drives more change into disadvantaged and vulnerable neighborhoods. And those patterns of protection have been a significant contributor to the great disparities in wealth accumulation between Black, Brown, and White non-Hispanic households across our land.

7.5. Focus on Not Perpetuating the Unfair Outcomes of the Past

I hope the previous chapters have made the case that our current zoning practices have been a major contributor to disproportionately harmful impacts on health, opportunity, and living conditions in historically disadvantaged neighborhoods. In resolving the tensions between zoning changes needed to promote more sustainable development and affordable housing, we need to ensure that our decisions do not perpetuate those impacts. Instead, our decisions need to help dismantle those patterns of negative impacts. Too often, our focus on adopting new rules for sustainable redevelopment has not considered the impacts of those regulations on residents and businesses that occupy older buildings and have less financial ability to maintain or improve their properties when those new rules apply. And our critical need for more housing has led us to sometimes decide that "any housing is good housing," even if it displaces vulnerable households or legacy businesses that serve disadvantaged communities. Section 7.1 requires that we always ask, "Who is missing from this conversation?" This section requires us to ask, "How can we ensure that this change does not negatively affect our poorest and most disadvantaged residents and businesses?" There needs to be increased focus on the equity of zoning outcomes, not just more equitable opportunities to participate in the decision.

7.6. Focus on the Long-Term Outcomes

One of the key reasons why the planning profession exists is to keep our eyes on the long-term, cumulative impacts of land use and zoning decisions. Many residents may be unaware of those long-term goals or may feel that their opposition to a proposed change outweighs the need to pursue those goals in a specific case. Elected officials are supposed to think long term as well, and sometimes they do. But they can also be swayed to ignore how a proposed decision helps achieve long-term community goals when faced with a roomful of angry voters.

When it is performing its job well, the appointed planning commission is supposed to act as the conscience of the community to ensure that the focus on long-term goals is not lost, and its recommendations often give the elected officials the political cover they need to make good long-term decisions. The depth of our affordable housing crisis, the failure of our zoning decisions to consider indirect impacts on disadvantaged communities, and our continued approval of unsustainable development patterns are all results of our failure to focus on the cumulative impacts of our individual zoning decisions.

When proposed zoning changes provoke vocal opposition, that reaction is often based on a general reluctance to change. Citizens can adapt to changes in their neighborhoods, and the usually do. In my experience, even vocal opposition to a proposed zoning change disappears within a year after the change is adopted. This is partly because investment changes happen over time, so the feared "parade of horribles" does not show up right away. More importantly, as new types of development happen, most residents find that their lives are less affected than they thought they would be. As an aside, fears that allowing a wider variety of housing into a neighborhood will reduce the property values of single-family homes almost never turn out to be accurate.[1] In a nutshell, this is why short-term resistance to change should not be allowed to derail changes needed to improve zoning in the ways described in this book.

7.7 Mitigate the Short-Term Impacts on Vulnerable Communities

When, despite our best efforts, a thoughtful long-term balancing of interests results in a zoning change that negatively affects disadvantaged neighborhoods more than others, the city should mitigate those impacts. Negative impacts on historically disadvantaged populations should no longer be ignored or treated as the unfortunate but unavoidable outcomes of otherwise logical planning and zoning systems. They do not just happen; they are the result of the systems we design and the other governance choices we make.

Mitigation can come in the form of economic tailoring zoning regulations based on the income level of the community, as discussed in Section 4.2.2. Or it could come in the form of a new naturally occurring affordable housing (NOAH) overlay district, as described in Section 4.1.3. Or it could come in the form of requirements for relocation assistance. Or perhaps a program to amortize locally unwanted land uses in disadvantaged neighborhoods. At a minimum, if new regulations designed to promote sustainability or affordability would make some existing uses or buildings nonconforming, the code can clarify that they will be treated as conforming uses. Finally, when other forms of mitigation will not be effective, the nonzoning tools discussed in Section 6.3 can be used to mitigate zoning impacts.

CHAPTER 8

Five Key Principles for Better Zoning in General

Revising our zoning rules, procedures, and maps to promote greater affordability, equity, and sustainability is not easy. Difficult politics aside, it is technically difficult because the results of our current systems are so entrenched and because there are often tensions that prevent us from making progress on all three at the same time. Chapter 7 suggested six principles that can help resolve those tensions between the three key challenges that are the focus of this book.

But there are also some overarching principles that should guide the zoning codes that incorporate those changes. This chapter identifies five ways that zoning can be drafted to work more effectively and efficiently. They reflect lessons distilled from working with over eighty communities to update their development codes, and I recommend using them regardless of how many of the recommendations in Chapters 4, 5, and 6 you decide to implement.

8.1. Focus on the Basics of What Matters Most

The first key to better zoning is to avoid overregulation. That requires continual focus on the fact that zoning is a system of governance, not a way to project into the future the personal preferences of appointed or elected officials or individual planners. It also requires continual focus on the need to design zoning to balance the interests of *all* community residents and property owners. And it requires increased focus on the likely equity impacts of each regulation. Zoning rules that will require expensive studies, third-party certification of compliance, or professional consulting services are likely to discourage investment and compliance by disadvantaged and low-income residents and builders. Those types of rules should be particularly suspect.

One way to avoid overregulation is to focus on basics rather than details and add-ons that are nice but not essential. Ensuring that a framework of connected open spaces and parks are easily accessible to both privileged and less privileged neighborhoods is important. Ensuring that all those neighborhoods have good access to a safe and efficient street network is also important. Ensuring that a network of public service facilities is convenient to every neighborhood is important. Getting the basic building relationships to streets and open spaces is important. In some cases, the design of those frameworks is at least partially controlled by other parts of local government, such as the public works department, the parks department, or the public health department. If so, then planners are often in an advisory or coordinating role, and they can help ensure that permitted land uses and intensities of development reinforce and promote efficient use of those frameworks.

When compared with availability and usability of these basics and frameworks, the design of individual buildings and sites is less important. In most mature cities and counties even the most desirable neighborhoods and employment areas contain a mix of wonderfully designed and less wonderfully designed buildings and sites, and those areas work just fine for those who use them regularly. Requiring that each building and site meet strict design, landscaping, and lighting standards is not only potentially unnecessary, it is also expensive, and that has a disproportionate impact on poorer households, businesses, and investors. Remember the difference between "Places" and "places" described in Section 3.5.3 and draft accordingly.

Unfortunately, focusing on basics, frameworks, and fair access to the benefits of the community is hard. It is sometimes hard to envision how a particular zoning decision will reinforce those frameworks, and it is easier to visualize the impact of site-specific building and site design and landscaping and signage requirements. We should resist the temptation to get more detailed about the topics we can best visualize and keep the discussion focused on public interests. The more zoning addresses the details of individual buildings and sites, the greater the risk of overregulation and its unintended consequences.

8.1.1. Size and Scale

The basics begin with clear rules about the size and scale of new development and redevelopment. Functionally, the size and scale of development have to align with the transportation capacity needed to get human beings to and from the buildings where they live, learn, worship, recreate, or work. That includes sidewalks, streets, bicycle facilities, and transit services. That seems obvious, but the alignment of land use and transportation systems is one of the hardest jobs in zoning.

One key difficulty of getting size and scale right is that transit service may be financially unsustainable, and bicycle lanes and sidewalks may be very underused, until substantial development or redevelopment at higher densities happens. I have been in many meetings where well-meaning citizens demand that transit service and capacities be increased, or streets and sidewalks be expanded and improved, before new development is approved.

But that desire for "transportation improvements first" is almost never realistic. Most mature communities are in an eternal game of catching up with outdated and undersized infrastructure. They have difficulty prioritizing and funding even those improvements necessary to reduce risks to human life and safety, so the dream of "getting ahead of" transportation congestion is just that—a dream. In addition, in many cases it is the additional taxes and assessments created by new development that provide the funds to pay for transportation improvements. While a master developer with development control over a big parcel of land can sometimes borrow funds to install transportation capacity before development, that is not the norm. As noted above, most development is redevelopment, and most of it occurs through scattered small investments, none of which generate enough tax revenue to pre-construct added transportation capacity.

Size and scale are also two of the key building blocks of urban design and determinants of whether the new development "fits in" with either the current or desired fabric of the neighborhood. They are part of key zoning frameworks that should be addressed even if individual building designs are not. Fortunately, zoning rules are very effective at regulating the size and scale of development. They can regulate not only the maximum height of the development, but also the maximum lengths of buildings along street frontages, which together determine the maximum volume of redeveloped buildings. And both use-oriented and form-oriented zoning systems do this well. The choice is whether to use "Euclidean" building dimensional standards or more detailed building form standards to achieve that goal, and to avoid overly detailed regulations regardless of which one you choose.

In the past, many communities used floor area ratios (FARs) to regulate the maximum volumes of buildings in an area or zoning district, but that turned out to have major drawbacks. FARs are the ratio of the total floor area in a building to the surface area of the lot on which it is located. Although measuring and regulating FARs can help estimate how much traffic a building may generate, or how much water or sewer capacity is needed to serve it, it does not help produce good urban design. A building with an FAR of 1:1 could be a two-story building that covers 50 percent of the lot, or a four-story building that covers 25 percent of the lot, or a 10-story building that covers 10 percent of the lot. But one of those buildings might fit into the fabric of a given neighborhood much better than the others.

Form-based zoning advocates have correctly pointed out that if you instead define building envelopes (i.e. maximum building height and width and location on the lot), you can estimate traffic and water and sewer demands just as well as by calculating FARs while having much greater control over the resulting urban fabric. And once you have defined building forms and envelopes you rarely need the additional layer of FAR controls.

Incidentally, it is not just the size and scale of new buildings that matters, it is often the size of the businesses or establishments that are located in them, and zoning can also regulate that. This is particularly true for retail and service businesses. Even if the desired scale of development is a one-story building with a street façade no more than 100 feet long, it often matters whether that building is occupied by five small businesses or by one large business. Smaller businesses are less likely, and bigger businesses are more likely, to become destinations that draw shoppers from greater distances, and that often means more traffic and more pressure to provide parking. There is a huge difference between a big box Home Depot store and a neighborhood hardware store, and business size regulations can ensure that you do not get the one you do not want. By limiting the maximum size of retail and service users of commercial and mixed-use buildings, zoning can discourage the location or growth of businesses whose size would create unacceptable impacts.

8.1.2. Site Orientation and Location

In addition to regulating maximum size and scale, zoning can effectively regulate the basic elements of street orientation. It can require or not require that buildings be located near the streets and that their primary façades face those streets. Requiring street-oriented locations by adopting a maximum building setback from street lot lines, means that any on-site parking will need to be located behind or beside the building. That leads to less car-oriented streetscapes, fewer parking lots visible from the street, and increased likelihood that pedestrians will enjoy using the street and perhaps patronize the businesses. Although building location regulations are one of the fundamental tools of form-based controls, the use of maximum building setbacks long predates the use of that tool.

In their zeal to promote pedestrian-active streets, however, planners often overuse this tool. Many areas of the community might be better places if buildings helped "enclose" the street, but not all of them. Most mature cities have major arterial and collector streets with high traffic volumes whose major role is to move cars, trucks, and buses (and only incidentally bicycles) across long distances efficiently. Imagining a world where everyone rides public transit or bicycles to work does not change the fundamental function of those streets. And the arguments for forcing new buildings to be built close to those types of streets is weaker. The likelihood that citizens will choose to walk along a busy six- or eight-lane street to access retail businesses or services or offices when they have other choices is low regardless of whether new buildings are located close to that street. And in many cases that is unlikely to change. Even if the goal is to prevent parking lot–lined streets, high-volume streets probably deserve larger maximum setbacks than quieter streets.

I have seen many zoning ordinances where the same small maximum street setbacks are imposed regardless of whether the development contains housing (which generally deserves at least a little bigger setback) and regardless of whether the lot fronts a quiet or busy street. So, although zoning can easily regulate building locations on a site, there are situations where a light hand works better, as well as situations where street enclosure makes very little difference to the public interest.

8.1.3. Doors, Windows, and Wall Articulation

Zoning can also easily prevent new buildings with blank walls along the street by requiring a certain percentage of the building façade to be constructed with windows or doors. As an alternative, some zoning regulations simply set a maximum length or area of street façades that can be constructed without doors or windows. Others require that there be some form of inset, projection, or change in wall plane every so many linear feet of building street façade. All these tools aim to create visual interest and accessibility for passersby.

This is another framework tool that is often overused. Some building uses (e.g., ground-floor residential apartments) do not lend themselves to large windows and many doors. The same is true for research, fabrication, and assembly uses, which sometimes need privacy because of the confidential or proprietary nature of what goes on inside the building. And door and window requirements that work well on a flat site often don't work as well when the building is built on rising or falling terrain.

More seriously, some codes apply street-level door and window standards to retail buildings that are almost certainly going to be occupied by franchisees of national chain retailers, and many of those chains have design standards and rules that undermine the planner's desire for street activation. Some franchise rules require only a single point of pedestrian entry, to reduce shoplifting, and also require that entry to be facing the parking lot. While planners may be tempted to say, "So let them choose a store somewhere else," most retail chain locations are determined by market buying power and not by the design details in the zoning regulations. As a result the internal layout of the store may face the parking lot, the windows facing the street may be blocked by inventory shelves, and doors facing the street will remain locked. While some zoning ordinances try to require that the street-facing windows and doors remain unblocked and unlocked, those requirements are rarely enforced, simply because of the time, expense, and intrusiveness of doing so.

However, rigid door, window, and façade articulation requirements tend to produce lots of requests for variances and exceptions that could have been avoided through more thoughtful drafting and consideration of the wide variety of contexts where the regulation will need to be applied. Because the "pedestrian-friendliness" of a commercial or mixed-use block depends on the experience of the block as a whole, and not of every building on the block separately, these types of regulations should be drafted with substantial flexibility to respond to real-world constraints.

8.1.4. Know When to Stop

Our discussion of zoning frameworks has focused on these elements—size, scale, site location, street orientation, doors, windows, and façade articulation—not just because they are basic tools for good urban design but because the majority of my clients tell me those are all the building form controls they need. Many other elements of building design could be regulated, of course. Menus of building forms or design elements can address or require specific roof shapes, street-level arcades, porticos, stoops, balconies, primary building materials, accent building materials, building corner features, colors, or architectural styles, but most of my clients decline those options. They realize that the public interest decreases, the public expense of implementing the rules increases, and the likelihood that small and disadvantaged builders will decide to build decreases, with each new layer of zoning control.

Although size, scale, street orientation, and requirements for doors and windows can be embedded in a menu of permitted building forms, they do not have to be. Advocates of form-based zoning have correctly reoriented our thinking away from overregulating uses and toward caring about form, but that correction sometimes leads to overregulation of building forms as well. Each of the zoning framework elements described above has been implemented without being integrated into a defined menu of permitted building forms or building frontages. Overregulation of either building use or building form has serious impacts on the sustainability and affordability of the resulting development and equity of the zoning system. To avoid those results, code should focus on regulating the key parameters that are not based on trendy and changeable ideas of what is beautiful and that will be noticed ten years after the decision is made. Let's talk about each of these in turn.

Regulations based on changeable ideas of beauty are particularly troublesome. I call this the "green shag carpet effect." Believe it or not, there was a time when we thought those were beautiful, and they may yet come back into style, but it is lucky our zoning codes did not require green shag carpet to be installed in new homes. Although that example sounds silly, there are real zoning regulations that make the same mistake. Just because you believe masonry façades, columned porches, or a particular color palette is beautiful does not mean that your children will agree.

More importantly, it is not clear that trying to regulate toward a specific idea of beauty is a good use of the police power. If the result of public discussions is to require that new developments incorporate particular materials or styles or design features, we should be having serious discussions about whether those should apply to redevelopment projects in the same way. We should also consider whether the same levels of visual interest and image could be achieved while allowing the builder more flexibility, for example, through the use of point-based menus of possible design features. In addition to building design regulations, landscaping regulations, outdoor lighting regulations, and sign regulations are often much more detailed than they need to be in order to promote important community goals.

Finally, discussions about new regulations should always ask, "Will anyone be able to tell the difference ten years from now?" If not, then it is likely that the proposed regulation may not have much to do with advancing public welfare. As just one example, I have been involved in several lengthy debates about whether front setbacks in a particular urban neighborhood should be 0 feet, 5 feet, or something in between, and I am almost certain that few will notice the difference ten years from now regardless of which decision is made. In cases where the difference will be noticeable, it is still important to ask what material difference it will make to the livability or usability of the development or the street, as opposed to reflecting the personal preferences of the drafters and stakeholders.

Remember that many well-intentioned regulations make it difficult to get approvals for the types of innovative developments we need to improve sustainability and affordability. In addition, each additional word and requirement included in a zoning regulation complicates code administration and makes it more likely that builders (particularly those with less expertise or financial strength) will get hung up on a detail that sober reflection would show is not very important to the future of the community.

Making the changes recommended in Chapters 4, 5, and 6 and then attaching complex or expensive development standards is a lot like driving with one foot on the gas and one on the brake.

8.2. Focus on Redevelopment and Infill

Draft zoning regulations so that you are confident they will work for redevelopment and infill sites first, and then consider whether you want a different standard for greenfield sites, rather than the other way around.

8.2.1. Zone for What Is Going to Happen Most Often

Always remember that in mature cities most development is redevelopment, and that redevelopment has constraints that are not applicable in greenfield development projects. Also remember that historically disadvantaged communities disproportionately live in areas where redevelopment and infill, rather than greenfield development, is the norm. Avoid codifying blank sheet requirements in neighborhoods where existing utilities, site conditions, motor vehicle traffic levels, or neighboring development make the redevelopment puzzle nothing like a blank sheet.

When it comes to redevelopment and infill, almost every site is unique. That means that the types of development regulations that are detailed enough to allow administrative approvals also need to allow staff defined levels of flexibility to respond to unique site constraints. In discussing redevelopment with an innovative builder in Pennsylvania a decade ago, I was told "Redevelopment is spear fishing, not net fishing. You have to see a potential reuse of the property that others did not see." That means it is unlikely to match someone's preconceived idea about how that site would or should redevelop.

8.2.2. Avoid Perfection Thinking

In my experience, few people are opposed to redevelopment or infill development in the abstract, but that support is often based on an assumption that the resulting building will be just like those near it. But that is very unlikely. If the site could be easily developed for what has already been approved around it, that would have already happened. There is something about the site that calls for an innovative solution, and that means it will be different, which means that our ideas of contextual redevelopment need to be more flexible. Not only should the word *contextual* not appear in development regulations (it is far too vague unless it is carefully defined), but criteria for redevelopment approval should allow for innovative uses and forms of development that do not exactly match the surroundings, and the public should be educated about the fact that that is likely to happen.

Because redevelopment and infill projects are so unique and so constrained by existing site conditions, it is also hard to design incentives that will work for them. Discussions of possible development incentives should focus on whether they will be usable by and valuable to redevelopment and infill projects. If they will not, then their disproportionate use by greenfield developers will actually undercut efforts to create more sustainable communities. Remember that incentives allowing more development height or intensity in areas are not helpful where the market is not demanding those things. If the market does support them, then of course they are valuable, and they should be available based on objective standards without the need for negotiations. We may need to design separate incentives that respond to the unique challenges of redevelopment and infill projects, and those may include exempting smaller sites from some of the site design standards that apply to larger sites. Or they may include exemptions from environmental or traffic study requirements that apply to greenfield projects. Or they may include administrative approval of projects that would otherwise require a public hearing.

If you really want infill and redevelopment to promote sustainable development and to generate economic activity in disadvantaged communities, you have to make it easier than other forms of development. Yes, there will be tradeoffs, and the zoning code should clarify that those tradeoffs are acceptable rather than debating them anew each time an innovative sustainable or affordable redevelopment project is proposed.

8.3. Use the Wonder Bread Approach

Removing outdated and unhelpful zoning regulations is often more important than drafting new ones.

8.3.1. What Can We Let Go?

A long time ago, I was touring Ireland and stopped to visit an old cathedral that had been recently renovated and refreshed. My guide emphasized how light and airy the sanctuary looked now that centuries of soot, smoke, wax residue, and pollution had been removed from the wall and ceiling stonework. He also emphasized that they had achieved that result without the use of harmful or toxic chemicals that could have damaged the centuries-old structure. When I asked how it was done, he said "Wonder Bread. The workers used thousands of loaves of bread. They pressed them against the stone and held them there until the bread absorbed all of the centuries of dirty deposits."

I suggest a similar approach to revising zoning regulations. Instead of asking, "What new regulations would better promote greater affordability, equity, and sustainability?" the first question should be, "What current regulations should we remove, because they perpetuate unsustainable patterns of development, or drive up housing prices, or continue to directly or indirectly harm historically disadvantaged neighborhoods?" New and better regulations may also be needed to achieve the community's goals, but don't add them until you have removed what is no longer needed or is counterproductive.

Most of the undesired consequences of current zoning regulations are caused by rules drafted by humans, and sometimes the simplest way to change zoning outcomes is to erase the regulations that produce those consequences. Many outdated regulations that should be erased are listed in the preceding chapters. All too often, my review of a development code finds that it is overly complex because new regulations were added to modify old regulations when the community should have simply repealed the old regulation. Remember that every unneeded zoning rule complicates development of the housing and commercial facilities that we need (particularly for smaller and less well-financed builders), but it also complicates administration of the code.

8.3.2. Innovation Requires Room to Maneuver

One key theme of this book is that achieving more sustainable and affordable communities will require innovation. It will require us to accept new forms of development that do not meet our past expectations about what will probably happen on that vacant site or what should probably replace that older building when the site is redeveloped. Early in my career I was asked to draft a set of design standards to address expected new development but to offer builders several options about acceptable designs. So I worked with an experienced architect and urban designer, and for each key design theme we drafted a design intent sentence and then drew three examples of what we thought were good designs that fit the intent for that type of building or building element.

Then, just to show that we were open-minded, we drew a fourth empty box and said, "Feel free to propose something similar to those three examples." And of course, every one of the early developments proposed a design that did not match any of the examples. No surprise there. The surprise was that the suggested designs were so very different from any of those examples that neither of us had even considered that they could meet the design intent. But they did. The lesson is that if we really want more affordable housing and more sustainable buildings, we need to allow them room to think further outside the box than we anticipated. Erasing detailed design and use regulations is a good place to start.

8.4. Embrace Reality

8.4.1. Get Flexible About Vacant Buildings

One additional way to improve the effectiveness of zoning is to allow more vacant buildings to be reused, and then reused again. Recall that the greenest building is the one that is already built. Effective zoning for the adaptive reuse of existing buildings involves thoughtful reviews of both zoning regulations and building codes. Because some existing buildings have significant structural problems or electrical or plumbing systems that cannot be effectively brought up to the same standards applicable to new buildings, many building codes now include special provisions that allow more flexibility and in some cases apply different standards to those buildings.[1] This process of updating building codes to address existing buildings will no doubt continue, but that discussion is beyond the scope of this book.

Assuming that an existing vacant building could be brought into compliance with applicable public health and safety standards, the focus shifts to zoning regulations that prevent the building from being reused. Three common situations demonstrate key opportunities to improve sustainability of our built environment through better reuse of existing buildings. The first occurs when an existing retail or commercial building is vacant because the services it used to provide are now provided by a newer, better-designed facility nearby or because of the rise of online retailing. The second occurs when an existing office building is vacant because of declining demand for office space, particularly in the wake of the COVID-19 pandemic. The third occurs when a school, religious institution, or other institutional building is vacant because of declining birthrates, declining attendance at religious worship services, or the failure of a nonprofit institution.

All three are common situations in many communities. The good news is that the role of zoning in keeping the building vacant is easy to fix. Most of the fix involves allowing a broader mix of uses, as discussed in Section 4.3.2. Some cities have responded to this challenge by drafting and adopting special base or overlay adaptive reuse zoning districts,[2] but that is often not necessary. Instead, the first step should be to review the list of permitted and conditional uses available in the zoning district where the vacant building is located to ensure that there are no additional uses that could be added.

Where the reason for excluding a possible use of the property is not apparent, it should be added as a permitted use if possible, and if not then as a conditional use. But the difference between the two is important. The added time, cost, and uncertainty of going through a public hearing process are enough to dissuade some investors from pursuing an adaptive reuse project. Missing uses should be added as permitted uses if at all possible, even if the use is subject to objective standards designed to mitigate the impacts of the new use on surrounding areas.

In addition, the review of permitted uses available to vacant buildings should include a review of the use-specific or performance standards applicable to each available use. These are the "ifs, ands, or buts" that limit the size, location, or conditions under which the use is permitted. While applying use-specific or performance standards to a permitted use is usually better than requiring a public hearing for approval, those standards often do not reflect the differences between new and existing buildings. The standards were often written as if the application was to construct a new building; they require all the desirable features and limits the community would like to see when something new is built. But if the existing building cannot comply with those use-specific standards or can be brought into compliance only at great expense, then the standards themselves can kill an adaptive reuse project. The answer is to revise the use-specific standards so that only those that clearly protect public health and safety (note I did not include public welfare) are applicable if the use is located in an existing building. If public health and safety are protected, then the public welfare might best be promoted by putting the building back to productive use rather than by applying desirable but not essential quality standards. The important question is not "What type of use do we wish would occupy this building?" but "What additional uses can we accept as being better than having the building remain vacant?"

There are several variations to this basic "review the possible uses and add the missing ones" strategy to promote adaptive reuse. One is to limit the applicability of the expanded building uses to a defined geographic area, usually one where the large stock of vacant buildings is having significant negative impacts on the surrounding area or where increased investment is particularly needed. In that case, drafting the changes as part of a new base or overlay zoning district may be needed. In my experience, however, the outcome of the permitted use review often shows that the expanded list of uses could be made available throughout the community with few if any negative impacts.

A second variant is to target only vacant schools, religious institutions, and institutional buildings, since those are often particularly difficult to reuse. They are often very visible in residential neighborhoods, and their vacancy is an important source of neighborhood frustration. Even communities that believe, or hope, that the market can find reuses for vacant retail and commercial buildings often understand that it is less likely in the case of institutional buildings. Schools and religious institution buildings were built for a specific use, and the number of possible market-driven reuses of those properties is often small. So some communities have broadened the list of possible reuses to include small offices, studios, trade schools, galleries, child and adult day care providers, and sometimes multihousehold housing even if those uses would not be available for new construction in the zoning district where the building is located. While property-by-property rezoning of those sites to a new zone where these listed uses are available is an alternative approach, the additional investments of time and expense and the unpredictable outcomes of public hearings are often enough to dissuade investors from applying for the zoning change.

A final variation is to list some uses not as permitted uses or conditional uses but as "V" (for "vacant building") uses. A few cities, including Indianapolis, Indiana, and Aurora, Colorado, have used this tool to identify land uses that are normally not available in a given base zoning district but become available in buildings that have been vacant for a stated number of years.[3] For example, a city or county faced with vacant commercial strip center buildings and a hope that they will eventually be reused for commercial purposes could revise the base zoning district regulations to list multihousehold dwellings as a "V" use that becomes a permitted use if the building has remained vacant for five years. Few property owners are willing to keep a property vacant for five years just to allow that amount of time to elapse so that new uses become available, when they could instead apply for a rezoning to a zone where the additional uses are permitted. But the passage of five years indicates that the property is probably not going to be put back into commercial use, and the "V" designation avoids the need for the landowner to seek a rezoning to get some additional community-supported uses that could have been made available without a rezoning.

8.4.2. See the Potential in Nonconforming Uses and Buildings

Yet another way to improve zoning performance is to rethink age-old approaches to nonconforming uses, buildings, lots, and site features. A nonconformity is something that was created legally and that complied with the law in effect when it was created but that no longer complies with the law because of some action by someone other than the property owner --usually a government agency. Examples include a building that is taller than would be currently allowed because the local government reduced the maximum height in that district, or a car repair business that would no longer be permitted in that location because the local government rezoned the area from a commercial to an office zoning district.

To strike a balance between the desire to avoid punishing a property owner who had done nothing wrong and the need for zoning to help change the future trajectory of neighborhoods as plans and markets change, early drafters of zoning rules came up with a sort of "zoning parole." Nonconforming uses and buildings would be allowed to continue in operation indefinitely (and could even be sold or leased to new owners and operators) but would not be allowed to expand or to restart in the same location if they went unused for a period of time. They also could not be rebuilt in the same location if they were significantly damaged by a fire or other natural disaster. Nonconformities were allowed to continue to exist and operate in the same way they existed and operated at the time the law was changed to create the nonconformity, but they were not given the same abilities to expand, restart, or rebuild as other permitted or conditional uses in the same zone district. When the property owner chose to redevelop the property for another building or use, of course, the development would have to comply with the then-current zoning rules.

In theory, this would slowly lead to the elimination of nonconformities as business that needed to expand their building or operation moved to districts where those were permitted, those interested in starting a new business found that they could not do that in a vacant building where a nonconforming business had stopped operations, and owners of buildings that had burned or flooded found they needed to take their insurance settlement and buy or build where those uses were now permitted. However, this balancing of public interests ignored several things.

First, it ignored the environmental benefits of reusing buildings that have already been built. Allowing those buildings to be reused (even after they have been damaged or after the business that operated there have gone out of business) acknowledges the value of the materials, energy, and labor that went into constructing the building and avoids the need to reinvest those resources just to allow a business or housing development to continue in another location. For nonconforming buildings, the question is not whether functionally obsolete buildings should be taken down but whether the local government should restrict the continued use of a building that could be reused.

In addition, early approaches to nonconformities ignored the human costs of forcing establishments to move when they could have expanded in their location or when they could have rebuilt after an accident or damage from natural causes. Business relocations often result in employees losing their jobs if they cannot travel to the new location easily and reliably. When housing is rebuilt elsewhere after accidental damage, residents often lose their homes. When a housing structure is rebuilt in a different location, it rarely provides housing for the same person who lived there before the damage, because people generally want and need to live near their jobs and schools.

Finally, early nonconformity theory ignored the fact that neighbors may have gotten used to and may even value the services provided by the nonconforming use or building. Although zoning may have changed to no longer allow hardware stores in the zone district, neighborhood residents may be very happy that the current hardware store is there. The same is often true with neighborhood convenience stores, grocery stores, or car repair shops. In theory, they do not belong there under current zoning regulations, but in practice they are neighborhood assets because their presence reduces the need for neighborhood residents to walk, drive, or bike longer distances to get the same services in a zone where those uses are permitted.

For all these reasons, many newer zoning regulations take different approaches to nonconformities. Some allow expansions of nonconforming buildings in ways that do not increase the degree of nonconformity. For example, a building constructed too close to the north lot line (because the minimum setbacks were changed after it was built) may be allowed to expand toward the south as long as that expansion does not encroach on the building setback for the south lot line. Or a building that is too tall (because it predates the zoning that established the height limit) is allowed to expand as long as the addition complies with the new maximum height limit. Sometimes the building expansion is limited to 15 or 20 percent of the size of the original footprint to limit the impacts on neighbors, but sometimes it is not.

As another example, a building that has been damaged by natural causes may be allowed to rebuild regardless of the degree of damage done, because of the housing or jobs it represents and the need for housing or jobs in the neighborhoods where the damage occurred. Early examples of this came from California, where housing developments that were too big or that contained too many units for their current location were allowed to replace all of the preexisting housing units when the damage was repaired, simply because the state could not afford to lose existing housing units if the building could be repaired and occupied safely.[4]

Some new zoning codes have increased the permitted time to restart a discontinued nonconforming use. Many older codes provide that if a nonconforming use is not operated for one year, that use cannot be restarted, but some newer codes have extended that period to three years, just to allow the owners of the property more time to find a new user for what may be a very specialized property. This time extension was often first granted for schools and religious institution properties, because they are specialized buildings and it is often difficult to find a new buyer or operator willing to occupy the structure. The question is not whether these types of institutional structures should be allowed to change to a new use; of course they should. The question is whether, if no one is putting them to an alternative use, they should be able to be reused as they were previously.

Other newer codes go further. Instead of saying that a nonconforming use may not restart after one year of inactivity and that the new use of the property must be a permitted or conditional use in that zoning district, they allow the property to be used for another nonconforming use with fewer neighborhood impacts. In some cases, a new nonconforming use can be installed if the zoning administrator determines that it has less negative impact on the neighborhood than the prior nonconforming use. In other cases a planning board or board of adjustment must make that determination.[5]

As an example, in older cities some corner retail stores in residential zones predate the residential zoning that now applies. If the corner store goes out of business for more than one year, older codes would require that the building be used only for housing. And although a creative architect might be able to do that, many commercial buildings are difficult or expensive to repurpose for housing. A newer code might say that the building can be used for other less-intensive neighborhood commercial uses such as a gallery, studio, or office, each of which is likely to have fewer patrons coming and going and fewer deliveries than the previous retail store. The question is not "What future use would fit in best with what is around this building?" but "Would a different nonconforming use allow us to reuse the building while producing fewer neighborhood impacts than the previous building use?"

Finally, some newer codes have redefined nonconformities. Instead of including any legally created building, use, or site feature that does not meet current zoning rules, they add "and that creates a material adverse impact on public health and safety." Note, again, that they do not say "health, safety, or welfare." These newer zoning ordinances reflect a determination that the public welfare requires that nonconforming buildings and uses be allowed to continue, expand, restart, and rebuild just like conforming uses *unless* the continued occupancy of the building or operation of the use is likely to physically harm someone on the site or in the surrounding neighborhood. In one code, nonconformities that do not threaten public health or safety are termed "benign" nonconformities and are given the same rights as conforming uses and buildings, whereas those with likely public health or safety impacts are termed "significant" and are subject to the same restrictions on expansion, restarting, or rebuilding applied to nonconforming properties in the past.[6]

Although most of the sustainability benefits of rethinking nonconformities come through more flexible approaches to buildings and uses, it is also important to rethink zoning treatments of nonconforming lots and site features. Nonconforming lots are almost always the result of government action to increase the minimum size or width of new lots in a specific zoning district. When two or more of these "too small" lots are owned by the same person, some local and state governments require that they be treated as if they were consolidated into fewer lots that each complies with minimum required dimensions. For example, the owner of two adjacent 2,500-square-foot lots in a zoning district that now requires 5,000-square-foot lots is treated as if they own one conforming lot, and they will be issued one building permit (not two) for that consolidated lot. However, some states now prohibit this type of consolidation over the objection of the property owner. As a result, many communities have numerous lots that cannot be developed unless a zoning variance is first obtained.

In general, the answer to nonconforming lots is to allow them to be developed with the same types of uses and structures available on conforming lots, and if possible, without first going through a variance process. Almost by definition, owning a legal lot that cannot be developed because of the actions of the local government is a hardship that would support the issuance of a variance. The better practice is simply to allow the development of the lot, subject to standards that ensure that it is a good neighborhood to the conforming development around it, without a variance.

In a few cases, standards applicable to "too small" lots require that the maximum size of the building be reduced proportionate to the degree of nonconformity. For example, on a lot that is only 80 percent as big or as wide as required in that location, the building can only be 80 percent as large as the maximum size of a building on a conforming lot. In other cases, cities and counties have encouraged development of undersized lots by reducing the minimum side or rear setbacks or by increasing the maximum permitted lot coverage above that allowed on nearby conforming lots. In general, the answer to nonconforming lots that cannot be consolidated with neighboring lots is to find a way to remove the barriers that are preventing development that does not require a separate public hearing each time.

Finally, a word about nonconforming site features. Almost all older zoning codes discuss only nonconforming uses and buildings (and often conflate the challenges of and solutions to those very different situations). But nonconformities can also involve site features such as parking, landscaping and tree canopy, outdoor lighting, or access points. More specifically, even if the use of the property is permitted and the building meets all zoning requirements, the amounts and locations of each of these site features may not meet current zoning requirements. Most communities do not intend to restrict redevelopment or reuse of the property because of these shortcomings until the site is completely redeveloped with a new building or use, in which case the current zoning requirements must be met. However, their zoning regulations do not say that, and confusion occurs when an application is filed to expand or reconfigure or change the current use or building without completely redeveloping the site. The key question then is whether those actions require that parking, landscaping, and lighting be brought into conformance with current requirements. In some cases that can be difficult or expensive even if the change to the use or building is minor. For example, expansion of a building may occupy portions of the site that are needed to bring the landscaping up to code.

Newer zoning regulations generally respond to this question in one of two ways. One is to say that only complete redevelopment of the site requires that all site features come into conformance with the new requirements. This is administratively easier, but it means that some important sustainability requirements, such as expanding the number of carbon-absorbing and earth-cooling trees, may not occur for decades after those requirements have been added to the code. Nevertheless, in my experience most newer codes adopt this approach just because the alternative is messy, as explained below.

The second approach is to adopt a sliding scale requiring that partial redevelopment of the site requires partial compliance with new site development requirements. Generally, sliding scale approaches exempt minor expansions of businesses or buildings (e.g., allowing a 15 or 20 percent increase in building size without the need to recalculate or redesign parking or landscaping). Above that allowance, and sometimes extending up to redevelopment of one half of the lot or a 50 percent expansion of the building, some improved effort at site compliance is required. If more than 50 percent of the site is redeveloped, or the building is expanded by more than 50 percent, full compliance is sometimes required.

While logical and easy to say, administering the middle tier between 20 and 50 percent site redevelopment is difficult. Is the property owner required to make proportionate progress toward compliance with all of the site design standards, or can they comply fully with some and ignore others? Because of the myriad ways in which partial compliance might be defined, and because some forms of compliance might be prohibitively expensive, the better practice is to allow the zoning administrator significant flexibility to determine what proportionate compliance is and to approve those types of site design improvements. The alternative is to slow down expansions and partial redevelopments that are consistent with community plans and that may significantly promote affordability, sustainability, and equity goals through infill, densification, and transit-friendly development because of noncompliance with secondary site quality standards.

8.4.3. Allow for Awkward Teenagers and Aging Grandfathers

There are two final reasons to embrace the reality of the current built environment. Since most development is redevelopment, most commercial and mixed-use areas contain a mix of buildings built long ago under different zoning rules and those built under current zoning. And they don't always fit together visually or functionally. New buildings built with small street setbacks to encourage pedestrian activity can be next door to older stores with parking lots in front. Even if the new rules are reasonable and well tailored, the result can look awkward, just because communities evolve and not everyone wants to redevelop at the same time. Live with it. Just like those awkward teenage years, they will pass.

The same is true for existing buildings that are way too big or so badly designed that they generate a bad image for the surrounding area. These are the aging grandfathers of our communities, and they should be accepted for what they are. Unless you are willing to condemn the property (which I would not recommend unless they create serious public health or safety concerns, or unless you have a wonderful redevelopment proposal in hand with financing in place), just accept it and make sure your zoning allows some viable continuing use or reuse of the building.

Remember that zoning regulations always require a balancing of competing public interests, including the right not to redevelop your property when the city wants you to. It is not about achieving a particular picture of what the block should look like. Zoning is part of the long game of local governance that cannot change the urban fabric on demand.

Finally, remember that many redevelopment projects do not involve replacing an entire building. They involve adaptive reuse of the existing building shell or maybe building an addition to the front, side, or rear of the building. In many cases, the basic building footprint is not changed very much, and the building is not moved. Strict form-based zoning controls should not apply to these types of projects. The building is where it is, and it is a waste of local government resources to try to force it into a shape or location when it was built under different rules.

Unfortunately, too few zoning codes pay careful attention to what level of investment or change triggers that applicability of the new zoning rules. In one community, I was asked to rewrite form controls that applied to every zoning permit and made no allowances for minor changes to existing buildings that were in the "wrong" location on the lot or were oriented the "wrong" way. And although the door and window requirements were reasonable for new construction, the load-bearing structures of existing buildings often made it hard to comply with those requirements. Every minor change to an older building required a variance or an exception.

To avoid this result, zoning controls should be drafted to exempt most changes to existing building structures from form or massing requirements that are inconsistent with existing structural components. Trying to apply expensive new requirements to reuse of existing structures often undermines the affordability, equity, and sustainability of zoning outcomes, all at the same time. This is another reason to be careful about zoning to a picture, because those pictures usually do not show the awkward teenage years or the aging grandfather situations when development is moving toward the desired outcome but has not gotten there yet.

8.5. Don't Win the Negative Trifecta

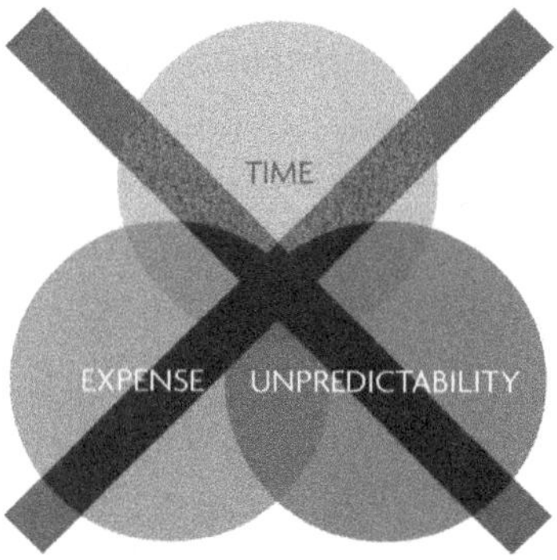

Remember the negative trifecta of time-consuming, expensive, and unpredictable development review procedures. In the course of partnering with cities and counties to update their development codes, I often hear, "Unfortunately, we need to design our standards and procedures for the least capable builders, or those who take every opportunity to cut corners." While there are no doubt builders in that category, it is not clear that more complex application review procedures will solve that problem or that it is fair to punish reasonable developers for the sins of others. We discussed earlier the need to avoid overly detailed development standards, and the same is true of complex review procedures. Adding steps to a development review procedure adds time, expense, and uncertainty, a trio of impacts that discourages development in general and innovations in sustainability and housing in particular.

8.5.1. Let Your Yes Be Yes and Your No Be No

Over the past decades I have also heard multiple builders say, "The code should just tell me what is required and allow staff to approve applications that meet those standards." I generally endorse this approach for most smaller projects, particularly for redevelopment and infill projects. Remember that the chilling effects of time, expense, and uncertainty fall most heavily on small and disadvantaged builders. Local governments see the challenges of local developers getting approvals under their current zoning. But they never see the more affordable and sustainable projects that were never submitted for approval because the developer was worried about the time, expense, and risk of getting an approval.

If the problem is that builders routinely file applications that do not meet code requirements, the solution is not to keep adding review steps and approval criteria; it is to provide training on the code requirements, clarify or revise those criteria if necessary, and then apply them consistently. The costs to builders of delays in the development design and approval process are so high that most builders adapt pretty quickly to avoid them. When it becomes clear that the regulations mean what they say and that staff will consider administrative adjustments for site conditions per the code but will not go further or waive other standards, most builders fairly quickly learn to submit applications that meet code requirements. Since you would not want to experience the negative trifecta of unnecessary time, expense, and uncertainty on your own projects, design review procedures that do not impose them on others.

8.5.2. Fight the Battles Once

Revising zoning procedures to make them shorter and more predictable is hard work, and you should expect a parade of "what if" questions based on the worst thing that might happen under a simpler approval. But the alternative to investing the time and hard work of improving your development review process is to invest far more time and effort on case-by-case discretionary reviews and arguments about what vague and subjective terms mean. The alternative to fighting the battle to fix the system once is fighting parts of it over and over again, at great cost to taxpayers and developers.

Fortunately, I have seen many cities and counties win this battle. In fact, almost all of my clients have managed to make their procedures simpler and their review criteria clearer and more objective. Some by a lot and some by a little, but improvement nonetheless. One reason is that developers, neighbors, and appointed and elected officials can draw on their best instincts about how government should work when they are not faced with a specific controversial project in a specific location. During the zoning reform process, the need for reasonable compromises can focus on shared values rather than being driven by the personal preferences or personalities of the developer, neighbors, or elected officials, which often happens when these debates happen on a site-specific basis. Do yourself a favor and do the hard work once.

CHAPTER 9

Make the Commitment

I want to end this book where I started. Zoning is not easy. But it is very powerful. And better zoning is essential to the future of our communities. To meet some of the key challenges of the twenty-first century, we will need to use zoning differently than we have in the past. More importantly, we will need to think differently about how zoning works than we have in the past. To illustrate these final points I'll draw on some of my favorite quotes, ones that make you think harder about the decisions you make.

First, we need to think about both direct and indirect impacts. We need to think through not only whether a zoning change will have the intended effect in the areas where it will apply but what indirect impacts it will have elsewhere. We have a long history of focusing on what we want to happen in some neighborhoods and not looking very hard at what the market will do in other neighborhoods in response. And too often, that focus has been driven by the preferred outcomes of our wealthier and Whiter residents.

Each time we exclude a land use or a permitted type of building from one neighborhood or raise the required quality or cost of development in a wealthier area, the market demand for what is excluded winds up somewhere else. To pretend that it will just go away is foolish. And to hope that it will land in the community next door is selfish. One of the more thought-provoking questions I have heard is, "What are you pretending not to know?" When it comes to zoning, I think we pretend not to know that the market will respond to exclusion by raising prices or landing somewhere else and that those who will bear the cost were probably not in the room when the decision was made.

Second, we need to think about cumulative impacts. Failure to do that is one of the key reasons for the current affordable housing shortage, our unsustainable development patterns, and the vast disparities in wealth in different parts of our communities. No project-specific zoning decision by itself created those outcomes, but over the years the cumulative impacts of individual decisions to restrict housing or to limit the redevelopment or reuse of existing sites created exactly those outcomes. Polish author Stanislaw Jerzy Lec once wrote, "No snowflake in an avalanche ever feels responsible," and that is sometimes how we think about zoning decisions. We ignore the cumulative impacts of our decisions at our peril.

Third, we need to focus on achieving long-term goals rather than avoiding short-term political pain. This is one of the toughest challenges facing planners. When we draft comprehensive plans we often bring out the best instincts of our residents. That is why the plans are so inspiring. They articulate the better world we want and make it seem achievable. But when we make individual zoning decisions, public comments are often driven by a general desire to avoid change or short-term inconvenience.

I say "short-term" because people, markets, and neighborhoods all adapt to change. Go back to a neighborhood that was the site of a controversial zoning approval consistent with the comprehensive plan ten years later and see whether it did indeed result in the bad outcomes predicted in the approval hearing. Most of the time the answer is "No," not just because people sometimes exaggerate to make a point when they have the floor in a public hearing, but because once the change was made it turned out to be acceptable. Writer Michael Lewis once said, "Everywhere you turn you see Americans sacrifice their long-term interests for a short-term reward," and I think that is very true in zoning. Our culture urges us to reach for short-term rewards every day, but true leaders focus on the long term and inspire others to do the same.

Finally, planners and the appointed and elected officials who draft and administer our zoning codes need to think courageously. Changing zoning is difficult, and the most meaningful changes are often the most difficult. Investments have been made and expectations established based on the current zoning rules and map. And no matter how much and how honestly you engage everyone in the community, someone will inevitably turn up at the final hearing, claim to have known nothing about the proposed change, and demand that the process start over again, which gives elected officials a reason to delay or avoid making hard decisions. That is when courageous leadership needs to show up and be counted.

By definition, zoning changes cannot make everyone happy, because someone always benefits from the current system. Courageous leaders focus on whether the process of drafting the change has been honest and inclusive and whether the result will help achieve difficult long-term goals of the community, and if that is the case they vote yes. Supreme Court Chief Justice Earl Warren famously quipped, "Everything I did in my life that was worthwhile, I caught hell for," and that is sometimes true in zoning.

Changing the way we think about zoning powers, and then changing how we use them, can make a big difference in the future of our communities. It can dramatically improve the affordability of housing by increasing housing supply and protecting naturally occurring affordable housing; it can prevent the disproportionately negative impacts on historically disadvantaged Americans who have borne most of the costs of our current exclusionary zoning; and it can require development that is more sustainable and resilient to the impacts of climate change. I hope at least some of you will rise to the challenge and lead our cities and counties to adopt at least some of the changes recommended in this book. And I hope that you will do so with the determination to prevent the disproportionately negative zoning impacts that our historically disadvantaged residents have often suffered from our current zoning systems. Your children's children will thank you.

Acknowledgments

Most of what I know about zoning—and, more importantly, how to think about zoning and alternative ways of using the power of zoning—I have learned from my almost thirty years with Clarion Associates. For over three decades, Clarion has attracted talented professionals interested in innovating, researching, writing, and sharing their knowledge of planning and zoning to improve communities throughout the United States and beyond. I am grateful to have been associated with the firm throughout that time, and I am particularly grateful for the leadership provided by firm directors Chris Duerksen, Craig Richardson, Ben Herman, Matt Goebel, Darcie White, Elizabeth Garvin, and Leigh Anne King. Although this book does not reflect the opinions of anyone at Clarion other than me, it could not have been written without the experience I gained working with them.

I also acknowledge the many lessons I have learned from the local government planners, attorneys, and administrators I have worked with on over 250 zoning-related projects. They include Alan Greenberger and Eva Gladstein in Philadelphia, Tamara Tracy in Indianapolis, Suzanne Lubar and Mikaela Renz-Whitmore in Albuquerque, Terri Porter and Scott Robinson in Bloomington, Cindy Steinhauser and Ryan Yetzer in Rochester, Andrea Tuning in Boise, Kim Bowman and Peter Fahey in Allen County, Carmen Bishop and Casey Judge in Fairfax County, Peter Wysocki and Morgan Hester in Colorado Springs, Rory Bolger in Detroit, Chris Spenser and Brad Glass in Albany, and others too numerous to mention. I enjoyed learning from all of them, and many of them became friends.

In addition, I thank the seven other co-authors of the American Planning Association's *Equity in Zoning Policy Guide*: Charnelle Hicks, Jordan Exantus, Richard Ezike, Gabby Hart, Jenny Baker, David Henning, and Paul Donegan. Many of their insights on that important topic have influenced the recommendations in this book.

Finally, I acknowledge and thank Holly White, the talented graphic artist who prepared the images used to illustrate key concepts in this book.

Notes

Chapter 1

1. M. Nolan Gray, *Arbitrary Lines: How Zoning Broke the American City, and How to Fix It* (Island Press, 2022).
2. Richard Rothstein, *The Color of Law: The Forgotten History of How Our Government Segregated America* (Liveright, 2017).
3. National Zoning Atlas, https://www.zoningatlas.org (accessed January 13, 2024).
4. Rothstein, *The Color of Law*.
5. *Buchanan v. Warley*, 245 US 60 (1917).
6. *Village of Euclid v. Ambler Realty Company*, 272 US 365 (1926).
7. US Census Bureau, https://www.census.gov/data/tables/2024 (accessed January 13, 2025).
8. American Planning Association, *Planning for Equity Policy Guide* (APA, 2019).
9. American Planning Association, *Equity in Zoning Policy Guide* (APA, 2022).

Chapter 3

1. See, for example https://www.dsm.city/departments/development_services/permit_and_development_center/building_permit_activity_reports.php#outer-5499 (accessed June 6, 2025).
2. David Carlin, "40% of Emissions Come from Real Estate; Here's How the Sector Can Decarbonize," *Forbes*, April 5, 2022, https://www.forbes.com/sites/davidcarlin/2022/04/05/40-of-emissions-come-from-real-estate-heres-how-the-sector-can-decarbonize/ (accessed March 10, 2025).
3. Carl Elefante, "The Greenest Building Is . . . One That Is Already Built," https://carlelefante.com/insights/the-greenest-building-is/ (accessed January 29, 2025).
4. National Trust for Historic Preservation, "The Greenest Building: Quantifying the Environmental Value of Building Reuse," 2011.
5. Chris Shildt, Naomi Cytron, Elizabeth Kneebone, and Carolina Reid, "The Subprime Crisis in Suburbia: Exploring the Links Between Foreclosures and Suburban Poverty," Federal Reserve Bank of San Francisco Working Papers, 2013, https://www.frbsf.org/research-and-insights/publications/community-development-working-papers/2013/02/

subprime-crisis-suburbs-foreclosures-suburban-poverty. See also Pew Research Center, V. "Foreclosures in the U.S. in 2008," May 12, 2009, https://www.pewresearch.org/race-and-ethnicity/2009/05/12/v-foreclosures-in-the-u-s-in-2008/ (accessed February 6, 2025).

6. Chris Chantrill, "The Fight Against Sprawl," *American Thinker* (February 28, 2007), https://https://www.americanthinker.com/articles/2007/02/the_fight_against_sprawl.html (accessed June 26, 2025).
7. Reid Ewing and Shima Hamidi, *The Costs of Sprawl* (Routledge, 2017).
8. Cody Hochstenbach and Sako Musterd, "Gentrification and the Suburbanization of Poverty: Changing Urban Geographies Through Boom and Bust Cycles," *Urban Geography* 39, no. 1 (2018), https://www.tandfonline.com/doi/full/10.1080/02723638.2016.1276718.
9. See Haewon Ma, "How Nonprofits Are Using Accessory Dwelling Units as an Affordable Housing Strategy," Joint Center for Housing Studies of Harvard University, 2024, https://www.jchs.harvard.edu/blog/how-nonprofits-are-using-accessory-dwelling-units-affordable-housing-strategy; and Common Good News, "ADUs: A Growing Solution to Housing Affordability Challenges in the US," November 10, 2024, https://commongoodnews.org/economy/adus-a-growing-solution-to-housing-affordability-challenges-in-the-us/, (accessed January 13, 2025).
10. California Government Code, Title 7, Division 1, Chapter 13, Article 2, Section 66323.
11. See, for example, Connecticut HB 6106 (2021), Massachusetts H 4977 (2024), Washington EHB 1337 (2023), Vermont S.100 (2023), Montana SB 528 (2023), and Rhode Island H 7062 (2024).
12. Kevin Lynch, *The Image of the City* (MIT Press, 1960).

Chapter 4

1. Nolan Gray, *Arbitrary Lines: How Zoning Broke the American City and How to Fix It* (Island Press, 2022).
2. Scott Breyer, "The Verdict Is In: Land Use Regulations Increase Housing Costs," *Forbes* (September 30, 2016), https://www.forbes.com/sites/scottbeyer/2016/09/30/the-verdict-is-in-land-use-regulations-increase-housing-costs/ (accessed January 29, 2025).
3. City of Portland, Oregon, Bureau of Planning and Sustainability, "Residential Infill Project Internal Conversion Report," October 17, 2016.
4. Marc Perry, Brian Mendez-Smith, and Lynda Laughlin, "National Archives Will Soon Release 1950 Census, Offering a Look at a Defining Time in

Modern U.S. History," US Census Bureau, March 28, 2022, https://www.census.gov/library/stories/2022/03/1950-census-records-window-to-history.html (accessed January 29, 2025).

5. US Census Bureau, "QuickFacts Denver County, Colorado; Denver City, Colorado," https://www.census.gov/quickfacts/fact/table/denvercounty-colorado,denvercitycolorado/HSD310223 (accessed January 29, 2025).
6. B. Erin Cole, "R-0: Race, Sexuality and Single-Family Zoning in Denver's Park Hill and Capitol Hill Neighborhoods, 1956–1989" (PhD diss., University of New Mexico, 2014), https://digitalrepository.unm.edu/hist_etds/14.
7. *Moore v City of East Cleveland*, 431 US 494 (1977) and *City of Cleburne v. Cleburn Living Center, Inc.*, 473.US 432 (1985).
8. Kristi Synder, "35 Top E-Commerce Statistics," *Forbes*, March 28, 2024, https://www.forbes.com/advisor/business/ecommerce-statistics/#general_e_commerce_statistics_section (accessed January 29, 2025).
9. Tony Semerad, "New Database Gives Widest Look Ever at LDS Church Landholdings. See What It Owns and Where," *The Salt Lake Tribune*, April 5, 2022, https://www.sltrib.com/religion/2022/04/05/new-database-gives-widest/ (accessed January 29, 2025).
10. University of California, Terner Center for Housing Innovation, "Mapping the Potential and Identifying the Barriers to Faith-Based Housing Development," Policy Brief, 2020.
11. Ricj Reinhard, "Affordable Housing: YIGBY (Yes in God's Backyard) Movement Seeks to Counter NIMBY Movement," *Urban Land*, https://urbanland.uli.org/property-types/housing-affordable-and-workforce/affordable-housing-yigby-yes-in-gods-backyard-movement-seeks-to-counter-nimby-movement (accessed January 29, 2025).
12. "City Council Unanimously Adopts Mayor's YIGBY Housing Reforms," December 17, 2019, https://www.sandiego.gov/planning/programs/housing/newsrelease191217 (accessed January 29, 2025).
13. OECD Affordable Housing Database, November 11, 2024, https://www.oecd.org/en/data/datasets/oecd-affordable-housing-database.html.
14. Ibid.
15. Ibid., "PH4.1 Public Spending on Support to Social Rental Housing," November 11, 2024, https://webfs.oecd.org/Els-com/Affordable_Housing_Database/PH4-1-Public-spending-social-rental-housing.pdf.
16. Ruoniu Wang and Sowmya Balachandran, "Inclusionary Housing in the United States: Prevalence, Practices, and Production in Local Jurisdictions

as of 2019," Grounded Solutions Network, 2019, https://groundedsolutions.org/resources/inclusionary-housing-united-states/.

17. See, for example, Diane K. Levy, Zach McDade, and Cassie Dumlao, "Effects of Living in Mixed-Income Communities for Low-Income Families: A Review of the Literature," Metropolitan Housing and Communities Center, 2010, https://www.urban.org/sites/default/files/publication/27116/412292-Effects-from-Living-in-Mixed-Income-Communities-for-Low-Income-Families.PDF.
18. Grounded Solutions Network, "Best Practices in Geographic Scoping and Tiering of Inclusionary Housing Policies," 2016, https://www.inclusionary-housing.org/wp-content/uploads/2016/08/Geographic-Scope-and-Tiering-of-Inclusionary-Housing-Policies_b.pdf (accessed January 31, 2025).
19. Consumer Financial Protection Bureau, "Manufactured Housing Finance: New Insights from the Home Mortgage Disclosure Act Data," https://files.consumerfinance.gov/f/documents/cfpb_manufactured-housing-finance-new-insights-hmda_report_2021-05.pdf (accessed January 31, 2025).
20. City of Fort Collins Land Use Code, "Use Standards," https://www.fcgov.com/planning-development-services/files/article-4-use-standards.pdf?1721227449 (accessed January 31, 2025).
21. City of San Jose, "Mobilehome Park Protection & Redesignation Project," https://www.sanjoseca.gov/your-government/departments-offices/planning-building-code-enforcement/planning-division/citywide-planning/mobilehome-parks-general-plan-amendments (accessed January 31, 2025).
22. Donald Elliott, "Do Planners Always Have to Make the Neighborhood 'Better'? Rethinking the Disturbing Tensions Between Redevelopment and Equity," Georgia State University College of Law, *Journal of Comparative Urban Law and Policy* 5, no. 1 (2022).
23. US Census Bureau, "Income in the United States: 2023," September 10, 2024, https://www.census.gov/library/publications/2024/demo/p60-282.html (accessed January 31, 2025).
24. USAFacts, "Wealth Inequality Across Race: What Does the Data Show?," April 6, 2023, https://usafacts.org/articles/wealth-inequality-across-races-what-does-the-data-show/ (accessed January 31, 2025).
25. US Department of Labor, "Sex Earnings Gaps by Age and State," https://www.dol.gov/agencies/wb/data/Sex-Earnings-Gaps-by-Age-State (accessed January 31, 2025).
26. Federal Reserve Bank of St. Louis, https://www.stlouisfed.org/open-vault/2022/jul/benefits-of-supporting-working-moms (accessed June 6, 2025).

27. 42 USC 3604 and CFR 100.304.
28. 42 USC 61 and 49 CFR Part 24.
29. Kenneth Barr, "Protections of (Im)mobile Home Owners from the Consequences of (Im)mobile Home Park Closures," *Pennsylvania Law Review* 128, no. 3 (2024): 779, https://www.pennstatelawreview.org/wp-content/uploads/2024/05/3.-Baar-1.pdf.
30. Habitat for Humanity, Portland Region, "A Decade Later: Portland's N/NE Preference Policy Sees Progress, Challenges Ahead," December 21, 2023, https://habitatportlandregion.org/a-decade-later-portlands-n-ne-preference-policy-sees-progress-challenges-ahead/ (accessed January 31, 2025).
31. Marlene Thornton and Katherine Bowers, "Poverty in Older Adulthood: A Health and Social Crisis," *Journal of Issues in Nursing*, January 31, 2024, https://doi.org/10.3912/OJIN.Vol29No01Man03.
32. *Larkin v. Michigan Department of Social Services*, 89 F.3d 285 (1996). See also Brian J. Connolly and Dwight H. Merriam, *Group Homes: Strategies for Effective and Defensible Planning and Regulation* (American Bar Association, 2015).
33. ORS 197.665, 667, and 670.
34. Doug Saunders, *Arrival City: How the Largest Migration in History Is Reshaping Our World* (Knopf Doubleday, 2012).
35. See, for example, Jane W. Seymour, Daniel E. Polsky, Elizabeth J. Brown, Corentin M. Barbu, and David Grande, "The Role of Community Health Centers in Reducing Racial Disparities in Spatial Access to Primary Care," *Journal of Primary Care and Community Health* 8, no. 3 (2017): 147–52, doi:10.1177/2150131917699029.
36. See, for example, Denver Housing Code 27-226(b)(3).
37. Mariana C. Arcaya and Alina Schnake-Mahl, "Health in the Segregated City," NYU Furman Center, October 2017, https://furmancenter.org/research/iri/essay/health-in-the-segregated-city%20 (accessed January 31, 2025).
38. Christine Clark, "Poor and Minority Communities Suffer More from Extreme Heat in U.S. Cities," University of California, July 22, 2021, https://www.universityofcalifornia.edu/news/poor-and-minority-communities-suffer-more-extreme-heat-us-cities (accessed January 31, 2025).
39. *Friends of East Fork v. Clark County*, No. 33422-4-II, 2006 WL 1745032, at *1 n.1 (Wash. Ct. App. June 27, 2006).
40. *Colo. Dep't of Health v. The Mill*, 809 P.2d 434 (Colo. 1991) and 887 P.2d 993 (Colo. 1994).

41. Jim Holway, Don Elliott, and Anna Trentadue, "Arrested Development," Lincoln Institute of Land Policy, Policy Focus Report, January 2014.
42. See, for example, Federal Emergency Management Agency, "Floodproofing Non-Residential Buildings," Report P-936, 2013; and Federal Emergency Management Agency, "Hurricane Sandy in New Jersey and New York: Building Performance Observations, Performance, and Technical Recommendations," Mitigation Assessment Team Report P-942, 2013.
43. See, for example, City of Boise River System Overlay District, Boise Development Code §11-02-07.3.E.
44. Maui County, "Three Strategies for Sea Level Rise Adaptation," https://climateadaptation.hawaii.gov/wp-content/uploads/2016/06/Maui-County-SLR-Story-Final.pdf (accessed January 16, 2025).
45. "Building a Better Norfolk: A Zoning Ordinance for the 21st Century," adopted January 23, 2018, updated February 25, 2025, https://www.norfolk.gov/DocumentCenter/View/35581/Adopted-Zoning-Ordinance?bidId= (accessed January 16, 2025).
46. Pitkin County Land Use Code §3-40-20 RR (Rural and Remote).
47. County of Hawai'i, "Toolbox and Strategies for Multi-Hazard Mitigation Through Land Use Reallocation," June 2020, https://records.hawaiicounty.gov/Weblink/1/edoc/134462/Toolbox%20%20Strategies%20for%20Mulit-Hazard%20Mitigation%20thru%20Land%20Use%20Reallocation%20-%20Clarion%20(2020).pdf (accessed January 16, 2025).
48. US Environmental Protection Agency, "Fast Facts on Transportation Greenhouse Gas Emissions," https://www.epa.gov/greenvehicles/fast-facts-transportation-greenhouse-gas-emissions (accessed January 13, 2025).
49. Sustainable Development Code, "Chapter 3.1: Development Patterns and Infill," https://sustainablecitycode.org/brief/street-connectivity-minimums-4 (accessed January 31, 2025).
50. Ilya Chernyakhovskiy, Tian Tian, Joyce McLaren, Mackay Miller, and Nina Geller, "U.S. Laws and Regulations for Renewable Energy Grid Interconnections," National Renewable Energy Laboratory Technical Report NREL/TP-6A20-66724, September 2016, https://www.nrel.gov/docs/fy16osti/66724.pdf.
51. Franziska Spitzler and Katherine Marengo, "21 Reasons to Eat Real Food," *Healthline*, 2021, https://www.healthline.com/nutrition/21-reasons-to-eat-real-food (accessed January 13, 2025).
52. Francesco Tubiello, "Food Systems Account for Over One-Third of Global Greenhouse Gas Emissions," United Nations Food and Agriculture

Organization, 2021, https://news.un.org/en/story/2021/03/1086822 (accessed January 13, 2025).

53. US Environmental Protection Agency, "Framework for Metals Risk Assessment," 2007, https://www.epa.gov/sites/default/files/2013-09/documents/metals-risk-assessment-final.pdf.
54. 45 U.S.C. Ch 42, §3604.
55. Civil Rights Division, US Department of Justice, "The Fair Housing Act," https://www.justice.gov/crt/fair-housing-act-1?a=2e7eff20-2e26-4d52-85b1-2f784f107cdb.

Chapter 5

1. Donald L. Elliott, *A Better Way to Zone* (Island Press, 2008).
2. *Village of Willowbrook v. Olech*, 582 US 562 (2000).
3. *Pennsylvania Coal Company v. Mahon*, 260 US 393 (1922).
4. *Tahoe-Sierra Preservation Council, Inc.*, 535 US 302 (2002); *Keystone Bituminous Coal Ass'n v. DeBenedictis*, 480 US 470 (1987); *Murr v. Wisconsin*, 137 S.Ct. 1933 (2017).
5. *Lucas v. South Carolina Coastal Council*, 505 US 1003 (1992).
6. *Nollan v. Cal. Coastal Commission*, 483 US 825 (1987).
7. *Dolan v. City of Tigard*, 512 US 374 (1994).
8. *Sheetz v. County of El Dorado*, 601 US 267 (2024).
9. *Koontz v. St. Johns River Water Management District*, 570 US 595 (2013).
10. *Kaiser Aetna v. United States*, 444 US 164 (1979).
11. 42 USC 2000cc.
12. American Planning Association, *AICP Code of Ethics and Professional Conduct* (APA, 2021).
13. American Planning Association, *Equity in Zoning Policy Guide* (APA, 2022).
14. Florida Statutes 380.0651(3), Exemptions for Dense Urban Areas, 2016.
15. Connecticut General Statutes 8-2(d)(10).

Chapter 6

1. Housing Act of 1937, 42 USCS 1437 et seq.
2. Sima Namin, Yuhong Zhou, Wei Xu, Emily McKinley, Courtney Jankowski, Purushottam Laud, and Kirsten Beyer, "Persistence of Mortgage Lending Bias in the United States: 80 Years After the Home Owners' Loan Corporation Security Maps," *Journal of Race, Ethnicity and the City* 3, no. 1 (March 8): 70–94. doi:10.1080/26884674.2021.2019568.

3. Rashawn Ray, Andre M. Perry, David Harshbarger, Samantha Elizondo, and Alexandra Gibbons, "Homeownership, Racial Segregation, and Policy Solutions to Racial Wealth Equity," Brookings Institution, September 1, 2021, https://www.brookings.edu/articles/homeownership-racial-segregation-and-policies-for-racial-wealth-equity (accessed February 3, 2025).
4. See, for example, *Kasper v. Town of Brookhaven*, 142 A.D.2d 213 (N.Y. App. Div. 1988).
5. Patrick Hain and Rosanna Mulcahy, "Cities Are Addressing the Past and Building Futures Through Reparations," National League of Cities, February 10, 2023, https://www.nlc.org/article/2023/02/10/cities-are-addressing-the-past-and-building-futures-through-reparations/ (accessed February 3, 2025).

Chapter 7

1. For example, see Yonah Freemark, "Upzoning Chicago: Impacts of a Zoning Reform on Property Values and Housing Construction," *Urban Affairs Review*, 1 2019. https://yonahfreemark.com/wp-content/uploads/2019/01/Freemark-Upzoning-Chicago.pdf
   See also Daniel Herriges, "What Would Mass Upzoning *Actually* Do to Property Values?," Strong Towns, January 19, 2022, https://www.strongtowns.org/journal/2022/1/18/what-would-mass-upzoning-actually-do-to-property-values (accessed February 3, 2025).

Chapter 8

1. International Code Council, International Existing Building Code, 2021.
2. See, for example, Leicester, Massachusetts, Zoning Bylaws §5.10, Adaptive Reuse Overlay District (AROD).
3. Indianapolis–Marion County, Indiana, Zoning Ordinance, §743-203 Permitted Where Vacant.
4. California Government Code, Title 7, Division 1, Chapter 654, California Housing Crisis Act of 2019.
5. See, for example, Rochester, Minnesota, Unified Development Code, §60-500-080.E.3, Change of Nonconforming Use.
6. Youngstown, Ohio, Youngstown Redevelopment Ordinance, 2013, https://youngstownohio.gov/sites/default/files/forms/Youngstown%20Final%20Adopted%20Published%20Version%204-13.pdf (accessed February 3, 2025).

Suggested Reading

Alexander, Michelle. 2012. *The New Jim Crow*. New Press.

Blaesser, Brian, and Alan Weinstein, 1989. *Land Use and the Constitution*. Planners Press.

Bronin, Sara. 2024. *Key to the City*. Porchlight.

Bruegmann, Robert. 2005. *Sprawl: A Compact History*. University of Chicago Press.

Connolly, Brian, and Dwight Merriam. 2015. *Group Homes*. American Bar Association.

Desmond, Matthew. 2017. *Evicted*. Crown.

Desmond, Matthew. 2024. *Poverty by America*. Crown.

Duerksen, Christopher, and Cara Snyder. 2005. *Nature-Friendly Communities*. Island Press.

Elliott, Donald. 2008. *A Better Way to Zone*. Island Press.

Ewing, Reid, and Shima Hamidi. 2017. *The Costs of Sprawl*. Routledge.

Florida, Richard. 2017. *The New Urban Crisis*. Basic Books.

Friedman, Thomas. 2009. *Hot, Flat, and Crowded*. Picador.

Garreau, Joel. 1992. *Edge City*. Knopf Doubleday.

Gray, M. Nolan. 2022. *Arbitrary Lines*. Island Press.

Herold, Benjamin. 2024. *Disillusioned*. Penguin.

Jacobs, Jane. 1961. *The Death and Life of Great American Cities*. Random House.

Kahlenberg, Richard. 2023. *Excluded*. Public Affairs.

Kendig, Lane. 2019. *Using the New Performance Zoning*. Book Baby.

Kunstler, James. 1993. *Geography of Nowhere*. Touchstone.

Levine, Jonathan. 2005. *Zoned Out*. Routledge.

Lynch, Kevin. 1960. *The Image of the City*. MIT Press.

McHarg, Ian. 1995. *Design with Nature*. Wiley.

Mumford, Lewis. 1961. *The City in History*. Harcourt.

Neuwirth, Robert. 2011. *Stealth of Nations*. Pantheon.

Nivola, Pietro. 1999. *Laws of the Landscape*. Brookings Institution Press.

Parolek, Daniel. 2020. *Missing Middle Housing*. Island Press.

Rothstein, Richard. 2018. *The Color of Law*. Liveright.

Saunders, Douglas. 2012. *Arrival City*. Knopf Doubleday.

Shoup, Donald. 2005. *The High Cost of Free Parking*. APA Planners Press.

Talen, Emily. 2005. *New Urbanism and American Planning*. Routledge.

Trotter, Joe. 2024. *Building the Black City*. University of California Press.

Waldon, Roger. *Planners and Politics*. 2006. American Planning Association.

Wilkerson, Isabel. 2020. *Caste*. Random House.

Index

Page numbers indicating tables are in **bold type**. Page numbers indicating photos are in *italics*.

About the Author

Author photo by Eric Lee.

Donald L. Elliott, FAICP, Esq., is a senior consultant with Clarion Associates, LLC, a national land use consulting firm. Don's practice focuses on land development regulation, fair and affordable housing, and international urban development issues. He has assisted over eighty US communities to update plans and regulations related to housing, zoning, subdivision, fair housing, and land development. Don is the author of *A Better Way to Zone* (Island Press, 2008), co-author of *The Rules that Shape Urban Form* (APA, 2012), and *The Citizen's Guide to Planning* (APA, 2009) and served as the editor of *Colorado Land Planning and Development Law* for thirty years. Don teaches a graduate-level course on land use regulation at the University of Colorado at Denver School of Architecture and Planning and is a former member of the Denver Planning Board.

He has a bachelor's degree in urban planning and policy analysis from Yale University, a law degree from Harvard Law School, and a master's degree in city and regional planning from the John F. Kennedy School of Government at Harvard.